Perspectives on Revolution
and Evolution

Richard A. Preston is W. K. Boyd Professor of History and Director of Canadian Studies, Duke University. Among the many books he has written and edited are *The Influence of the United States on Canadian Development, Contemporary Australia, The Defense of the Undefended Border,* and *Canada and Imperial Defense.*

Perspectives on Revolution

and Evolution

Henry S. Albinski   Claude Bissell

James W. Ely, Jr.   Seymour Martin Lipset

John Porter   Robert Presthus

Richard A. Preston   André Raynauld

Guy Rocher   A. J. M. Smith

Robin W. Winks

Edited by

Richard A. Preston

Number 46 in a series published for the
Duke University Center for Commonwealth and Comparative Studies
Duke University Press, Durham, N.C.

1979

© 1979 Duke University Press

L.C.C. card number 78-74448

I.S.B.N. 0-8223-0425-2

Printed in the United States of
America by Kingsport Press, Inc.

Preface

Recent interest in the American Revolution provided an opportunity for the study of the long-term effects of the Revolution on the development of the United States. As a contribution to the examination of that problem, the Canadian Studies Center at Duke University sought to organize an International Bicentennial Conference of American and Canadian scholars to explore the comparisons and contrasts in American and Canadian experience. Subsequently, the National Endowment for the Humanities provided funds for support of such a conference, and a special travel grant was given by the Ford Foundation to the Association for Canadian Studies in the United States.

Since one country had emerged as a result of a revolution while the other had moved later to nationhood and independence by a gradual process of evolution, it was assumed that parallel but different developments from somewhat similar backgrounds, and in somewhat similar environments, could produce material for comparative studies in which the Canadian experience would throw light on the nature and significance of the revolutionary factor in American life and society and on American cultural development and vice versa. The title of the proposed conference summed this objective up broadly: "Revolution and Evolution: Development in the United States and Canada." The conference was also to serve as an extraordinary session of the Association for Canadian Studies in the United States in the off year of its biennial series.

In accordance with a requirement of the National Endowment for the Humanities for organizing such conferences, a preplanning conference was convened at Quail Roost, North Carolina, in the spring of 1975 to explore the subject in its broad perspective, to advise the organizers on agenda and participants, and to give general guidance. A number of scholars from the United States and Canada, specialists in a variety of fields, were invited to meet with members of the Duke Canadian Studies Committee and with selected members of the Commonwealth Studies Committee. Those who attended received a preliminary statement of objectives in an agenda divided into the following topics: a broad overview, internal political development, external outlook, economic development, sociocultural development, intellectual-cultural development, and a summary. Consecutive sessions of the full preplanning conference were chaired by appropriate members of the Duke Canadian Studies Committee to deal with each of these subtopics in turn.

The preplanning conference proved to be a most exciting intellectual experience for all involved. Without presentation of researched papers, discussion ranged widely over the whole field and was fertile with ideas, concepts, comparisons, contrasts, and suggestions for research and analysis; yet it retained a remarkable integrity and coherence. The preplanning discussions revealed enormous interest in a theme that offered most useful possibilities for drawing deeper conclusions from detailed and specialized investigations. With the aid of a grant from the Canadian Embassy in Washington, a digest of the proceedings of the preplanning conference was printed and was circulated to all those who were invited to present papers and also to all those who planned to attend as auditors.

Discussion at the preplanning conference demonstrated that the scope of the topic was huge, far greater than could be covered in a brief conference. In order to secure depth, it would be necessary to select a very few rather limited topics for investigation; in the brief time available many broad areas would have to be omitted. A series of case studies within a few selected areas, rather than broad overall coverage, seemed to be the best means of opening up a vast area for future study. But it was hoped that discussion at the Bicentennial Conference of the implications of these selected special studies and the subsequent publication of its proceedings would permit preliminary conclusions and would suggest areas for further inquiry and research.

An announcement of the proposed conference was issued through various learned journals in the United States and Canada, especially through the *American Review of Canadian Studies,* the official organ of the Association for Canadian Studies in the United States, and by circulation from the Canadian Embassy in Washington. The Bicentennial Conference was held at the Ramada Inn in Durham on 14–16 October 1976. Inquiries and applications had been received from 157 persons. Those who actually attended numbered 125. Abstracts of the papers were circulated in advance, and copies of the complete texts were available for distribution when the conference opened. After oral summaries had been presented and prearranged discussants had commented, general discussion was vigorous.

Because the grant received from the National Endowment for the Humanities did not cover publication, the manuscripts from the conference were sent to the Duke Commonwealth Studies Committee with a view to inclusion in its Commonwealth series of publications. At the same time, a small panel of appraisers, some of whom had not attended the Bicentennial Conference, was convened under the chairmanship of Dr. Dale Thomson, a former director of the Canadian Studies Center at the School of Advanced International Studies in Washington, to assess the impact of the conference. The Commonwealth Studies editorial committee, chaired by Dr. John Cell, two anonymous readers for the Duke University Press, and the panel of appraisers selected those papers for publication that in their opinion, contributed most to the exploration of the theme of the conference, "Revolution and Evolution."

Finally a meeting of the members of the preplanning conference was reconvened at Quail Roost in late spring of 1977 to assess to what extent the conference had achieved the objectives established by the preplanning. A thorough discussion of individual papers and of general conclusions to be drawn from them provided supplementary material to be included by the editor in the eventual volume.

I am therefore personally indebted not only to those who presented papers. who acted as discussants, or who participated in general debate, but also to a large number of others who assisted in the difficult problem of selection and in the formulation of an analysis, especially in fields remote from my own. The thanks of the Canadian Studies Committee at Duke are also due to the National Endowment for the Humanities, to the Association for Canadian Studies in the United States (and through it to the Ford Foundation), to the Duke Commonwealth Studies Center, and to the Duke University Press who collectively made this volume possible.

RICHARD A. PRESTON

Gananoque, Ontario
July 1977

Contributors

Henry S. Albinski, Professor of Political Science, Pennsylvania State University, specialized in comparative politics. He was a Fellow at the Australian National University. He has published *Asian Political Processes* (1971), *The Australian Labor Party and the Aid to Parochial Schools Controversy* (1966); *Australian Policies and Attitudes Toward China* (1965), *European Political Process* (1967), *Politics and Foreign Policy in Australia* (1970), and *Canadian and Australian Politics* (1973).

Claude T. Bissell, born in Meadford, Ontario, is a University Professor of English, University of Toronto and a past president of Carleton University and of the University of Toronto. He has served as Chairman of the Canada Council. His publications include *Canada's Crises in Higher Education* (1967), *Great Canadian Writing* (1968), *Halfway Up Parnassus: A Personal Account of the University of Toronto* (1974).

James W. Ely, Jr., teaches American legal history in the School of Law, Vanderbilt University. His primary academic interest is in American legal history of the Revolutionary War period.

Seymour Martin Lipset, born in New York City, graduated from CCNY and Columbia and taught at the University of Toronto, Berkeley, Columbia, and Harvard before moving to the Hoover Institute, Stanford University. He is now Professor of Political Science and Sociology and a Senior Fellow, Hoover Institution on War, Revolution, and Peace, Stanford University. His publications include *Agrarian Socialism: The Cooperative Commonwealth Federation in Saskatchewan* (1950), *Political Man* (1960), *Revolution and Counterrevolution* (1968), *The First*

New Nation (1963), *Rebellion in the University* (1971), *The Politics of Unreason* (1970), and (with I. L. Horowitz) *Dialogues on American Politics* (1979).

John Porter, Professor of Sociology, Carleton University, born in Vancouver, B.C., is author of *The Vertical Mosaic: An Analysis of Social Class and Power in Canada* (1965), *Canadian Society: Sociological Perspectives* (1961, 1965), *Towards 2000: Post-Secondary Education for Post-Industrial Ontario* (1972), and other books and articles.

Robert Presthus, University Professor of Political Science, York University, born in St. Paul, taught at Southern California and Michigan State, Cornell and Oregon before moving to York University where he became Chairman of the Political Science Department and University Professor. He published among other books *Men at the Top: A Study in Community Power* (1964), *The Organizational Society* (1963), *Elite Accommodation in Canadian Politics* (1973), and *Elites in the Policy Process* (1976).

Richard A. Preston, W. K. Boyd Professor of History and Director of Canadian Studies Program, Duke University, was founding president of the Association for Canadian Studies in the United States and was awarded the first Donner Memorial Medal for Promotion of Canadian Studies in the United States. He taught previously at the University of Toronto, University College, Cardiff, and the Royal Military College of Canada. His publications include *Canada and "Imperial Defense"* (1967), *Canada's RMC* (1969), *The Defence of the Undefended Border* (1977), and he edited the *Influence of the United States on Canadian Development* (1972).

André Raynauld, Chairman of the Economic Council of Canada, formerly served as Director and Professor of Economics, Université de Montréal. He has held numerous governmental advisory appointments. Born in Ste-Anne-de-la-Pocatière, PQ, he was President of the Economic Council of Canada at the time of the conference and he is now a Liberal member of the Quebec General Assembly. His publications include *The Canadian Economic System* (1967) and various other books and articles.

Guy Rocher, Professor of Sociology, Université de Montréal, born in Berthierville, PQ, is a Ph.D. from Harvard in Sociology and is Professor Titulaire at the Université de Montréal. He taught at Laval University and was a member of the Parent Commission on Education in Quebec. His publications include *Famille et Habitation* (collab., 1960) and *Introduction à la Sociologie Générale* (1960). Dr. Rocher is now in the Executive Council Office of the Government of Quebec.

A. J. M. Smith, Professor Emeritus of English, Michigan State University, born in Montreal, is a specialist in Canadian poetry and prose. He served as Michigan State's poet-in-residence for many years. He founded the *McGill Fortnightly Review* in 1925. He taught in various American universities and published many books of poetry and anthologies including *The Oxford Book of Canadian Verse in French and English* (1960) and *Modern Canadian Verse* (1967).

Robin W. Winks, Professor of History, Yale University, born in West Lafayette, Indiana, graduated from Colorado and Johns Hopkins and has taught at Yale since 1957. He was Cultural Attaché to the American Embassy in London in 1969–71. His publications include *Recent Trends and New Literature in Canadian History* (1959), *Canada and the U.S.: Civil War Years* (1960), *Historiography of the British Empire-Commonwealth* (1965), and *The Blacks in Canada* (1970.).

Contents

Perspectives on Revolution
and Evolution

Introduction

Richard A. Preston

The celebration of the Bicentennial of the American Revolution in 1976 was regarded as something more than a commemoration of the natal day of the Republic. For, as Robin Winks argued in the opening address to the International Bicentennial Conference on Revolution and Evolution in October 1976, the Revolution, while primarily a secession of the thirteen colonies from the British Empire, was different from all other revolutions. "The United States was founded squarely on the right of revolution and on the right to alter or abolish government."[1] The French Revolution is sometimes credited with having introduced that concept of popular sovereignty into western society by the overthrow of one of Europe's oldest and most powerful monarchies in the name of "equality, liberty, and fraternity." But Seymour Martin Lipset reminded the Bicentennial Conference that the American Revolution had been an important factor in sparking the French Revolution.[2] Furthermore, the American Revolution had preceded by almost half a century Britain's Reform Bill of 1832, which brought a limited degree of parliamentary democracy to replace the oligarchy of the Hanoverian period and established Britain as an example for liberal constitutional development. Meanwhile, the American Revolution and the drafting of the Constitution had already founded a national state that was stable and durable. The American Revolution was thus a landmark in the history of human society, the first successful anticolonial

1. See below, p. 14.
2. See below, pp. 24–25.

revolt against imperial control in modern times. It gave concrete form to a principle potentially applicable throughout not only the Americas but also in Europe itself and by European nations. That principle was popular sovereignty: that the people of a nation should govern themselves and not be governed from above by a monarch, an oligarchy, or upper class. The Revolution had become not only a symbol for popular self-government but also an inspiration for those people subjected to foreign imperial rule, autocracy, and dictatorship.

In view of this universal significance of the Revolution in America, it is not surprising that it is widely accepted as more than a secession that enabled divergent development in the United States on radically different lines. The act of revolution had laid down principles for a new form of society and government. Indeed, the principle of revolution itself was considered a virtue. In a letter in 1787, Thomas Jefferson, recalling his Declaration of Independence, wrote, "I like a little rebellion now and then. It is like a storm in the Atmosphere."[3] If he is to be taken literally here, it would seem that he favored revolution as a recurring phenomenon in a radicalized society. Today this concept is preached only by the radicals of the "New Left." But it was not always so. Commenting on Jefferson's Declaration of Independence, President Abraham Lincoln said, "All honor to Jefferson—the man who in the concrete pressures of a struggle for national independence by a single people had the coolness, forecast, and sagacity to introduce into a merely revolutionary doctrine an abstract truth, applicable to all men and all times, and so to embalm it there that today and in all coming days that it shall be a rebuke and a stumbling block to the very harbingers of reappearing tyranny and oppression."[4] Lincoln's opponents in the Confederacy could have echoed these thoughts, but with a different tyranny in mind.

3. Jefferson to Abigail Adams, 22 February, 1787, in Lester Cappon, *The Adams-Jefferson Letters* . . . (Chapel Hill, N.C.: The University of North Carolina Press, 1959), 2 vols., 1:173.
4. Dumas Malone, *Jefferson and His Time*, vol. 1, *Jefferson the Virginian* (Boston: Little, Brown, 1948), p. 226.

William Tyler Page, a clerk in the House of Representatives, quoting from Lincoln's Gettysburg Address when the United States was launched on what was believed to be a crusade against German autocracy, drafted a resolution for the House of Representatives that became known as the American Citizens' Creed.

I believe in the United States of America as a government of the people, by the people, for the people; whose just powers are derived from the consent of the governed; a democracy in a republic, a sovereign Nation among sovereign states; and perfect Union one and inseparable; *established upon those principles of freedom, equality, justice, and humanity for which American patriots sacrificed their lives and fortunes.* I therefore believe it is my duty to my country to love it, to support its Constitution, to obey its laws, to respect its flag, and to defend it against all enemies.[5]

The wheel had apparently come full circle since Jefferson had lauded revolution as a necessarily recurring phenomenon, but the idea of a heritage laid down in 1776 had survived. Presidential candidate Wendell Willkie, in a speech during World War II, defined the principles of the American Revolution to demonstrate their all-encompassing benefit. "American liberty is a religion. It is a thing of the spirit. It is an aspiration on the part of the people for not alone a free life but a better life."[6] Willkie thus attributed the affluence of American society to the spirit that had been inherited from the Revolution. A government guide for the celebration of the Bicentennial also praised the revolutionary tradition. "1776! A year to remember in our Nation's history. America in those days caught the imagination of the world. Not because she was strong and rich, but because the young nation stood for something far more important. It had a flaming idealism, a high purpose, and a free spirit that has come to be called the 'Spirit of '76' . . . the Revolution proclaimed two centuries ago is a great American legacy and the focal point of our birthday."[7] The

5. Charles Hurd, *Words that Inspire: A Treasury of Great American Quotations* (Chicago: J. G. Ferguson, 1964), p. 253. Italics introduced.

6. Hurd, *Words that Inspire*, p. 299.

7. [Department of Health, Education, and Welfare], *We're Having a Birthday: Let's Celebrate: The American Revolution Bicentennial 1776–1976* (Washington, D.C.: Department of Health, Education, and Welfare, 1976), p. 5.

Revolution is thus in the eyes of many people the foundation of the American way of life and of the American character.

It is not necessary here to discuss the semantics of the word *revolution* or to establish precisely what is meant by it, whether it must necessarily include a resort to violence or to what degree it must bring about radical change. Nor do we need to discuss theories of revolution—for instance, that successful revolutions were often engineered by groups with special interests, using the grievances of a majority only to seize ultimate power for themselves by introducing a dictatorship. Charles Beard, in his study of the Constitution, suggested that by a similar process the American Revolution had led to conservative stability rather than to radical democracy.[8] We are concerned with the persistence of the revolutionary tradition despite the possibility that it may have been in some respects denied by later events and circumstances. As some of the quotations cited here suggest, it was possible for the tradition of the Revolution to remain operative even though it may not necessarily have applied in precise detail to every circumstance.

What was to be discussed in the Bicentennial Conference was therefore not only the consequences of the Revolution but also the belief that the United States is a product of principles established in 1776. What was to be explored was the extent to which that belief has shaped, and still shapes, American attitudes, American policies, and the nature of American society. For it is clear that since 1789 the United States has become a stable society, rather than one undergoing continual radical change. Some may regard the Civil War as a second resort to violence over principle of a kind usually associated with revolutions; but the verdict of that war was on the side of stability rather than change. Others may regard the upheavals of our own time caused by the manifest grievances of large minorities of the American people as another stage in resort to the principles of the Revolution laid down in 1776. Like the Southern cause in the Civil War,

8. Charles A. Beard, *An Economic Interpretation of the Constitution of the United States* (New York: Macmillan, 1973).

but on very different premises, these movements can be rationalized as a protest in keeping with certain of the principles of 1776. But these later examples also confirm that the mythology of the Revolution was and is frequently a continual factor in rationalizing, if not entirely explaining, the American outlook on the problems of society. What we need to determine is whether that rationalization is based on reality, i.e., whether the act of revolution had an important consequence, or whether in fact, despite popular belief to the contrary, the United States developed as it did merely because separation from the British Empire and from Europe for over a century permitted development along new and radical lines. If the inheritance of revolutionary principles, or a belief in that inheritance, is in fact found to apply, even if only intermittently, we need to know in what circumstances, in what areas, and to what effect.

The American Revolution created two nations in North America, a fact too often forgotten. For Canada was, of course, as much the product of the events of 1776 as was the United States. But Canada emerged by virtue of the rejection of the secession and of the principles the Americans had espoused and became independent by a continuing process of evolution. Some Americans have admired that stability and decorum of Canadian society, which they assume to have resulted from this development by evolution; others are still inclined to regard Canada as an inflexible society retaining its colonial bonds. But most Americans have probably never thought of Canada's development at all. It has been left mainly to Canadians, therefore, to accept the fact that, insofar as they have evolved a distinctive identity along with independence and sovereignty, it has been achieved, at least in part, by the absence or rejection of revolution, not by experiencing it.

From time to time Canadian utterances have attributed certain Canadian qualities and virtues to the way in which their country developed by evolution. George Brown, a great Liberal newspaperman whose adherence to Confederation in 1867 was crucial, said in Toronto two years earlier, "The world no longer believes in the divine right of either kings or presidents to govern wrong;

but those who seek to change an established government by force of arms assume a fearful responsibility—a responsibility which nothing but the clearest and most intolerable injustice will acquit them for assuming."[9] Sir Robert Borden, who had been the Conservative prime minister during World War I, wrote in his book *Canada in the Commonwealth* in 1929: "The political instinct of the [Canadian] race is practical rather than logical, and one observes an invariable tendency to avoid change until its necessity is manifest."[10] Although Agnes MacPhail, a Canadian socialist, told the Canadian Club on 4 March, 1935, "Canadians can be radical," she added, "but they must be radical in their own peculiar way, and that way must be in harmony with our national traditions and ideals."[11] Frank Underhill, an iconoclastic historian, suggested to the Canadian Historical Association in 1946 that the view of Canadians as the heirs of a nonrevolutionary tradition was deliberately cultivated. "In Canada we have no revolutionary tradition; and our historians, political scientists, and philosophers have assiduously tried to educate us to be proud of this fact. How can such a people expect their democracy to be as dynamic as the democracies of Britain, France, and the United States have been."[12] Despite Canada's growing maturity, or because of it, the myth of a distinctive tradition is still powerful. In a symposium on twentieth-century Canadian culture held in Washington in 1977, Robertson Davies, Canadian playwright, novelist, and newspaper editor, quoted sympathetically an unidentified poet of the previous century who had extolled the virtues of Canadian conservatism. He said that the growth of what is excellent is slow. "Cabbages can be grown quite quickly; an oak takes longer, and I do not think my country should be contented with a cabbage culture."[13] Qualities inherited from the rejection of the Revolution

9. Robert M. Hamilton, *Canadian Quotations and Phrases: Literary and Historical* (Toronto: McClelland and Stewart, 1952), p. 199.
10. Robert Borden, *Canada in the Commonwealth: From Conflict to Cooperation* (Oxford: Clarendon, 1929), p. 86.
11. Hamilton, *Canadian Quotations*, p. 183.
12. Canadian Historical Association, *Report, 1946*, p. 12.
13. "Dark Hamlet with the Features of Horatio: Canada's Myths and Realities," Judith Webster, ed., *Voices of Canada* (Burlington, Vt.: Association for Canadian Studies in the United States, 1977), p. 46.

and developed by a continuing process of evolution are thus seen by many Canadians to be something very different from the spirit of '76 inherited by their American neighbors. That the striking difference between the American and Canadian self-images shown in the two sets of quotations detailed above must not be underemphasized was the theme of three essays that emerged from a Canadian-American session of the American Historical Association and were published in Sydney F. Wise and R. Craig Brown, *Canada Views the United States.*[14] Those who generalize about national characteristics must, however, always be aware that these are in part a figment of the imagination or even a conscious creation. The National Portrait Gallery's bicentennial volume states that "Jefferson, *in writing what was intended as a piece of propaganda,* enshrined at the heart of American political philosophy the great principle of equality and human dignity."[15] Nevertheless, Jefferson could not have done it had there not been a basis of fact on which to build. Myth is, of course, not necessarily untruth. It is built up of concepts that are based on tradition rather than on observed experience or similar evidence. The fact that national character is to some extent mythical, fictitious, or invented is immaterial. What is important in using Canada as a control to examine American development is not merely the contrast between the facts of revolution and evolution but also the contrast between broad concepts that are widely accepted as the basis of national distinctiveness and between the contrasting mythologies of their origins.

Discussion at the preplanning conference uncovered complications other than whether particular features of American society had developed as post hoc or propter hoc consequences of the Revolution and whether they were the result of fact or myth. One obvious circumstance that would have to be taken into account was that the two countries had developed in different periods.

14. Seattle: University of Washington Press, 1957.
15. Lillian B. Miller, ed., *"The Dye is Now Cast"*: *The Road to American Independence, 1774–1776* (Washington, D.C.: National Portrait Gallery, Smithsonian Institute Press, 1973), p. 273.

The time-lag in Canadian development might thus explain dissimilarities that might otherwise be wrongly attributed to variation in the process of development. Furthermore, there were some differences between the two environments. Canada's more northerly location and other geographic features were unlike those of the United States and would have to be taken into the reckoning in some instances. The continuing connection with Britain and differences in the nature of immigration were also important points of difference, but these could to some extent be attributed to the different processes of development by later parturition, if not to the absence of revolutionary change. A more difficult problem that was revealed was the fact that few scholars have studied the same elements in both American and Canadian development and also that different areas of inquiry would inevitably need different treatment. It might not always be possible to produce directly contrasting papers.

It thus became obvious that the conference would not be able to pursue what had at first seemed a simple problem of contrasting the results of revolution with the results of evolution. Indeed, as was pointed out by the preplanners, the United States, like Canada, could be described as a product of evolution in certain aspects of its development. So, quite apart from the fact that in many fields basic research still needed to be done, there could be no simple cut-and-dried answer to the comparison between the effects of revolution and evolution. Indeed, the result of these various complications would mean that papers presented at the conference would often need to establish a groundwork of circumstance that would differ from field to field and from topic to topic and would make a simple answer to the problem difficult.

Finally, since the conference was to be multidisciplinary in the broadest possible sense and was to motivate cultural as well as social and political discussion, it was obvious that papers to be presented could not be narrowly specialized. What they could provide would be something quite different; a broad interdisciplinary intellectual experience around an intriguing theme that was ripe for further exploration when general conclusions had been drawn. Meanwhile, the papers presented by specialists based on their own research would have indicated certain hypotheses about the contrasts between the two countries, and at the point where general conclusions among them differed, future inquiry could begin.

Two of the presentations at the conference were philosophical talks rather than research papers: Robin Winks's opening address, which he preferred not to call the keynote speech, and Seymour Lipset's concluding summary. The former had not been available when the papers were written and the latter could not, at such short notice, be a definitive detailed summary of the results of the conference. Both talks were, however, thoughtful and useful discussions of the theme of the conference and lent it valuable perspective. Accordingly, these two contributions are published in this volume separately from the research papers. Their wisdom is a valuable addition to the material from which general conclusions can be drawn about the value of using Canada's evolutionary experience as a means of making possible a better understanding of the significance of the American Revolution and of its impact on the life of America.

2

Cliché and the Canadian-American Relationship

Robin W. Winks

For this well-nigh impossible task I have divided what I want to say into three categories. The first I call a few ground rules. If we are not to spend the next two-and-one-half days in one grand waffle of "hands across the border," "five thousand miles of undefended frontier," etc., etc., some rules on rhetoric must apply. This conference ought to be able to get past those kinds of phrases and down to what I understand is called in the South the "nitty-gritty."

As one ground rule, we should try to avoid cant phrases. For instance, in the preplanning conference summary that was distributed to all conference participants, someone said that Canadian literature had in some way been restrained by the "yoke of Imperialism," presumably British and American. If we are going to use that kind of phrase, let us define the words for each other before they are used—otherwise let us avoid them altogether. For some of us may think that imperialism at certain stages and for certain societies was not without its benefits, and that the word therefore carries little agreed analytical meaning. Let us refrain from using such words loosely.

Second, we are gathered here to consider certain hypotheses related to the Bicentennial. But what are those hypotheses? We must remember that the object of the world of ideas as a whole is not to portray reality—that would be an utterly impossible task—but rather to provide us with an instrument for finding our way more easily. To carry this out usefully I suggest that we speak more about the present and the future than about history and that we try to avoid abstractions. In particular, let us not mire ourselves in this conference in a debate over the meaning of the words "revolution" and "evolution," the concepts we are here to discuss. Let us simply agree that it is in terms of the contrast implied by these two words that our two nations view themselves. Whether they are or are not revolutionary, whether they have or have not turned their backs upon the Revolution, Americans believe themselves to be a revolutionary people. Let us not quibble over that belief. And whether they are or are not, Canadians believe themselves to be a people shaped by evolution. Surely we can accept that what people believe to be true of themselves is what is important in understanding them.

As another important guideline or ground rule, I would like to suggest further that we ruthlessly purge ourselves of the sentimental baggage of predisposition that we ordinarily bring to a conference called "Canadian-American." Let us not get mixed up in false sentiments and pointless fears of wounding. Let us avoid debating clichés. Let us not discuss whether one people is more ignorant of the other, for that debate would go on forever. Let us not talk about "the golden hinge" and the "linchpin," and whether this is, or is not going to be, the Canadian century, and whether the last century was the American century. Let us all avoid using the theme of "revolution" for rhetorical, political purposes.

Thus we come to the favorite theme of any Canadian conference, a theme (usually expressed as a question) that we should also eschew—although if we do, some of you will feel there is no conference left. Let us not ask whether Canada is a nation in search of its identity. Can we try to avoid searching out that identity in this conference and get down to some of those dull facts that help define actual identity?

Then too, I would suggest that a certain robust cynicism about the notion that both of us are in a state of crisis would be helpful. If we begin to get bogged down in a debate over the rather natural inability of many people in a democracy to contend with the challenges, demands, and discipline that a democracy entails, we will find ourselves discussing Political Science 101 and not discussing Canada and the United States at all. I am reminded, for example, of a very facile comparison that was popular not too many years ago in Canada, contained in a book that you will remember, *The White Niggers of America.* Pierre Vallière thought it useful to compare the French-Canadian situation in Canada to the black situation in the United States. Such facile comparisons lead to nothing except the raising of temperatures.

What does all this leave if we accept such ground rules?

First, I would remind you that we are here (with mild apologies if this strikes some Canadians as a blatantly patriotic statement) because we are engaged in the celebration of the American Bicentennial. We are probing an event and positing a connection more causal than casual between that event and differences that we can discern between the United States and Canada. For that reason it would be useful for us not to debate at great length the meaning of the American Revolution today, but merely to begin by accepting the view that it was primarily a secession from the British Empire. But the American Revolution was, of course, different from all other revolutions. The United States was founded squarely on the right of revolution and on the right to alter or to abolish government. No other people had previously asserted the right to revolution in precisely this manner and it is correct to view the 1770s as a unique genesis of a nation. Tom Paine put it this way: "The revolution is not the affair of a city, or county, or a province, or a kingdom, but of a continent. Not the concern of a day, a year, or an age, because posterity are virtually involved."[1]

Now, of course, rooted in that kind of sentiment are the roots of American imperialism. Paine's reference to the continent must fall jarringly upon Canadian ears. But let us accept that political rhetoric is often nothing more than rhetoric. We need not necessarily examine the American Revolution as the first stage in an effort to dominate the entirety of the North American continent.

Second, we are here to celebrate not just the Revolution but the Bicentennial itself. When one compares the Canadian Centennial with the American Bicentennial we realize that Canadians

---

1. Henry Steele Commager, *The Empire of Reason* (Garden City, N.Y.: Doubleday, 1977).

quite often *do* do things rather better than Americans. The Canadian Centennial was a great success from which Americans could have learned much in planning their own Bicentennial, but didn't. Canada did not open its Centennial, as we did our Bicentennial, with a beleaguered president—ultimately two beleaguered presidents—urging a nation to recall two hundred years of history with pride while the Army choir sang "America the Beautiful" on television. Canada so often does do things the right way—and then reminds Americans of this, which is an annoying habit. Canada did not attempt to create the largest flag that had ever flown, as we did, only for it to be promptly, or symbolically, whipped to pieces by the high winds above the Verrazano Strait.

Third, a number of us are here to explore the idea of comparative history, comparative politics, comparative studies in a variety of disciplines. We need not be Canadianists at all to want to see whether this most logical of all comparisons can lead to new approaches in comparative methodology. We should, therefore, take care to distinguish between comparisons and arguments by analogy. We should recognize that all disciplines engage in comparisons and that some comparisons are false. Comparisons that try to cast against each other two utterly different societies operating under the impact of utterly different technologies are not legitimate. Yet, I would argue, if comparative studies are to have any future, surely it can be in the comparison of the United States and Canada. These two nations became separate and independent under the impact of much of the same body of European-transported ideas, with a population made up of much the same people, under the impact of a technology changing roughly at the same rate of speed, and in an environment roughly similar.

Fourth, we are here to exploit ways in which different disciplines argue from cause to effect. We can ask, did *this* development result because one country has a revolutionary tradition, and did *this* event result because another country has an evolutionary tradition? We might produce results that will be helpful to those who are not interested in the comparative technique as such, but simply in the application of logic. To follow such a course is to explore how disciplines have changed. I am reminded, for example, of the way in which many scholars initially viewed slavery as a system in direct contradiction of the principles of the American Revolution. This contradiction, they said, produced the tension within American society that led to the Civil War. More recently, another body of scholars, led by Edmund S. Morgan, has argued that the Revolution could not have taken place had there been no slavery—that slavery was not a contradiction but a natural result of the logic inherent in the way in which independence and freedom for the rest of the population were defined.

Finally, and most important to be sure, we are here to examine two specific nations and their experiences by dwelling at times upon what the planning paper called dull facts within the context of certain theoretical constructs listed by Professor Preston. He suggested that we accept these constructs for purposes of this conference. One theory holds that the study of past revolutions suggests that revolutions are often brought about by middle-class exploitation of underprivileged groups that are utilized to carry out the violence sometimes necessary to successful revolution, but that these agents do not reap the fruits of the victory. It follows that a resort to violence often introduces conditions that lead to authoritarian rule or dictatorship. A revolution is then often followed by a degree of stability that brings new changes, which may lead people to feel thát the principles of the revolution have been betrayed. This theorètical construct, then, sees revolution in a series of discrete stages. Perhaps one can identify and compare specific stages of the American Republic in its revolutionary experience and contrast those stages to specific stages in Canada's evolutionary experience. The alternative—a continual process of revolutionary change, as advocated by some modern radicals, with its concomitant condition of continual resort to violence leading ultimately to anarchy and continual disorder—should be kept in mind.

On the other hand, in theory an evolutionary process implies growth, although perhaps at the expense of preserving vested interests that obstruct the legitimate claims of underprivileged groups in society. Is this the Canadian story? I pause here merely to make the point that these phrases obviously contain value judgments. They happen to be value judgments that I share. Many wish to see certain vested interests broken; yet as those interests break down, they ironically feel that the sense of community is breaking down as well. Did the American Revolution inaugurate an age of violence in world affairs? Did it teach other nations that violence can be successful? (The best example I can think of is the Irish, who most directly copied the Americans.)

Within the revolutionary tradition, American historians embarked upon describing a phenomenon that we now call *exceptionalism*. This term embraces the idea that Americans were different and were intent upon showing themselves to be different. American scholars took it as given that the United States was a different society, and rather than question this conclusion, they set out to explain the American difference from other societies. There is the pervasive attempt by Frederick Jackson Turner to account for America's exceptionalism through the significance of a frontier. (There was also an attempt by Canadian scholars to find a similar frontier in Canada that would give them the same source of excitement, the "shoot-out at the O.K. Corral," for themselves.) There was the attempt by David Potter to explain America's uniqueness or exceptionalism on the basis of a unique abundance—the fact that there was always more to be had—which made Americans an optimistic, materialistic, and philanthropic people. Canadians were not slow to point out that this interpretation of abundance did not apply in a Canadian society that was dependent upon staples and that quite often was under the thumb of the United States in terms of world markets. Potter meant that there were options, many options, open to Americans. Canada did not have nearly so many options.

Another exceptionalist view, put forward by C. Vann Woodward, is now referred to as the idea of *free security*. He argues that Americans were unique, exceptional, optimistic, because their security came free of charge without any moral compromise or real expense. Hence, unlike the nations of Europe that had to spend large sums of money on defensive establishments, the United States could put that same money into its industrial revolution and could overtake Europe with unexpected speed. Canada, on the other hand, had constantly to compromise itself, to sell itself on the block of Anglo-American harmony. (This is one of the great clichés of Canadian history. I am not suggesting that clichés are not true, of course; it is often by their truth that they become clichés.) Instead of being able to act independently, Canada had constantly to compromise its own sense of independence, tempering its desire to move away from Britain by keeping Britain as a sheet anchor against the possible danger of an invasion from the United States. Canadians are very different from Americans because the factors that Americans deeply believed influenced them in fundamental ways were not operative in Canada. Canada did not have the options of economic abundance; it did not have free security; and it certainly did not have a frontier in the way in which Turner meant it.

Canadians, of course, put their own special mythology in the place of this American triumvirate. There is, for example, the Canadian assumption about "northernism"; there is the Canadian assumption about monarchy; there is the Canadian assumption about biculturalism. Often it is said that Canada stands as a nation uniquely identified through these three elements. One could argue that northernism was as effective in Scandinavia; one could argue that monarchy had little real significance in Canadian thought, that biculturalism was yet to be proven and was at risk. Yet are these not basic to the evolutionary process?

Let me suggest three other elements in the Canadian experience that set Canada apart not only from the United States but from the rest of the Commonwealth nations as well. Two of these elements arise from deeply held Canadian notions. One is that Canadian history is in many ways embedded in the history of every Commonwealth member nation. One cannot study the history of Africa—of Nigeria, for example—without knowing Canadian history. (I would argue, too, of course, that one cannot study the history of Canada without knowing United States history.) Canada, as the Mother Dominion, through its actions or through the problems it gave Great Britain and through Britain's responses, set virtually all the constitutional precedents that were later applied by Britain to the process of decolonization in the African and Asian colonies. If one wants to understand the principles that administrators attempted to apply in East Africa, one must understand the mythology (not necessarily the reality) of the Durham report. If one wants to understand how the Ghanaians or Sinhalese quoted the British against themselves, one must know the Canadian precedents. In this sense Canada internationalized its history and participated through its evolutionary process in the formulation of the rules of the game of decolonization. And decolonization is surely one of the grandest and most pervasive evolutionary processes of recent times. Canadians knew that they had to embrace the world to understand themselves because, through their particular role as the Mother Dominion, they had played a world role.

I also would argue that Canadians approach most problems, especially in the Canadian-American relationship, in what might best be described in geriatric terms. By the geriatric approach, I mean that Canadians like old problems. They would prefer to have no solution to the problem at all than to have a third-rate solution. As one reads Canadian history, it becomes repetitive—some say boring—with an element of monotony, as the same problems arise time and again. This monotony may well be evidence of that elusive evolution we seek here. As a result, Canadians have a different scripture, a different attitude toward their origins. Americans know exactly when they became a nation—after all, we have just been celebrating it. We all "know" that on 4 July 1776 the United States was born in the twinkling of an eye, at a precise moment in time. The scripture of the Declaration of Independence, of the Constitution, of the Federalist Papers, of Washington's Farewell Address, have been so embraced by Americans that we return to them over and over. We were independent the moment we said we were. We are not celebrating 1783, the moment in which the world affirmed that we were independent; Americans are celebrating the moment we *willed* ourselves to be independent.

Canadians, on the other hand, do not really know when they became independent, and many may not care. I have often taught summer school in Canadian universities, and my favorite opening-day gambit is to ask the students, who are largely teachers of Canadian history from Canadian high schools, "When did Canada become independent?" I never receive fewer than four conflicting dates. Many, of course, will say 1 July 1867. But we all perfectly well know that Canada did not become independent in 1867. Some others will give dates in 1911, 1919, 1931, perhaps even 1939. The point is important here only to throw light on the nature of evolutionary independence.

Canadian nationalism came to be expressed best in internationalism, whereas American nationalism was perhaps best expressed in a form of free-trade imperialism. Some of us, who in that liberal phase of the 1950s and the 1960s thought that internationalism was a desirable goal, may look with a little sadness on the apparent present Canadian desire to turn their backs upon their internationalized nationalism. But it is significant, at least, that Canada, in its evolution, has waited this long to do so.

Let me conclude with a final suggestion. It seems to me that too often, for too long, too many other people have expected too much of the United States. If it is a revolutionary society, it is still undergoing evolutionary change. Europeans, in particular, often have disliked Americans for not becoming what they wished them to be. Once European intellectuals thought that Americans might achieve the *beau sauvage*, avoid the Leviathan, rise above the great and entrammeling state, and become the first truly free republic in the world. Americans were to *achieve* theory by bringing it into practice. Disappointingly, Americans proved not to be capable of doing just that. They went on being Americans, and doing their own thing, and becoming what they were. Thus it is not quite fair play to criticize the United States for being the United States. If it is itself to become truly independent it must be what it is and what its people wish it to be, not what others wish for it. It would be healthy if, in this conference, we were to discuss the realities of what it is—a large, powerful, technologically expanding nation—and if we were to discuss the realities of what Canada is, without the assumption that somehow Americans have disappointed Canadians by not becoming what they wished Americans to become.

Perhaps it would also be useful not to hear about the large man and the small boy, or the elephant in the bed, or any of those other clichés about how Canada finds it difficult to share the same bed with Americans because Americans are such heavy (or is it light?) sleepers. It strikes me that this conference might best achieve its purpose if it focuses squarely upon how we might most fruitfully study each other in the future, the realization that revolution produced some differences, evolution produced others, but that many of the differences we will detect arose from events that came after the fact of revolution or evolution and are not to be credited to a putative evolutionary or revolutionary tradition.

Wallace Stevens, the poet, tells us of thirteen ways of looking at a blackbird. In implying his fifth way of looking at the blackbird, he says, "I do not know which to prefer, the beauty of inflections, or the beauty of innuendo."[2] I think we all may learn a great deal from each other if we recognize that the inflections and innuendo of the Canadian-American experience are ambiguous, exciting, and important. They matter, and very much. What more can one ask?

2. Wallace Stevens, *The Collected Poems of Wallace Stevens* (New York: Knopf, 1973), p. 93.

3

Revolution and Counterrevolution—Some Comments at a Conference Analyzing the Bicentennial of a Celebrated North American Divorce

Seymour Martin Lipset

The editor has given me what I knew would be a very difficult assignment: to try to pull together everything that has been written here. I have dutifully read all the papers and made detailed notes, but I finally decided that it would be impossible to do justice to them in one paper. What I have done, therefore, is to comment on the general theme of the conference, revolution and evolution, and also to deal with some of the methodological problems of comparative analysis that are raised in some of the chapters.

The way people think about Canada and the United States has changed drastically over time. This point, to which I shall return, may be best illustrated by a comment made by a late nineteenth-century European visitor to Canada. This foreign traveler wrote, "One imagines that one is in Europe again [he was writing about Canada after spending some time in the United States] and then one thinks that one is in a positively retrogressing and decaying country. Here one sees how necessary the *feverish speculative spirit* of the Americans is for the rapid development of a new country. . . . [I]n ten years this sleepy Canada will be ripe for annexation . . . and they may tug and resist as much as they like, the economic necessity of an infusion of Yankee blood will have its way and abolish this ridiculous boundary line."

The maker of this statement is a man who together with his

principal intellectual collaborator now has many disciples in Canada—Friedrich Engels. This was his reaction to Canada on the only occasion that he visited North America. It is an interesting commentary. Marx and he actually had similar ideas about other countries, not only Canada. They thought that nothing should step in the way of economic progress, including nationalism, ridiculous boundary lines, and concern for linguistic and cultural autonomy. Marx believed that British rule was good for India; it would break down the caste system and eliminate many traditional institutions that inhibited economic growth. Engels's statement and others by Marx and himself on other areas indicate how much more catholic they were in their attitude to the factors that affected economic development than most of their latter-day "disciples." Development was not simply a function of economic factors; it also was linked to values and noneconomic institutions.[1]

Is the distinction between revolution and evolution an appropriate one? We are dealing with two nations, both of which stem from the same event, the American Revolution. In this bicentennial period, Americans and people around the world think of this event primarily as having given birth to the United States, ignoring the fact that it created two nations. The Revolution divided British North America into two political communities. The United States is the country that came out of the Revolution. Canada is the country that came out of the counter-Revolution. Part of it was Nova Scotia, which was part of New England before 1776. After 1783 it was the part of New England in which British rule remained. As we know, tens of thousands of United Empire Loyalists moved north.

In analyzing the two nations in articles I have written earlier, I have emphasized revolution and counterrevolution rather than revolution and evolution, much as Claude Bissell and others have

1. Engels to Sorge, 10 September 1888, in Karl Marx and Friedrich Engels, *Letters to Americans* (New York: International Publishers, 1935), p. 204. For comparable comments on other countries by Marx and Engels, see S. M. Lipset, "Radical and Ethnic Tensions in the Third World," in W. Scott Thompson, ed., *The Third World: Premises of U.S. Policy* (San Francisco: Institute for Contemporary Studies, 1978), pp. 137–39.

done in the session on literature and culture here.[2] Both countries, of course, have developed through evolution. The two countries started out differently, but they have both evolved. The United States, in addition, had what some people called the Second American Revolution, the Civil War, but it would be wrong to say that the United States has remained a revolutionary nation; it has rejected Jefferson's advice that blood should flow every twenty years or so. Canada, of course, achieved its full independence through evolution. It never had a successful revolution, rebellion, or even triumphant left or populist movement. In looking at the two countries, I would like to discuss briefly the extent to which the varying formative events still inform the character of the two nations, their politics, culture, and the like.

The Revolutionary Background of the U.S.

The question was raised at the conference that engendered this book of how revolutionary the American Revolution was. Kenneth McNaught discussed the issue and Michael Parenti also mentioned it in passing. This is a topic on which there are numerous books and articles, and we could have devoted the entire conference to the matter. To argue that the American Revolution was a real revolution requires going into the question of how one defines revolution. Two indicators of the extent of revolutionary change involve confiscation of property and expulsion of refugees. R. R. Palmer in his comparative studies of revolutions, in which he places the American Revolution in the same category as the various European late-eighteenth-century revolutions such as the French, notes, among other things, that as much property was confiscated in the United States on a per capita basis as in France, and that many more people emigrated—were political émigrés— from the United States than from France.[3] Also indicative of the

2. See S. M. Lipset, Revolution and Counterrevolution (New York: Basic Books, 1968), chap. 3; and "Radicalism in North America: A Comparative View of the Party Systems in Canada and the United States," Transactions of the Royal Society of Canada 14 4th ser., (1976): 19–56.

3. R. R. Palmer, The Age of the Democratic Revolution: The Challenge (Princeton: Princeton University Press, 1959), pp. 188–89.

truly revolutionary character of the American Revolution is its seeming impact on subsequent events in France. A study by Forrest McDonald of the effect of the American Revolution on the French found a strong correlation between the communities of residence of the eight thousand French "veterans of the land phase of the war for American Independence" and the centers of agrarian radicalism in France between 1789 and 1792. McDonald emphasizes, "On their subsequent discharge and return to their homes in France, these soldiers spread the idea they had seen in practice. When, in 1789, financial crisis, general discontent, and the weakness of the monarchy combined to make revolutionary action possible in France, these veterans formed the dynamic element in a movement which guaranteed the completion of the Revolution by the destruction of economic feudalism."[4]

But whether the American Revolution was revolutionary or not at the beginning is, I think, not terribly relevant to what happened subsequently. What is more pertinent is that the myth of the Revolution, or the populist image of what the Revolution stood for, was extrapolated over time, resulting in what Abraham Lincoln called the American political religion, or in more recent times what Gunnar Myrdal has referred to as the American Creed —a value system, a notion of the ideals of good society, whose basic contemporary content stems from egalitarian conceptions of the Declaration of Independence, of the radical meaning of the American Revolution.[5] The United States, as we know, was a slave society when its leaders declared that all men are created equal, but when Jefferson wrote this he consciously felt that the statement would undermine slavery. He knew or at least hoped (even though he himself was a slave owner) that once the idea of equality was proclaimed as a basis for American independence, it would have a continuing effect.

Like all revolutions, the American Revolution started with

4. Forrest McDonald, "The Relation of the French Peasant Veterans of the American Revolution to the Fall of Feudalism in France, 1789–1792," *Agricultural History* 25 (October 1951): 151–61.

5. See S. M. Lipset, *The First New Nation: The United States in Historical and Comparative Perspective* (New York: Basic Books, 1963; revised ed., New York: The Norton Library, 1979), pp. 74–98 and *passim*.

small demands, relatively unimportant ones, but as elsewhere, these deepened, not only during the Revolution, but afterwards. Revolutions, periods of turmoil, instability, have ways of extending themselves far beyond what those originally participating in them want. A good example of this is contained in the interesting correspondence between Abigail Adams and her husband concerning the rights of women. In the famous letter that Abigail wrote to John in Philadelphia in March 1776, she told him that when drafting the new code of laws,

> I desire you would remember the ladies and be more generous and favorable to them than your ancestors. Do not put such unlimited power into the hands of the husbands. Remember, all men would be tyrants if they could. If particular care and attention is not paid to the ladies, we are determined to foment a rebellion, and will not hold ourselves bound by any laws in which we have no voice or representation.
>
> That your sex are naturally tyrannical is a truth so thoroughly established as to admit of no dispute. . . . Why, then, not put it out of the power of the vicious and the lawless to use us with cruelty and indignity with impunity?[6]

John was a bit upset at receiving this letter and wrote back rejecting her advice, noting that the Revolution was disrupting all forms of authority.

> As to your extraordinary code of laws, I cannot but laugh. We have been told that our struggle has loosened the bonds of government everywhere; that children and apprentices are disobedient; that schools and colleges were grown turbulent; that Indians slighted their guardians, and negroes grew insolent to their masters. But your letter was the first intimation that another tribe, more numerous and powerful than all the rest, were grown discontented. . . . Depend upon it, we know better than to repeal our masculine systems.[7]

John Adams was opposed to a broad extension of equality, as were most of the people associated with him, but they had started something that was out of their control. It was not just out of con-

6. L. H. Butterfield et al., eds., *The Book of Abigail and John: Selected Letters of the Adams Family 1762–1784* (Cambridge, Mass.: Harvard University Press, 1975), p. 121.
7. Ibid., pp. 122–23.

trol in their period; it remained out of control, and I think still is. One has to remember that by the end of the first decade of the Republic, the conservative party, the first more right-wing party if you will, the party favored by the more elitist elements, the Federalists, which opposed the French Revolution, was declining and ultimately disappeared. The Jeffersonian Democrats who were ideologically more egalitarian and also pro–French Revolution, came to power and remained dominant. Succeeding more elite-based opponents of the Democratic party, the Whigs and the Republicans chose names that identified them with the revolutionary and Jeffersonian traditions.

The continued weakening of conservative forces and institutions may be exemplified by changes in the religious arena. British America had church establishment at the time of the Revolution, and the policy continued in many states after independence. But church establishment disappeared, and the principle of separation of church and state was accepted all over the United States. The struggle took as much as a half a century to win out. Church establishment lasted in New Hampshire until 1833.

The success of the struggle to extend manhood suffrage to all, one that succeeded in almost all the states long before any other country, indicates the strength of egalitarian and populist values in early-nineteenth-century United States. One of the best examples of the vigor of such sentiments may be found in the history of a party or a movement that failed, the Workingmen's party. It was the first party anywhere in the world that called itself a labor or workingmen's party, and it emerged in the United States. The party existed in New York, Philadelphia, Boston, and other coastal cities in the late 1820s and early 1830s.[8] It gave to Karl Marx the idea that the workers would come to class consciousness. That is, Marx developed his beliefs about working-class consciousness and the possibilities of socialism by reading about the Jack-

8. Edward Pessen, *Most Uncommon Jacksonians* (Albany: State University of New York Press, 1967), pp. 183–89; Walter Hugins, *Jacksonian Democracy and the Working Class* (Stanford: Stanford University Press, 1960), pp. 13, 18–20, 132–34.

sonian United States.[9] In later years he reminded Europeans that the United States had had socialist movements since the 1820s.[10] The Workingmen's party, of course, lasted only a few years, although it received between 15 and 20 percent of the vote in some cities. Within a few years it merged with the Democrats. (It was the first of many leftist third parties that ended up walking down the road to the Democratic party; from 1830 to 1978 that pattern seems to have been repeated almost like an invariant necessity.)

The most interesting fact about the Workingmen's party, in my judgment, is not that it was the first labor party in the world, but its radical egalitarian stance with respect to the family, one that makes the Maoist Communists appear conservative. The Workingmen were not socialists, they did not propose nationalization of property, but they sought to institutionalize extreme forms of equality of opportunity. In their documents they argued, back in the late 1820s, that given the fact of rich and poor, cultured and uncultured people, it is impossible to speak of equality of opportunity for children who start life in different family environments. They contended that equality of opportunity could not be secured by sending children to the same school, what then was called a common school, what we now call an integrated school. They said that it was not enough to send the children of the rich and the poor to the same school, since their home life remained very different and their cultural background varied greatly. The party's proposal, therefore, was to nationalize the children. That is, they proposed that *all* children, rich and poor, be required by law to attend state-supported boarding school from the age of six on, so that regardless of family background, all would have a common environment for twenty-four hours a day. They felt that this was the only way to guarantee true equality of opportunity in the race for success, although they were in favor of having a great variation in achieved income and status. This proposal ob-

9. Lewis S. Feuer, *Marx and the Intellectuals* (Garden City, N.Y.: Doubleday-Anchor Books, 1969), pp. 198–209; Maximilien Rubel, "Notes on Marx's Conception of Democracy," *New Politics* 1 (1962): 84–85.

10. Karl Marx and Friedrich Engels, *The German Ideology* (New York: International Publishers, 1960), p. 123.

viously did not have much popular appeal, but the fact that the party received as much as 15 percent of the vote in the 1820s indicates the extent to which sophisticated concerns for egalitarianism were current then, were real then—it wasn't just a "get rich quick" materialistic society.

Canada: The Counterrevolution

To turn to Canada, to what was happening north of the new border, we must first note that although not independent, it maintained continuity with North American society and polity before 1776, since the colonies had had self-government, and the population of the various provinces had absorbed tens of thousands of political emigrés.

As the country that had made the great refusal, that had refused to join the Revolution, whose peoples (some of whom were still alive in the early nineteenth century) had marched north, Canada then and Canadians ever since, to some degree or another, have had to justify the great refusal, to explain why they did not join the Revolution. Not to do something (or to do something—to look at it positively) presumably reflects a belief that the decision to refuse was morally preferable, superior to what others had done. Canadians felt that their decision or that of their ancestors was right, that there was something wrong with what the Americans had done, that there was something wrong with what the United States was like and was coming to be. Canadian spokesmen, politicians, and intellectuals emphasized the crudity of American "mobocracy," the advantages gained from liberty as distinct from democracy, subsumed in the whole complex of English values that has been referred to as elitism, but which can be seen as necessary to protect minority rights from populist excesses, an issue that also concerned Tocqueville.

Some years ago when I gave a talk at the University of New Brunswick under the title of "Rebels and Loyalists," I discovered that this ideology still lives. One of the discussants was a woman leader of the United Empire Loyalists of Nova Scotia, who very adamantly argued that her ancestors were right, that McCarthyism, political intolerance, and discrimination in the United States all were consequences of the American Revolution, that in a society with unlimited popular rule repression must occur. According to her, the British and the American Tories had fought for the protection of the right of law, of traditional values, including the rights of minorities, and of individual creativity. (She also took me to task for my limited knowledge, saying that she found it peculiar that all the people I cited in my talk were from Upper Canada. I had not realized that. The next day, much to my surprise, some students came to me and also wanted to know why I had referred only to works written by Upper Canadians. It was clear that some minority cultures still continue in Canada, even into the 1970s.)

If early American history can be written as a triumph for the more leftist Jeffersonian-Jacksonian tendencies, Canadian historians and sociologists such as S. D. Clark, A. R. M. Lower, Frank Underhill, John Porter, George Grant, and many others have suggested that the conservative forces continued to win out north of the border, up to and including the events that led up to Confederation.[11] Canada, of course, was no more homogeneous politically than the United States, but its populist reform wings lost while the equivalent groups of Americans were winning. It is interesting and important to note that in Canada many of the more populist, more democratic, more egalitarian, and proindependence groups that took various forms, such as the Mackenzie and Papineau rebellions, tended to be pro-American. The proindependence groups in Canada saw America in positive terms. They were often republicans and were in effect saying "our ancestors had made a mistake."

11. See S. D. Clark, *Movements of Political Protest in Canada* (Toronto: University of Toronto Press, 1959); idem, *Canadian Society in Historical Perspective* (Toronto: McGraw-Hill Ryerson, 1976); Frank Underhill, *In Search of Canadian Liberalism* (Toronto: The Macmillan Co. of Canada, 1960); idem. *The Image of Confederation* (Toronto: Canadian Broadcasting Corp., 1964); A. R. M. Lower, *Colony to Nation* (Toronto: Longman's, 1964); George Grant, *Lament for a Nation* (Princeton: Van Nostrand, 1965); and John Porter, *The Canadian Mosaic* (Toronto: University of Toronto Press, 1965).

National Identities

There were two nineteenth-century national self-images, the Americans on one hand glorying in the tradition of Revolution as defended or argued for in the Declaration of Independence, the Canadians defending a tradition, it must be said, of counter-revolution, of a linkup with a mother country, Britain, of elitist values. These images existed not only within North America but outside, too. In Europe the United States was looked upon as a center of what may be described as left-egalitarian populist values for much of the nineteenth century and into the early twentieth. Even various Marxists, including Marx and Engels themselves, saw the United States as the most progressive country in existence. Until World War I, the general assumption among socialists and Marxists was that the first socialist country in the world would be the United States, partly because of its democratic political background, partly because of its advanced level of economic development.[12] Lenin, for example, argued as late as 1912 that the reason socialists did so badly in the United States was that they had no issue other than socialism around which to organize support, that other political problems had been solved. He stressed, as did other radicals, that socialist parties had been built in Europe by fighting for democratic rights, for trade-union rights, for the suffrage, and the like, but that these issues did not exist in the United States.[13] American socialists, therefore, were faced with seeking support for a new abstract social system, socialism, whereas socialists in Europe won mass backing for a long program of concrete demands for democratizing their respective nations.

In discussing national images, to be honest one would have to

12. S. M. Lipset, "Why No Socialism in the United States?" in *Sources of Contemporary Radicalism*, ed. S. Bialer and S. Sluzar (Boulder, Col.: Westview Press, 1977), pp. 32–33, 48–50.

13. V. I. Lenin, "Preface to the Russian Translation of 'Letters by J. Ph. Becker, J. Dietzgen, F. Engels, K. Marx and Others to F. A. Sorge and Others,'" in V. I. Lenin, *On Britain* (Moscow: Foreign Languages Publishing House, n.d.), p. 51; *Capitalism and Agriculture in the United States of America* (New York: International Publishers, 1934), p. 1.

say that Canada did not have much of an image abroad, beyond the idea that it was a British colony, owned by Britain or controlled by Britain. Thus, the United States was seen as an independent democratic and egalitarian country, while Canada was somehow an overseas Britain. In this context, as A. J. M. Smith notes in his paper in this volume, the kind of settlers who went to the two countries, the immigrants, were probably different. Unfortunately, we know very little about this subject. There should be more research on this for both the nineteenth and the twentieth centuries. Who went to Canada compared with who went to the United States, and why? I suspect that political and value orientations were involved, particularly for people from the British Isles. Obviously many choices were unrelated to these factors —somebody you knew from your village or town lived in Toronto or Buffalo, or you had heard something about opportunities in one place or another, or you happened to know somebody who might help you out in a particular community. But a fair amount of emigration to Canada may also be related to the desire of some people from the British Isles still to be under the Queen. And conversely, others went to the United States, in part, because they were not concerned with the Queen one way or the other, or because they were interested in *not* being under the Queen. I would hypothesize that the varying national images affected the kinds of people who settled in the two countries long after their formation by rebels and tories.

There are, of course, other sources of ideological variations between the United States and Canada, which have been debated by comparative analysts of North American society. Perhaps the best-known one is *The Liberal Tradition in America,* Louis Hartz's interpretation of the United States as a nation formed in the image of late-eighteenth-century liberal conceptions, one that never developed a socialist response to industrial capitalism, because it lacked a European statist conservatism. Hartz contended that the absence of a traditional European Right in America transmuted the liberal doctrines that had formed the Revolution into conservative dogmas quite different from those of the Old World. It is impossible to build an ideological Left in the United

States because there has been no hereditary aristocracy against which to rebel and because the philosophical bases on which an ideological Left might be founded were institutionalized as part of the received liberal tradition of the country.[14] In a subsequent work, which also deals with Canada, *The Founding of New Societies*, Hartz and his protégé, the Canadian historian Kenneth McRae, treat English Canada as a liberal Enlightenment society that is not very different from the United States.[15] Hartz acknowledges, however, that Canada has a "tory touch," and McRae refers to Canadian behavior derivative from a "tory streak coming out of the American revolution."[16] More recently, Canadian political scientist Gad Horowitz, in challenging Hartz, has emphasized that unlike American antistatist, laissez-faire right-wingers, whose views reflect a liberal tradition, "Canadian Conservatives have something British and non-liberal about them . . . a touch of the authentic tory aura—traditionalism, elitism, the strong state, and so in."[17]

Some socialist writers have gone much further than Hartz in emphasizing the distinct political orientation of American society. They present a variant of the thesis, argued by Marx, Engels, and Lenin, that the United States has been the most modern, purely bourgeois culture and also the most democratic one. As the American socialist theoretician Michael Harrington has stressed, implied in the writings of Marx and others is the thesis that one of the difficulties in building socialism in America has been that "America was too socialist for socialism."[18] Harrington has called for renewed attention to the writings of an American socialist intellectual of the 1930s, Leon Samson, who in seeking to explain the weakness of socialism in America suggested that American values derived from the Revolution are, with one major exception,

14. Louis M. Hartz, *The Liberal Tradition in America* (New York: Harcourt, Brace and World, 1955).
15. Louis M. Hartz, *The Founding of New Societies* (New York: Harcourt, Brace and World, 1964), pp. 1–48.
16. Ibid., pp. 34, 239.
17. Gad Horowitz, *Canadian Labour in Politics* (Toronto: University of Toronto Press, 1968), p. 20.
18. Michael Harrington, *Socialism* (New York: Saturday Review Press, 1972), p. 111.

identical to those fostered by socialists. Samson argued that the emphasis on egalitarianism, on classlessness, and on equal social relations in the United States has meant that property relations apart (which is a big apart, obviously, for socialists, Marxists, or anybody else), the Americans think they already have what socialists want. He suggested that this is the reason for socialists' difficulty in the United States.[19] That is, the image of a good society that socialists project, property relations apart, is the image that Americans have of what their society is like, an argument that Michael Harrington accepts.

To appreciate the general thesis that the United States has been a liberal society, that it lacks a conservative segment, it is important to recognize that the term *conservatism* relates to a traditional meaning in the European and British sense, different from the way it has been used in America. Conservatives were not simply people who supported laissez-faire free enterprise against a high-tax, welfare, and planning state, but rather conservatism in its European and British origins represented the political point of view of aristocracy, monarchy, and church, of the throne-altar relationship in eighteenth- and nineteenth-century Europe, which was collectivist, corporatist, and statist. In Europe three orientations emerged, or were perpetuated, in the nineteenth century. The first was a conservative, statist, collectivist, aristocratic, noblesse oblige, tory-socialist one, which became the Bismarck-Disraeli pattern; the second was liberal in the classic Manchester liberal sense—laissez-faire, antistatist, bourgeois, competitive free enterprise and business-related; and third was the socialist, welfare-state, trade-unionist and working-class-based collectivist syndrome.

Political Developments

A perceptive effort to account for the weakness of socialism in the United States, outlined by the Fabian socialist H. G. Wells in

19. Leon Samson, *Toward a United Front* (New York: Farrar and Rinehart, 1935), pp. 1–90; see also Hermann Keyserling, *America Set Free* (New York: Harper and Brothers, 1929), pp. 237–39, 244–52.

1906, stressed that the country not only lacked a strong socialist party, but also failed to have a true conservative or Tory party. A half century before Louis Hartz, Wells linked the failure of socialism in America to the absence of conservatism. He formulated what has come to be known as the Hartz thesis, saying, "[I]t's not difficult to show, for example, that the two great political parties in America represent only one English party, the middle-class Liberal party. There are no Tories to represent the feudal system and no Labor party. . . . [T]he New World [was left] to the Whigs and Non-Conformists." He went on to argue that the absence of feudalism meant that "America is pure eighteenth century. . . . Its spirit was essentially Anarchist—the antithesis of Socialism. It was the anti-State."[20] The dominant value system, the political orientation of both major political tendencies, American political philosophy, is antistatist and individualistic. As a result, the Left in the United States has repeatedly advocated Jeffersonian individualism. Many of the Americans who are seen as leftist in the modern socialist sense turn out, when you look more deeply at them, to be antistatist. In Canada, however, which has had a statist tory tradition, twentieth-century laborites and radicals have been socialists.

Until the 1930s, the American trade union movements in both their radical (IWW) and moderate (AFL) forms were syndicalist and antistatist. Both gave expression to forms of anarchism or libertarianism, except that Samuel Gompers, the long-time head of the AFL, called it Jeffersonianism. In Canada, however, the TLC (Trades and Labour Congress), although affiliated with the AFL, has supported welfare, statist, and planning measures since early in the present century.

The most recent mass expression of American leftist protest, the New Left of the late sixties and early seventies, contained important components of antistatism and antibureaucratic individualism. Its ideology and organizational structure were closer to those of the anarcho-syndicalist IWW than to socialist or Com-

20. H. G. Wells, *The Future in America* (New York: Harper and Brothers, 1906), pp. 72–76.

munist movements. One of the most revealing episodes of that recent period, which is not widely known, occurred when New Left spokespersons such as Noam Chomsky, Marc Raskin (head of the Institute for Policy Studies, the left-wing think tank in Washington), Karl Hess, then an editor of the leftist magazine *Ramparts*, and other leftist intellectuals joined conservative (laissez-faire) economists such as Milton Friedman and Henry Hazlitt in an organization that called for reducing the size and power of the state as much as possible and for sharply reduced taxes, especially the income tax, so that people who contributed money to charity could take it straight off the taxes—that is, they could deduct 100 percent from their tax bill. These American New Leftists apparently agreed that the way to deal with the financial problems of the poor was to encourage the rich to contribute, that voluntary donations to charity are better than involving the state in welfare. So, here in the 1970s we find this kind of antistatist philosophy linked to a kind of anarchistic sentiment. It is a tribute to, or a reflection of, the continued power of individualist liberalism in the eighteenth- and nineteenth-century sense in contemporary America.

This is not to say that the United States is still a liberal society in the classic sense of the term. It is obvious that welfare-planning policies have been increasingly accepted since the 1930s. The AFL has, of course, dropped its opposition to welfare-statist policies and in many ways has become social-democratic in its orientation to economy and polity. A "Tory-Elite" as well as a social-democratic movement has emerged in the United States, but because of the nature of our party system both are within the Democratic party. One of the incongruous things about the United States has been that the Democratic coalition (that is, with a capital *D*) includes both the Tories and the Social-Democrats. It logically does so because they are both welfare statist, while the alternative Republican coalition remains more individualistic and antistatist. The problem for the Republicans is, of course, that pure individualism has declined greatly because almost everybody now wants something from the state. But emotionally many Americans still like to think they are individualists, so that Republicans still have some chance of getting elected occasionally.

In Canada, the Great Depression helped give birth to a socialist party (the Co-operative Commonwealth Federation, CCF) of some significance. But, as we know, after some forty years or more, its successor (NDP) still is a weak third party, getting about 18 percent of the vote, which is what the CCF received in 1945. But socialism, in terms of control over provincial governments and of electoral support, is much stronger in Canada than in the United States, as is traditional conservatism, in the European sense. Presthus's studies of members of legislatures, mentioned in discussion at this conference, show clearly the difference between the two countries. He finds that Canadian Conservatives, as well as Liberals, are much more favorable to using the state than are Americans comparably located on the political spectrum. This emphasis on the continued differences in values and political orientations between Canada and the United States does not, however, and is not meant to, suggest that they vary much in practice. Both countries have adopted much of the welfare-state planning policies advocated by social democratic parties in Europe.

More significantly, given the concerns of this volume, there has also been a considerable change in the self-perceptions of the two countries. Evolution has resulted in crucial changes in both countries. Earlier I suggested that the United States was perceived until World War I, and to some extent until World War II, as a center of egalitarian, populist, leftist support for democratic movements of social change, fighting what was conceived as reaction. But this image of the United States basically was challenged by the Russian Revolution. Among other things, the Russian Revolution clearly ended the Marxist assumption that the United States would be the first socialist country. It also destroyed the belief that socialism as a movement would come to power first in advanced industrial countries.

Following the Russian Revolution, the United States shifted, not only from being first in line to last (the Communists began seeing it as probably the last country that would go socialist), but also from being viewed as a leader of the Left to being seen as a defender, an exemplar, of reaction and as a leader of the Right. The criticism of the United States by people outside of it changed in direction, though often not in content. In Canada and Latin America the principal supporters of the United States before the Russian Revolution and for some time after it, tended to be the more liberal Left groups. In Canada, the CCF was largely pro-American and anti-British in the 1930s, the classic Left position, similar to that of Canadian rebels a century earlier. The Conservatives were the pro-British, anti-American party, the defenders of the great refusal. In Latin America before 1917, the conservatives, the *pensadores,* those identified with Catholic traditional thought, were very anti-American. The democrats, the liberals, the socialists were pro-American. Conservatives, north and south, criticized the United States as a crude, vulgar, materialistic, mechanical, technologically oriented society, which was unconcerned with high culture, the finer things of life, the decent things.

Today much of the criticism is the same, except that the arguments that once were advanced by conservatives are now voiced by leftists. But in their criticisms leftists do not blame populist democracy and vulgar popular taste; they hold capitalism responsible. Conversely, conservatives increasingly defend the country and culture their forebears used to attack. Many Americans, however, are either unaware of or reject this change in image. They still prefer to see themselves as citizens of a nation that defends liberty and equality against reaction, against authoritarianism. When the authoritarian threat was fascism that position was easy to hold; now that it is communism, it has become more difficult, since the Left is seen as progressive and Communists are further left than liberals. America is constantly thrust into an international role as the defender of the status quo.

There is currently an ambivalence in the American psyche as a result of confusion about itself. I think the United States is having much more of an identity crisis than Canada; however, unlike Canadians, Americans do not think in these terms. They do not ask: What is our identity? Are we a leftist nation, a rightist nation, a reformist nation, a defender of the status quo? But fundamentally, I think, many Americans are very confused about what the United States is and what it stands for abroad. This in turn affects internal domestic politics, where people line up, and how they see the potentialities for reform and change within the United States.

Canada, of course, has also changed. It was once a country whose intellectual leaders proudly identified as conservatives and elitists, on the model of Britain, which, as Claude Bissell and A. J. M. Smith have noted, rejected Whitman and accepted Wordsworth as literary models. Recently, however, many Canadians have come to see their country as being to the left of the United States. That is, they think of Canada as less elitist, less capitalist, less reactionary, less stratified. They would like to think that this is as it should be. Many Canadians increasingly are critical of the United States from the left, a fact that affects their orientation and notions of what Canada is and what Canada should be.

The Comparative Approach

I would like to end briefly with just a few points related to the value of Canadian-American comparative research for Americans. One of the advantages of being a Canadian is that willy-nilly, if you are a social scientist, a historian, or a student of culture, you are a comparativist. It is impossible for anyone to grow up and live in Canada without intimately knowing two countries, and possibly, although less likely, two linguistic cultures. The latter has clearly been less necessary than the first. Many English-Canadians and some French-Canadians do not know each other's cultures, but in general, most Canadians know almost as much, and in many cases much more, about the United States than Americans do. Hence, whenever Canadians write about Canada they are to some degree or other also contrasting Canada to the United States. If the pattern or institution with which they are dealing is different in Canada from in the United States, they are aware of the difference and they may have some hypothesis, hunch, notion, as to why it varies. If they are writing about Canadian history they know what happened in American history, in two countries whose ecological characteristics are similar, whose majority populations have common cultures, and so on. If they are interested in Canadian law, they know about American law.

Unfortunately, the reverse is not true except for a very tiny number of people, Americans who know something about Canada. I would reiterate what I have urged on many occasions, although in this volume it may look like carrying coals to Newcastle —the importance of Canadian-American comparative research. I say this although I agree with Maurice Pinard's methodological warnings about the problems of case studies. It is important to recognize that there are significant advantages in close comparisons, in comparing nations or other units that are very similar to each other, for in a certain sense it is possible to hold a number of things constant, to assume that certain aspects are almost identical. When comparing a variety of nations that have very discrete cultures, it becomes almost impossible, or it is impossible, to control enough factors, to be able to generalize about the impact of a given variable. There are not enough countries and the countries vary too much to permit the analyst to focus on a few elements. But in close two-country analyses, it is possible to compare the legal systems, to compare the police systems, to contrast the literature, to analyze family systems, and to link hypotheses about variations to assumptions about other aspects of the two cultures.

We can learn much by comparing English Canada to the United States, since these two societies are probably as close to each other culturally as any two in the world, although still different. The discussion here on the legal system would have benefited by a more detailed comparison of legal institutions and behavior of Britain, Canada, and the United States. Although as indicated by Professor Ely, the British and North American legal systems were similar after the Revolution, fairly soon afterward, the United States had many more lawyers than the British today. We have many hundreds of thousands of lawyers, while the British have fewer than fifty thousand. We have five times as many homicides as the British do, and about two and one-half times as many as the Canadians. On a number of related indicators of attitudes toward law, crime rates, use of lawyers, litigiousness, and the like, the British are low, the Americans are very high, and the Canadians are somewhere in between, varying somewhat on each indicator but still in the same relationship. It is clear that they are not like the Americans or the British; that they fall in the middle may be an example of the fact that Canadian culture and Canadian law draw on both Britain and the United States.

There are, of course, many other indicators of social structure, which similarly vary consistently in the three countries. Americans have always devoted substantially more of their resources to education than Canadians, who in turn have been more dedicated to learning for large numbers than the British. These differences continue to show up today with respect to the percent of the relevant age cohort in each country who graduate from high school or enroll in higher education. Indicators of family stability also reveal comparable variations, the most instability in the United States and the least in the United Kingdom, with Canada in the middle.[21]

The method of close comparisons may, of course, be applied to analysis of internal variations within countries. The Scots, Welsh, Irish, and English vary greatly within the British Isles. The Scots are most like North Americans, the Welsh next, with the English and Irish differing most on various dimensions. Thus, although Scotland has been much poorer than England, a much larger proportion of Scots than Englishmen have completed high school and gone to universities for a long time. Persons of Scottish descent in overseas countries differ considerably from those of English ancestry, a fact that opens another comparative dimension.

The fact of two linguistic cultures inside one Canadian nation within the environment of the Americas also offers an important

21. See my discussion in *Revolution and Counterrevolution*.

arena for comparative research, which has been largely over-
looked by the international and American scholarly world. A
cursory examination of the literature seeking to explain how and
why Quebec differs from English Canada in economy and polity
indicates that many of the explanatory hypotheses closely re-
semble, on the one hand, those suggested until recently to account for differences between France and England, and on the
other, the interpretations of the variations between Latin America
and Anglophonic North America. Studies of French-Canadian
businessmen, based on interviews, report their economic value
orientations in terms very reminiscent of analyses of Latin-
American entrepreneurs.[22] Although clearly not as unstable as
most of Latin America, Quebec has long exhibited greater symp-
toms of political instability than the English-speaking provinces.
Quebec, like the countries south of the Rio Grande, is certainly
Latin and Catholic, if these terms have any general analytic or
descriptive meaning. Writing nearly three decades ago, Pierre Elliott Trudeau noted, "French Canadians are Catholics; and Catholic nations have not always been ardent supporters of democracy.
They are authoritarian in spiritual matters; and since the dividing
line between the spiritual and the temporal may be very fine or
even confused, they are often disinclined to seek solutions in
temporal matters through the mere counting of heads."[23] Others
have pointed to the differences in the economic development of
the two Canadas, as an example of the thesis of Max Weber that
Catholic values and social organization are much less favorable
to economic development than Protestant ones have been. S. D.
Clark has suggested that "in nineteenth-century Quebec religion
was organized in terms of a hierarchy of social classes which had
little relation to the much more fluid class system of capitalism,
and sharp separation from the outside capitalist world was main-

22. See S. M. Lipset, "Values, Education and Entrepreneurship," in *Elites in
Latin America*, ed. S. M. Lipset and Aldo Solari (New York: Oxford University
Press, 1967), pp. 11–12.
23. Pierre Elliott Trudeau, "Some Obstacles to Democracy in Quebec," in
Canadian Dualism, ed. Mason Wade (Toronto: University of Toronto Press,
1960), p. 245.

tained through an emphasis upon ethnic and religious differences and through geographic isolation."[24]

Within North America, we ought to study the extent to which certain common patterns exist across the border, north-south as compared to east-west. I was talking to Martin Robin of the University of British Columbia recently, and he stressed the fact that British Columbia has the oldest tradition of strong radical socialist labor movements in Canada. But in the United States in the 1930s (here is something Canadians and Americans usually do not know), socialist factions controlled the Democratic party in Oregon, Washington, and California. In Oregon and Washington, the group that dominated the Democratic party was called the Cooperative Commonwealth Federation, a name you may have heard of. In California it was the EPIC (End Poverty in California) movement led by Upton Sinclair, who had previously run for office as a socialist. More recently, extreme left and right tendencies have both been stronger with the California Democratic and Republican parties than is true in other states. North of the border, of course, a right-wing Social Credit party confronts a left-wing New Democratic party. It seems evident that the West Coast of the United States politically has been to the rest of the United States as British Columbia has been to the rest of Canada. In like manner Saskatchewan is the home of the first elected socialist government; to the south is North Dakota, the home of the Non-Partisan League. The NPL was formed by socialists who decided in 1917 that they could do much better running within primaries of the major parties than as an independent third party. The NPL elected governors, legislators, senators, and congressmen in the 1920s and has had recurrent electoral revivals running within Republican primaries until the 1950s and within the Democratic since. The difference between the North Dakota NPL and the Saskatchewan CCF in ideology, program, and policies when in office is so slight that I defy you to demonstrate a fundamental difference, except that the Non-Partisan League

24. S. D. Clark, *The Canadian Community* (Toronto: University of Toronto Press, 1962), p. 161.

rarely uses the word *socialist*. But it nationalized property and it established the state-owned Bank of North Dakota. Dakota-Maid Flour is state owned, and there are more cooperatives in North Dakota than there are in Saskatchewan.[25]

In 1952 United States Senator William Langer, NPL leader, who first served as governor of North Dakota and was then elected for three terms to the Senate as a Republican, told Adlai Stevenson, whom he was supporting against Dwight Eisenhower, that this was the first time he had backed a Democrat for president, since previously he had always voted for Norman Thomas. Further south in the Wheat Belt, we may note that the two senators from South Dakota are named McGovern and Abourezk. As you know, these are the two most left-wing senators.

On another level, Quebec and the American South offer possibilities for comparative analyses. Both are "conquered provinces," which have perceived themselves as socially, economically, and politically oppressed by a more powerful and more numerous cultural group. Each may be described as a subculture that, compared to the dominant one, has been relatively underdeveloped economically, has lacked a stable democratic system, and has had special and peculiar relations to the national two-party system. But there the obvious similarities end, since one is French and Catholic, the other Anglo-Saxon and Protestant; the climates and agricultural systems vary; and the black-white relationship within the South, with blacks the numerical minority, is different from the English-French one in Quebec where the economically weaker group is in the majority. Yet there are enough similarities in the cultural, economic, and political behavior of French Canada and the American South to suggest that comparative research on these two "conquered" regions could contribute much to our understanding of the reactions of cultural minorities within complex societies.

There is a clear similarity between the relative position of regions in Canada and the United States. Canada has five dis-

25. S. M. Lipset, *Agrarian Socialism: The CCF in Saskatchewan* (Berkeley: University of California Press, 1950, rev. ed. 1971).

tinct regions, which are very different from each other. The United States has regions that (except for the South and North) do not look as different, but still, as the Dakota and West Coast examples suggest, comparable elements of social and economic structure and other aspects, produce common patterns within the two countries. It is possible, therefore, to extend a comparative analytic framework as well as evidence by looking north and south of the border, at units that are comparable.

The chapters in this volume well illustrate some of the advantages of comparative North American scholarship. Unfortunately, however, Canada still remains the unknown country to most American scholars. Not enough has been done to take advantage of the magnificent comparative laboratory that the Americas provide social scientists and humanists. Let us hope that those who gather a hundred years from now to analyze three centuries of revolution and counterrevolution will be overwhelmed by the intellectual abundance that can be found in Canadian-American studies.

4

Law in a Republican Society: Continuity and Change in the Legal System of Postrevolutionary America

James W. Ely, Jr.

Reformers of the Jacksonian period had no difficulty in singling out the survival of English laws in the United States as a major grievance. "Instead of living under British laws after we had thrown off the government which produced those laws," Frederick Robinson declared, "we should have adopted republican laws, enacted in codes."[1] Such complaints echoed the cry of an influential Boston pamphleteer in 1786: "Why should these States be governed by British laws? Can we suppose them applicable to the circumstances of this country? Can the monarchical and aristocratical institutions of England be consistent with the republican principles of our constitution? Why should a young Republic be ruled by laws framed for the particular purpose of a monarchical government. . . ?"[2] Similarly, Governor John Tyler of Virginia complained to his state's legislature about "the unfortunate practice of quoting lengthy and numerous British cases; the time of the court being taken up in reconciling absurd and contradic-

---

The author wishes to acknowledge the research assistance of Simon Kimmelman, a student at Vanderbilt Law School.

1. Frederick Robinson, "An Oration Delivered before the Trades Union of Boston," in *Social Theories of Jacksonian Democracy*, ed. Joseph L. Blau (New York: Hafner Pub. Co. 1947), p. 331. See also Frances Wright, *A Course of Popular Lectures* (New York: Office of the Free Enquirer, 1829), and Stephen Simpson, *The Working Man's Manual* (Philadelphia: Thomas L. Bonsal, 1831), pp. 35–37.

2. Honestus, *Observations on the Pernicious Practice of the Law* (1786), reprinted in *American Journal of Legal History* 13 (1969): 244, 257.

tory opinions of foreign judges which certainly can be no part of an American judge's duty."[3]

To these commentators the republican character of American society seemed threatened by the lingering influence of English law once political independence had been achieved. Critics of English law drew upon the heady nationalism of the postrevolutionary period, which produced a natural suspicion of foreign authority in the United States. This was fused with a reformist concern to simplify the law so that it could be more readily understood.

In a sense such concern was misplaced. Most legal historians would agree with William E. Nelson's view that there is no evidence that any of the men who led America into the Revolution intended to change fundamentally the legal system.[4] On the contrary, many Americans saw the Revolution as a struggle to affirm, not overthrow, traditional English legal guarantees. Still, revolutionary movements do not always proceed as anticipated and the currents of popular unrest might well have been expected to engulf English law as a relic of monarchy. The purpose of this paper is to explore the impact of the American Revolution upon the legal system of the newly independent United States. We shall first consider the effect of the Revolution upon the substantive content of the law and then probe the consequences for the legal profession.

Substantive Law

Changes occurred in many areas of law following the Revolution, but one should take care not to overstate the degree of alteration or even to attribute that alteration necessarily to the Revolution. Legal experimentation and innovation had taken

---

3. Lyon G. Tyler, *The Letters and Times of the Tylers,* 2 vols. (Richmond: Whittet & Shepperson, 1884), 1:260.
4. William E. Nelson, *Americanization of the Common Law: The Impact of Legal Change on Massachusetts Society, 1760–1830* (Cambridge, Mass.: Harvard Univ. Press, 1975), p. 67.

place during the colonial period and doubtless would have continued even without a revolution.

There was considerable interest in constructing a new system of penal law. Criminal prosecutions for sexual offenses grew less frequent—a trend that had first appeared in the late colonial period—and the authorities turned their attention to crimes against property.[5] This de-emphasis of prosecutions for immorality reflected a decline in the sense of community responsibility for personal transgressions. Another result of the Revolution was heightened concern for procedural due process in criminal cases; courts construed technical requirements strongly in favor of the accused. "The Revolutionary leaders," Lawrence M. Friedman stressed, "quite naturally identified oppression with abuse of criminal law, and identified the rights of man with basic rights to fair criminal trial."[6] During the postrevolutionary period, Pennsylvania led a movement to revise the widespread reliance upon capital and corporal punishments as criminal sanctions. Pennsylvania reduced the number of capital crimes, established degrees of murder, and introduced confinement in a penitentiary as a substitute punishment.[7] Other states gradually followed Pennsylvania's lead, but a few, headed by South Carolina, resisted the reform drive and adhered for decades to the eighteenth-century scheme of punishments.[8]

To what extent the Revolution produced this shift in the penal laws and enforcement attitudes cannot be determined with certainty, but it appears that other factors were more influential. Pennsylvania's Quakers had long stressed the redemptive possibilities of criminals, and as early as 1682 William Penn unsuccessfully sought to abolish capital punishment except for the

5. Ibid., 110–11.

6. Lawrence M. Friedman, *A History of American Law* (New York, 1973), pp. 248, 133.

7. Edwin R. Keedy, "History of the Pennsylvania Statute Creating Degrees of Murder," *University of Pennsylvania Law Review* 97 (1949): 759; David B. Davis, "The Movement to Abolish Capital Punishment in America, 1787–1861," *American Historical Review*, 63 (1957): 23.

8. Jack K. Williams, *Vogues in Villainy: Crime and Retribution in Ante-Bellum South Carolina* (Columbia, S.C.: University of South Carolina Press, 1959).

crime of murder.[9] Then, too, the reform philosophy of Cesare Beccaria was popular among American intellectuals on the eve of the Revolution.[10] Probing the rationale for punishing criminals, Beccaria rejected retribution in favor of the deterrent effect that would result from the certainty of punishment. He urged a graduated scale of punishment commensurate with the harm done to society. Beccaria was cited frequently by proponents of a revised criminal law, with Robert J. Turnbull crediting "the small and invaluable gift of the immortal Beccaria to the world" as a major influence for reform.[11] Beccaria's impact, of course, was international in scope, with Catherine the Great, Maria Theresa, the Grand Duke of Tuscany, and Voltaire among those who were impressed by his analysis of criminal penalties. There was nothing unique in America's uneven progress toward reform. The Revolution removed the imperial veto that tied the colonies to the traditional English criminal sanctions and left Americans free to act in the area of criminal justice. Nonetheless, the intellectual and religious basis for reform was in the formative stage before the break with the mother country and received no more than a final push from the Revolution.

The law of real property was central to an eighteenth-century society in which land represented the primary source of wealth. This matter was particularly sensitive to the colonists, since many of them came to America in order to obtain greater access to land ownership. It is not surprising that much of English real-property law was transplanted to these shores. Thus, the English law of tenure, whereby, at least in theory, landholders held title under the king as overlord, was recognized in most colonies. There were also partially successful attempts to impose a quitrent system, under which an annual rent was imposed on the grant of a tract

9. Keedy, "Pennsylvania Statute," pp. 760–64.
10. Marcello Maestro, *Cesare Beccaria and the Origins of Penal Reform* (Philadelphia: Temple University Press, 1973), pp. 137–43; Comment, "The Eighth Amendment, Beccaria, and the Enlightenment: An Historical Justification for the Weems v. United States Excessive Punishment Doctrine," *Buffalo Law Review* 24 (1975): 783, 806–15.
11. Robert J. Turnbull, *A Visit to the Philadelphia Prison* (Philadelphia, 1796), p. i.

of land. More controversial was the introduction of primogeniture, a device designed to restrict land in favor of a single family heir, and the fee tail, a scheme to maintain land within family lines.[12] Historians differ over the extent to which colonists actually employed primogeniture and entail,[13] but such practices were repugnant to many Americans, who saw them as badges of the aristocratic land order they sought to escape.

Professor Friedman has aptly noted that "[l]and-law reform was well under way even before the Revolution."[14] New Englanders started the process of repudiating undesirable features of English law in the seventeenth century. They favored partible inheritance with an equal distribution of land upon death rather than primogeniture.[15] Moreover, the Massachusetts Code of 1648 declared that "all our Lands and Heritages" were free of such feudal incidents as fines, wardships, and escheats.[16]

With this background it was inevitable that the Revolution would stimulate a drive to eliminate the aristocratic features of real-property law. By statute or judicial decision most jurisdictions severed any tenurial relationship for American landowners and substituted allodial ownership, in which land was held absolutely in one's own right and not in that of any superior.[17] "The title of our lands," Judge Jesse Root of Connecticut boasted

12. James A. Casner, ed., *American Law of Property*, 7 vols. (Boston: Little, Brown 1952), 1:54–64; Richard B. Morris, *Studies in the History of American Law* (New York: Columbia University Press; London: King, 1930), pp. 69–125; Beverley W. Bond, *The Quit-Rent System in the American Colonies* (New Haven: Yale University Press, 1919); James Sullivan, *The History of Land Titles in Massachusetts* (Boston: I. Thomas and E. T. Andrews, 1801).

13. Some scholars have argued that entail and primogeniture were not in fact widely employed in Virginia and did not perpetuate a landed elite. See Robert E. Brown and B. Katherine Brown, *Virginia, 1705–1786: Democracy or Aristocracy?* (East Lansing, Mich.: Michigan State Univ. Press, 1964), pp. 80–92; C. Ray Keim, "Primogeniture and Entail in Colonial Virginia," *William and Mary Quarterly* 25, 3rd ser. (1968): 545.

14. Friedman, *A History of American Law*, p. 205.

15. George L. Haskins, "The Beginning of Partible Inheritance in the American Colonies," *Yale Law Journal* 51 (1942): 1280.

16. Max Farrand, ed., *The Laws and Liberties of Massachusetts* (Cambridge, Mass.: Harvard University Press, 1929), p. 32.

17. Robert Fowler, *History of the Law of Real Property in New York* (New York: Baker, Voorhis & Co., 1895), pp. 79–85; *Wallace v. Harmstad*, 44 Pa. St. Rev. 492, 500–503 (1863).

in 1798, "is free, clear and absolute, and every proprietor of land is a prince in his own domains, and lord paramount of the fee."[18] Following Virginia's lead in 1776,[19] most states that had not previously done so abolished fee tail and primogeniture. Although the importance of these steps was probably more symbolic than practical, such a conclusion does not denigrate their significance. Chancellor James Kent of New York perceived a connection between republicanism and the free alienation of land:

Entailments are recommended in monarchical governments, as a protection to the power and influence of the landed aristocracy; but such a policy has no application to republican establishments, where wealth does not form a permanent distinction, and under which every individual of every family has his equal rights, and is equally invited, by the genius of the institutions, to depend upon his own merit and exertions.[20]

At the same time, the abolition of certain features of English real-property law should not obscure the fact that the English concept of estates in land, dower, curtesy, the Statute of Uses, and technical rules governing future interests were readily accepted as the basis of American land law.

Another legal reform emanating from the Revolution was the initial movement to abolish slavery. A paradox of colonial society, Edmund S. Morgan has noted, was that American freedom and independence depended in large measure upon the coerced labor of others.[21] Of course, the Revolutionary War was not waged to end bondage, and many prominent slaveholders supported the patriot cause. The Declaration of Independence contained no mention of emancipation, and Thomas Jefferson proposed language to condemn King George for inciting slaves to rise against their masters.[22] Still, in the 1770s a growing number of Americans

18. Jesse Root, *Reports* (Conn., 1798), 1:39.
19. Virginia abolished entail in 1776, 9 Hening, *Statutes at Large of Virginia*, 226, and primogeniture in 1785, 12 Hening, *Statutes*, 138.
20. James Kent, *Commentaries on American Law*, 4 vols. (New York: O. Halsted, 1827–30), 4:20.
21. Edmund S. Morgan, "Slavery and Freedom: The American Paradox," *Journal of American History* 59 (1972): 5.
22. Julian P. Boyd, ed., *The Papers of Thomas Jefferson* (Princeton: Princeton University Press, 1950–), 1:426.

were bothered by the inconsistency between Negro slavery and allegations of a British conspiracy to enslave the colonies. Further, many felt that slavery was a serious blemish on the republican ideal. David Brion Davis cogently observed, "If the American Revolution could not solve the problem of slavery, it at least led to a perception of the problem."[23]

Nonetheless, historians must be careful not to exaggerate the force of antislavery sentiment. Most Americans were unconcerned about the philosophical conflict between revolutionary ideology and slavery, and southern planters did not relinquish their bondsmen. Indeed, widespread public hostility to a 1782 Virginia statute merely allowing private manumissions caused a strenuous effort to repeal the measure, and manumission continued to be unusual.[24] South Carolina retained its harsh slave code from the colonial period.[25] During the postrevolutionary era slavery was abolished in Pennsylvania and New England, never areas with a large servile population. Not only was antislavery success confined geographically, it was also limited by a commitment to gradualism, respect for the property rights of masters, and the general desire to discipline potentially disruptive behavior of freed blacks.[26] For example, Pennsylvania's 1780 emancipation statute appealed directly to the spirit of the Revolution—"in grateful commemoration of our own happy deliverance from that state of unconditional submission, to which we were doomed by the tyranny of Britain"—but adopted a gradual scheme. The law applied only to the future generation of slaves, born after its effective date, and then postponed freedom until the age of twenty-eight in order to reimburse their masters for the expense of raising them.[27] The ultimate end was freedom, but the process

23. David B. Davis, *The Problem of Slavery in the Age of Revolution, 1770–1823* (Ithaca, N.Y.: Cornell University Press, 1975), p. 285.
24. Fredrika Tente Schmidt and Barbara Ripel Wilhelm, "Early Proslavery Petitions in Virginia," *William and Mary Quarterly* 30, 3rd ser. (1973): 133.
25. James W. Ely, Jr., "American Independence and the Law: A Study of Post-Revolutionary South Carolina Legislation," *Vanderbilt Law Review* 26 (1973): 939, 952.
26. Davis, *Slavery in the Age of Revolution*, pp. 303–42.
27. *Laws of the Commonwealth of Pennsylvania* (Philadelphia: J. Bioren, 1810), 1:339; Robert M. Cover, *Justice Accused: Anti-slavery and the Judicial Process* (New Haven: Yale Univ. Press, 1975), pp. 62–67.

of emancipation and the judicial construction of the statute emphasized the master's property interests.

Nor was the situation much different in other northern states. The obscure path of emancipation in Massachusetts has long perplexed historians. The Massachusetts Constitution of 1780 declared, "All men are born free and equal, and have certain natural, essential, and unalienable rights," and three years later Chief Justice William Cushing instructed a jury that slavery was inconsistent with that constitution.[28] Although the effect of this case was to undercut the legal sanction for slavery, it did not lead to immediate abolition. Slavery evidently lingered in Massachusetts for several years.[29] Highlighting the caution of northern legislators, in 1788 New York, the most important slave state outside the South, enacted a new slave code, which renewed the legal basis for human bondage. Not until 1799 could reluctant lawmakers be persuaded to accept a gradual emancipation plan under which rights to existing slaves were protected.[30] In short, although there was unmistakable progress, a wide disparity remained between revolutionary idealism and social and economic reality, a gap reflected in the general conservatism of slavery statutes. Anthony Benezet, a Quaker reformer, lamented in 1783 that it was "sorrowfully astonishing that after the declaration so strongly and so clearly made of the value and right of liberty on this continent, no state but that of Pennsylvania and that imperfectly, have yet taken a step towards the total abolition of slavery."[31]

The Revolution also left a lasting imprint on American thinking about the relationship between law and extralegal force. Preceded by a decade of riots and mob activity, the Revolution was a striking example of violence as a purposive weapon of protest

28. Cover, *Justice Accused,* pp. 43–49; John D. Cushing, "The Cushing Court and the Abolition of Slavery in Massachusetts: More Notes on the 'Quock Walker Case,'" *American Journal of Legal History* 5 (1961): 118; Arthur Zilversmit, "Quock Walker, Mumbet, and the Abolition of Slavery in Massachusetts," *William and Mary Quarterly* 25, 3rd ser. (1968): 614.

29. Nelson, *Americanization of the Common Law,* p. 102; Arthur Zilversmit, *The First Emancipation: The Abolition of Slavery in the North* (Chicago: Univ. of Chicago Press, 1967), pp. 115–16.

30. Zilversmit, *First Emancipation,* pp. 146–52, 176–84.

31. As quoted in Davis, *Slavery in the Age of Revolution,* pp. 317–18.

and change.[32] Indeed, Richard M. Brown has maintained, "Among the intellectual bequests of the American Revolution has been the precept that violence in a good cause pays, a lesson that has been well learned by Americans. In our enthusiasm, we have found many good causes, and, in emulation of the Revolution, we have turned frequently to violence in our pursuit of them."[33] To be sure, the colonies had long manifested a rebellious and anti-authoritarian spirit, but the success of the Revolution solidified this sentiment into a permanent attitude. The revolutionary generation was particularly creative in fashioning an intellectual justification for violence, linking the concept of popular sovereignty by the majority to summary justice and the meanest sort of violence. The long history of vigilantes and extralegal force, either to supplement or to obstruct law enforcement, attests to the violent legacy of the revolutionary era.

Rather than maintain that the Revolution caused these shifts in law and legal thinking, one might more accurately conclude that the break with England terminated the royal negative and facilitated greater innovation in American law. The substantive areas in which the law was changed were those concerning which the colonists had long shared strong concern. Developments in other fields, such as the emergence of the business corporation after 1800, related more to changing economic circumstances than to revolutionary theory.[34] Indeed, corporate law grew from English provisions governing municipal and charitable institutions.

It seems evident that the colonists were not displeased with the bulk of English law and everywhere accepted it as the foundation of American justice. There were constant efforts to establish

32. Hillier B. Zobel, *The Boston Massacre* (New York: W. W. Norton, 1970); Pauline Maier, "The Charleston Mob and the Evolution of Popular Politics in Revolutionary South Carolina, 1765–1784," *Perspectives in American History* 4 (1970): 173.

33. Richard M. Brown, *Strain of Violence: Historical Studies of American Violence and Vigilantism* (New York: Oxford Univ. Press, 1975), p. 42.

34. J. Willard Hurst, *The Legitimacy of the Business Corporation in the Law of the United States, 1780–1970* (Charlottesville, Va.: University Press of Virginia, 1970), pp. 1–12; Joseph S. Davis, *Essays in the Earlier History of American Corporations*, 2 vols. (Cambridge, Mass., 1917), 2:3–6.

English law throughout the colonial period.[35] In fact, the revolutionary generation viewed itself as the legitimate heir of traditional English law and liberty in the fight against a corrupt king and Parliament.[36] The Continental Congress in 1774 resolved "That the respective colonies are entitled to the common law of England."[37] Immediately following the Declaration of Independence, most jurisdictions adopted new constitutions or statutes that carefully guaranteed the right to indictment by a grand jury, trial by jury, habeas corpus, and the privilege against self-incrimination.[38] Hymns to the common law regularly appeared in postrevolutionary legal literature. Declaring that "[t]he common law of England is a highly improved system of reason, founded on the nature and fitness of things, and furnishes the best standard of civil conduct," Zephaniah Swift of Connecticut observed in 1795, "At the late revolution, when we were separated from the British empire, the general consent and approbation of the people established the common law of England, as far as it is warranted by reason, and conformable to our circumstances, to be the law of the land."[39]

In a similar vein, the various states enacted provisions that governed the extent to which English law was henceforth to be binding. While reception measures varied, the Delaware Constitution of 1776 was fairly typical: "The common law of England, as well as so much of the statute law as has been heretofore adopted in practice in this state, shall remain in force unless they shall be altered by a future law of the Legislature, such parts

35. George Dargo, *Roots of the Republic: A New Perspective on Early American Constitutionalism* (New York: Praeger, 1974), pp. 53–76.
36. Bernard Bailyn, *The Ideological Origins of the American Revolution* (Cambridge, Mass.: Belknap Press, 1967), pp. 30–31.
37. Worthington C. Ford, ed., *Journals of the Continental Congress, 1774–1789* (Washington, D.C.: U.S. Govt. Print. Off., 1904), pp. 63–73.
38. A. E. Dick Howard, *The Road from Runnymede: Magna Carta and Constitutionalism in America* (Charlottesville, Va.: Univ. of Va. Press, 1968); Leonard W. Levy, *Origins of the Fifth Amendment: The Right against Self-Incrimination* (New York: Oxford Univ. Press, 1968), pp. 368–432; Richard D. Younger, *The People's Panel: The Grand Jury in the United States, 1634–1941* (Providence, R.I.: Brown Univ. Press, 1963), p. 37.
39. Zephaniah Swift, *A System of the Laws of the State of Connecticut*, 2 vols. (Windham, Conn.: John Byrne, 1795), 1:41–42.

only excepted as are repugnant to the rights and privileges contained in this Constitution."[40]

Unhappily, the status of English law in postrevolutionary America could not be settled so easily as such measures seemed to suggest. What did the English common law include? Which portions of common law were inconsistent with American constitutions and customs? The problem regarding English statutes was even more vexing. Widespread doubt existed throughout the United States over which English laws were in force and which were not.[41] "The laws," a South Carolina attorney complained, "are in a very confused and uncertain state—the best lawyer does not really know what is law at present."[42] So perplexing was the situation in Pennsylvania that in 1807 the legislature directed the judges of the Supreme Court to report "which of the English statutes are of force in this Commonwealth, and which of those statutes in their opinion ought to be incorporated into the statute laws of this Commonwealth."[43] Yet the overriding significance of the reception measures is their legal conservatism and continuity with the past. Even amid the turmoil of the Revolution, legislators decided to fashion American law from familiar English precedents.

Despite modification in some areas, the content of most of the substantive law supports the impression of stability in the law. Hence, the poor laws,[44] the regulations governing indentured

40. Article 25, Constitution of Delaware, 1776, in *The Federal and State Constitutions*, 7 vols., ed. Francis N. Thorpe (Washington: U.S. Govt. Print. Off., 1909), 1:566–67.

41. The most satisfactory examination of the reception of English statutes is Elizabeth G. Brown, *British Statutes in American Law, 1776–1836* (Ann Arbor, Mich.: University of Michigan Law School 1964); for Virginia's effort to define the laws in force, see Charles T. Cullen, "Completing the Revisal of the Laws in Post-Revolutionary Virginia," *Virginia Magazine of History and Biography* 82 (1974): 84.

42. Joseph W. Barnwell, ed., "Diary of Timothy Ford, 1785–1786," *South Carolina Historical Magazine* 13 (1912): 199.

43. *Statutes at Large of Pennsylvania* (Harrisburg: C. M. Busch, 1915), 18: 518–19; *The Report of the Judges of the Supreme Court*, 3 Binney's Reports (Pa. 1808), 593.

44. New York, for example, substantially reaffirmed colonial relief practices and endeavored to adapt the English poor laws to American conditions. Raymond A. Mohl, *Poverty in New York, 1783–1825* (New York: Oxford Univ. Press, 1971), pp. 51–61.

servants, debtor-creditor relations,[45] and the status of women[46] were unchanged by the Revolution. An effort to introduce French civil law as a supplement to, if not a substitute for, English law aroused the interest of a few intellectuals, but received scant support from the bulk of lawyers and judges.[47]

With such a heavy reliance on both the statute and the common law of England, the rulings of English courts would obviously furnish important decisional guides. Nevertheless, one is struck by the frequent, almost routine, citations of English cases by American courts of the postrevolutionary period. Virginia and South Carolina judges, for instance, commonly resorted to English decisions and treatises during this era.[48] Judge Spencer Roane of the Old Dominion remarked in an 1804 opinion that "the English law and ours are precisely the same on the subject: nay, I have even taken my ideas upon the subject entirely from the English authorities."[49]

Everyone agreed that English decisions since the Revolution had no binding force in American jurisprudence, but such rulings were influential with American courts as evidence of the principles of common law. This aroused the latent prejudice against foreign law. "The absolute authority of recent English adjudica-

45. A student of credit relationships in the United States recently concluded, "The Revolution did not change relationships between debtors and creditors in any fundamental respect" (Peter J. Coleman, *Debtors and Creditors in America: Insolvency, Imprisonment for Debt, and Bankruptcy, 1607–1900* [Madison: State Historical Society of Wisconsin, 1974], p. 16).
46. Nelson, *Americanization of the Common Law*, pp. 103–4.
47. Peter Stein, "The Attraction of the Civil Law in Post-Revolutionary America," *Virginia Law Review* 52 (1966): 407.
48. M. Leigh Harrison, "A Study of the Earliest Reported Decisions of the South Carolina Courts of Law," *American Journal of Legal History* 16 (1972): 51; William B. Stoebuck, "Reception of English Common Law in the American Colonies," *William and Mary Law Review* 10 (1968): 393, 423–26. I am indebted to a former student, Donald Morton, for his assistance in furnishing data on the use of English precedents in Virginia courts.
49. Read v. Read, 5 Call 160, 212 (Va., 1804); see also Roane's explanation of the role of English precedents in Baring v. Reeder, 11 Va. 154 (1806). In the same period Chancellor Kent observed, "But whatever may be our opinions on the point, as an abstract question, or whatever may be the decisions of the civil law, or the feudal and municipal law of other countries, we must decide this question by the common law of England" (Frost v. Raymond, 2 Caines [N.Y., 1804] 188, 191).

tions is disclaimed," C. J. Ingersoll lamented in 1823, "but they are received with a respect too much bordering on submission."[50] This attitude produced legislation that sought to curtail the citation of English decisions following the Revolution. Starting with New Jersey in 1799, several states passed statutes that prohibited attorneys from citing any English legal authorities since July 1776.[51] But recent English law was not easily banished, and such statutes were circumvented and finally repealed.

Nothing better illustrated the affinity of Americans for English law than the enormous popularity of British text writers, particularly William Blackstone, in the postrevolutionary era. In Blackstone's *Commentaries on the Laws of England* Americans found a readable and compact statement of English common law. Despite some failings, Blackstone skillfully presented the common law as a reasoned system that secured the public welfare. American editions of Blackstone appeared in 1771 and 1773, but copies of his work were available here earlier.[52] Since he familiarized Americans with their rights under English law, Blackstone unwittingly helped pave the way for the Revolution. His biographer observed, "It is one of the strange paradoxes of history that Blackstone, who believed so strongly in limited monarchy, should have aided a rebellion against his country and the establishment of republican government in America."[53] The Revolution notwithstanding, the *Commentaries* rapidly became the most widely used legal textbook in the United States, and a mastery of Blackstone was considered essential for the practice of law. Not only was Blackstone cited more frequently than any other author in the postrevolutionary period, but he impressed James Kent, John

50. C. J. Ingersoll, *A Discourse Concerning the Influence of America on the Mind* (Philadelphia: A. Small, 1823), p. 35.
51. Charles Warren, *A History of the American Bar* (Boston: Little, Brown, & Co. 1911), pp. 232–33; Friedman, *History of American Law*, pp. 97–98.
52. Julius S. Waterman, "Thomas Jefferson and Blackstone's Commentaries," *Illinois Law Review* 27 (1933): 629; David A. Lockmiller, *Sir William Blackstone* (Chapel Hill: Univ. of No. Car. Press, 1938), pp. 169–90; Dennis R. Nolan, "Sir William Blackstone and the New American Republic: A Study of Intellectual Impact," *New York University Law Review* 51 (1976), p. 731.
53. Lockmiller, *Sir William Blackstone*, p. 173.

Marshall, Joseph Story, and Daniel Webster, leaders of the bench and bar in another generation.

So pervasive was Blackstone's influence on the legal profession that Thomas Jefferson lamented that when "the honied Mansfieldism of Blackstone became the student's horn-book, from that moment, that profession (the nursery of our Congress) began to slide into toryism, and nearly all the young brood of lawyers now are of that hue."[54] Another Virginian, St. George Tucker, was induced to publish in 1803 a republicanized edition of Blackstone, which noted the references to obsolete and inapplicable English statutes.[55] While most Americans avoided Blackstone's monarchist leanings, his work popularized a traditional view of English law and insured its acceptance among attorneys and judges.

Nor was Blackstone the only English author cited by Americans in the years following independence. In 1788 Judge John F. Grimké of South Carolina asserted that "the respectable names of Coke, Hawkins, Hale, Bacon, and many others, who have written on the laws of England, must ever be revered in this State, for their sound doctrine and liberal philanthropic sentiments."[56]

The Legal Profession

Historians have often stressed the popular hostility toward the bar that surfaced in the wake of the Revolution. One can readily find expressions of antilawyer sentiment in the postrevolutionary era. In 1786 the town of Braintree, Massachusetts, adopted a resolution:

We humbly request that there may be such Laws compiled as may crush or at least put a proper check or restraint on that order of

54. Thomas Jefferson to James Madison, 17 February 1826, in Andrew A. Lipscomb and Albert E. Bergh, *The Writings of Thomas Jefferson*, 20 vols. (Washington: U.S. Govt. 1904), 16:156.
55. St. George Tucker, *Blackstone's Commentaries*, 5 vols. (Philadelphia: W. Y. Birch & A. Small, 1803); Charles T. Cullen, "St. George Tucker and Law in Virginia, 1772–1804," (Ph.D. diss., University of Virginia, 1971).
56. John F. Grimké, *The South Carolina Justice of the Peace* (Philadelphia: R. Aitken & Son, 1788), p. viii.

Gentlemen denominated Lawyers the completion of whose modern conduct appears to us to tend rather to the destruction than the preservation of this Commonwealth.[57]

Similarly, in his *Letters from an American Farmer*, Hector St. John Crèvecoeur, a Frenchman living in New York, declared:

Lawyers are plants that will grow in any soil that is cultivated by the hands of others, and when once they have taken root they will extinguish every vegetable that grows around them. The fortunes they daily acquire in every province from the misfortunes of their fellow citizens are surprising. The most ignorant, the most bungling member of that profession will, if placed in the most obscure part of the country, promote litigiousness and amass more wealth than the most opulent farmer with all his toil.[58]

There was also resentment against the domination of public office by attorneys. A Charleston resident warned his fellow citizens against electing attorneys in an 1786 municipal canvass, "Shun all lawyers, as they are more liable to corruption than other men; they being used to argue for Wrong, as well as Right, when paid for so doing."[59]

A more difficult task is to explain this negative attitude toward the legal profession and to assess its impact on the actual workings of the legal system. It is important to remember that lawyers have never been liked by the American public. As early as 1640, John Cotton, a Boston minister, reproached "unconscionable Advocates" who "bolster out a bad case by quirks of wit, tricks, and quillets of Law."[60] During the seventeenth century colonies from Massachusetts to Georgia attempted either to prevent or to limit the practice of law. A 1641 Massachusetts statute stipulated that attorneys could not receive compensation for advocacy, and the number of lawyers in seventeenth-century America was never

57. Charles Francis Adams, *Three Episodes of Massachusetts History*, 2 vols. (Boston: Houghton, Mifflin & Co. 1892), 2:897.
58. J. Hector St. John de Crèvecoeur, *Letters From An American Farmer* (London: J. M. Dent & Sons, Ltd., 1782; New York: E. P. Dutton, 1912), p. 196.
59. *Charleston Evening Gazette*, 25 August 1786.
60. Thomas Lechford, *Plain Dealing: or Nevves From New England*, edited by J. Hammond Trumbull (Boston: J. K. Wiggin & W. P. Lunt, 1867), p. 68.

large.[61] This antilawyer sentiment was muted during much of the eighteenth century but flared anew in the turbulent decade after 1783. Traditional explanations have emphasized the toryism of a large segment of the bar. While many prominent attorneys, John Adams and Alexander Hamilton among them, supported the Revolution, an estimated one-fourth of the prewar bar joined the Tory exodus. In addition, the unsettled economic conditions of the postrevolutionary period produced a flood of lawsuits to collect debts, enforce contracts, and foreclose mortgages. Public discontent with these economic problems was easily fastened upon lawyers as a class.[62] Maxwell Bloomfield has recently suggested another interpretation for the unpopularity of attorneys: "For in the face of a primitivist ideology, the lawyer of the early republic represented, above all else, the force of civilization. Armed with his Blackstone and Coke, he invaded the wilderness to impose artificial constraints upon the anarchy of nature, transferring to frontier areas all the machinery of coercion familiar to the most sophisticated European governments."[63]

Critics of the legal profession urged that arbitration or simplified court proceedings be substituted for litigation. In Massachusetts Benjamin Austin called for reformation of the legal system along the following lines:

1. Encourage parties to refer suits to referees for a binding determination.
2. "That instead of the numerous codes of British laws, which are now introduced into our Courts, we should adopt a concise system, calculated upon the plainest principles, and agreeable to our Republican government."
3. Encourage the parties to present their cases in person, but if a

61. W. H. Whitmore, *The Colonial Laws of Massachusetts* (Boston: Published by order of the city of Boston, 1889), p. 39; Warren, *History of the American Bar*, pp. 5–10.
62. Richard E. Ellis, *The Jeffersonian Crisis: Courts and Politics in the Young Republic* (New York: Oxford Univ. Press, 1971), pp. 112–16.
63. Maxwell Bloomfield, *American Lawyers in a Changing Society, 1776–1876* (Cambridge, Mass.: Harvard University Press, 1976), p. 41.

party wishes counsel, allow such individuals to be "heard by any friend they may choose to employ."[64]

Jesse Higgins of Delaware authored a widely read pamphlet, *Samson Against the Philistines*, in 1805. Stressing the delays, expense, complicated pleadings, and confusion of judicial proceedings, he advocated compulsory arbitration upon the request of either party to a dispute.[65]

Despite these hostile comments and reform proposals, one cannot help but concur with Bloomfield's assessment of "the general failure of antilawyer efforts to achieve enduring results in these years."[66] No state adopted the arbitration schemes popularized by Austin and Higgins, although Pennsylvania experimented to a limited extent with arbitration. Such reform proposals raised the sensitive issue of trial by jury, and many voices spoke out in defense of this prized institution. "The Trial by Jury," one contemporary argued, "was the Birth-right of our American ancestors; and is secured as a Constitutional Right, to every citizen of the United States."[67] Even as the legal profession was being assailed, lawyers were regularly elected to public positions and increasingly replaced lay judges on the bench. Moreover, attorneys never lacked vocal champions. In 1803 an anonymous Pennsylvanian asserted, "Nothing is more certain, then, that envy, resentment and malice, are the great sources of this hostility towards lawyers, and all that are connected with the courts of law in the administration of justice. And these hateful passions we know, are principally confined to weak and licentious characters."[68]

Some states made modest strides toward meeting the grievances

64. Honestus, *Observations*, p. 267.
65. Jesse Higgins, *Sampson Against the Philistines, or the Reformation of Lawsuits* (Philadelphia: William J. Duane, 1805); Henry C. Conrad, *History of the State of Delaware*, 3 vols. (Wilmington: Henry C. Conrad, 1908), 2:529–30.
66. Bloomfield, *American Lawyers in a Changing Society*, pp. 53–54.
67. *Observations on the Trial by Jury: with Miscellaneous Remarks Concerning Legislation and Jurisprudence* (Philadelphia: Brown & Bowman, 1803), p. 71. Similarly, a municipal court in Charleston was subject to frequent criticism because it sat without a jury. James W. Ely, Jr., "Charleston's Court of Wardens, 1783–1800: A Post-Revolutionary Experiment in Municipal Justice," *South Carolina Law Review* 27 (1976): 645, 656.
68. *Observations on the Trial by Jury*, p. 24.

against lawyers. For example, in 1785 and 1786 Massachusetts enacted statutes to limit the number of attorneys that a party could retain, presumably an attempt to reduce both the cost of litigation and the advantages of the wealthy. Yet all efforts to regulate lawyers' fees were frustrated during these years.[69] The judiciary helped to undercut reform legislation, and the attorneys retained their professional monopoly.

The outbreak of the Revolution only temporarily interrupted the professionalization of the bar. Bar associations had been established in the major cities during the colonial era and, despite some bitter criticism, they continued to flourish once independence was secured. Gerard W. Gawalt's study of Massachusetts lawyers noted the appearance of new county bar associations after the Revolutionary War.[70] These organizations sought to maintain the occupational monopoly of lawyers and to restrict entry into the legal profession. Seeking to fulfill its plan for a self-regulated profession of gentlemen, the Suffolk County Bar Association enforced educational requirements and limited the number of law students. Although opponents denounced the monopolistic character of bar associations and even alleged that such groups secretly decided the outcome of cases, the organized bars in Massachusetts easily triumphed over proposals to abolish them. The Revolution did not halt the legal profession's drive for greater status and autonomy.

In one area of professional concern the Revolution provided the impetus for an important reform. Judicial opinions in eighteenth-century America were neither collected nor published. Hence counsel were compelled to rely upon their loose recollections of earlier cases or upon reported English cases. This not only compounded the confusion in the law in the United States but also left attorneys and judges dependent upon English authorities. The growth of a distinctly American law was retarded by the absence of authoritative court reporting. William Cranch

69. Gerald W. Gawalt, "Massachusetts Lawyers: A Historical Analysis of the Process of Professionalization, 1760–1840" (Ph.D. diss., Clark University, 1969), pp. 55–57; Nelson, *Americanization of the Common Law*, p. 69.

70. Gawalt, "Massachusetts Lawyers," pp. 33–90.

spoke for many when he observed, "Much of that uncertainty of the law, which is so frequently and perhaps so justly the subject of complaint in this country, may be attributed to the want of American reports."[71]

The initial moves toward the establishment of court reporting in the United States took place in Connecticut. A 1784 statute required judges to file written opinions, and "thereby a foundation be laid for a more perfect and permanent system of Common Law in this State."[72] Four years later Ephraim Kirby, a former officer in the Continental army and a country lawyer, privately published the first collection of cases, known as *Kirby's Reports.*[73] Kirby's motives for this venture were varied. He hoped to secure professional recognition and reap a financial reward, but he had reform objectives as well. Kirby recognized that "[t]he uncertainty and contradiction attending the judicial decisions in this State have long been subjects of complaints."[74] Moreover, he desired to hasten a distinctly American system of jurisprudence by lessening dependence upon English precedents. Within a few years after the appearance of Kirby's volume, judicial decisions were published in Pennsylvania, Vermont, and Virginia.[75]

Conclusion

While stressing the ambivalence of the American revolutionary experience, R. R. Palmer pointed out, "it must be admitted that the Americans, when they constituted their new states, tended to reconstitute much of what they already had."[76] Palmer's comment

71. I Cranch (5 U.S.) iii.
72. "An Act Establishing the Wages of the Judges of the Superior Court," *Session Laws of Connecticut,* May 1784.
73. Alan V. Briceland, "Ephraim Kirby: Pioneer of American Law Reporting, 1789," *American Journal of Legal History* 16 (1972): 297.
74. Kirby, *Reports* (Conn. 1789), iii.
75. The problem of legal uncertainty was also reflected in the compilation and revision of state statutes during the postrevolutionary era. Charles M. Cook, "The American Codification Movement: A Study of Antebellum Legal Reform" (Ph.D. diss., University of Maryland, 1974), pp. 39–48.
76. R. R. Palmer, *The Age of Democratic Revolution,* 2 vols. (Princeton, N.J.: Princeton University Press, 1959), 1:232.

would seem to apply with full force to the legal system. Aside from a relatively few areas in which the law had long been viewed as inapplicable to American conditions or repugnant to the republican spirit, the American revolutionaries made no major changes in their legal code. A 1783 South Carolina statute neatly captured this fundamentally conservative philosophy: "That all fines and penalties inflicted, or made payable by any of the Acts herein before mentioned to the use of the King of Great Britain are hereby directed to be paid into the public treasury of this State for the use of the same."[77] Law in a republican society was remarkably similar to that of a monarchy.

77. Thomas Cooper, *Statutes at Large of South Carolina* (1836–1841) (Columbia, S.C.: John W. Denny, 1868), 4:542. In a similar vein, Richard B. Morris concluded, "Save for minor reforms, such as the abolition of slavery and a slight modification of the laws of descent and distribution, the War of Independence had virtually no effect upon the system of private law administered in New England" (Richard B. Morris, "Legalism versus Revolutionary Doctrine in New England," *New England Quarterly* 4 (1931): 195, 214).

5

Organized Politics and Political Temper:
Predisposing Factors and Outcomes

Henry S. Albinski

In contemporary nation-states, an important function of political parties is to provide linkages between individuals and groups on the one hand and centers of decision-making authority on the other. Parties can be regarded both as recipients and as donors in the political process. They are molded by the milieu from which they spring. In turn, through their own dynamic, they influence policy outputs and generally affect systemic outcomes. It is good to remember that parties do not behave as they do simply because they are outgrowths of the community's political culture. Giovanni Sartori has urged, "We should pay more attention to the manipulative aspects of politics, whereas we have recently yielded too much to the social-determinist and also to a somewhat cultural-determinist point of view. If we attempt to explain everything in terms of the political culture, then we are likely to reach the conclusion that what happens is, or was, inevitable."[1]

While bearing this caveat in mind, we shall nevertheless focus on the relationship between historical/cultural forces and the character and contributions of the Canadian and American party systems. We freely admit not only that other, "manipulative" factors have shaped these two party systems, but also that the tracing of linkages between predisposing historical/cultural forces

---

1. Giovanni Sartori, "European Political Parties: The Case of Polarized Pluralism," in *Political Parties and Political Development*, ed. Joseph La Palombara and Myron Weiner (Princeton: Princeton University Press, 1966), p. 166.

and party qualities is often an inferential enterprise, suggestive rather than firmly demonstrable. More particularly, we will take up the premise that America's revolutionary experience and Canada's evolutionary experience have mattered in coloring the two party systems. Our analysis will be informed not only by whether one nation sprang from revolution and the other from evolution, but also by the circumstances surrounding these ostensibly different developmental patterns.

The analysis will cover four party-system dimensions: growth and salience, character and scope of roles performed, style and appeal, and programmatic outputs and systemic outcomes. Initially, we will try to identify those dominant values and historical experiences that may be thought to underlie each of these four features of Canadian and American party life.

Party Growth and Systemic Salience

Assessing revolutionary-evolutionary influences upon party-system origins and consolidation helps to set the foundation for much that follows. There is no doubt that an identifiable party system materialized in the United States before one did in Canada, whether we calculate by a purely temporal criterion or by some such standard as rate of emergence following self-government. Parties are, in fact, widely regarded as an American invention. There were no modern, stable political parties in the American colonies, but existing factional groups already contained important, preparty properties.[2] An elaborate, fully articulated "second" American party system was built by the 1830s. But the displaced "first" system of Federalists and Republicans, and then Republicans essentially without effective opposition, had been a genuine system of parties in its own right as early as the presidential election of 1800. It is argued that the second, highly sophisticated

2. See, for instance, Alison G. Olson, *Anglo-American Politics 1660–1775: The Relationship between Parties in England and Colonial America* (New York: Oxford University Press, 1973), and Bernard Bailyn, *The Origins of American Politics* (New York: Knopf, 1968), pp. 59–105.

system was facilitated because "the first parties had been built upon a modern and rationalized basis rather than on traditional or merely personal foundations."[3] In Canada, both before and after the 1837 rebellions, and then after Union but before Confederation, politics were highly factional and groupings often proved ephemeral. It took some time for Nova Scotia and New Brunswick Members of Parliament to associate themselves with a mainstream party system, to abandon their roles as opponents of Confederation or simply as "ministerialists." Not until the 1878 election was there more or less a party system in place, with candidates seeking election on the basis of party pledges. Indeed, Frank Underhill does not identify the emergence of a "national" party system until the end of the nineteenth century, when Laurier's Liberals caught up with the Conservatives as a broadly competitive party.[4]

One explanation for these American-Canadian differences is basically noncultural but nonetheless related to contrasts in political growth. The American Revolution created a new nation-state. After a very brief flirtation with the Articles of Confederation, those who had made the Revolution and their immediate successors were able to build a constitutional system to their liking, and the system was retained thereafter. The Revolution and the Constitution became important symbolic underpinnings in popular American mythology. Canada, on the other hand, underwent up to five political orders before it entered sovereign nationhood. First was the representative government period from 1791 to Union; then the years following Union but still short of responsible government; then Union with responsible government; then Confederation, followed by many years before the achievement of sovereign status. Although the Maritimes acquired representa-

3. William N. Chambers, *Political Parties in a New Nation: The American Experience* (New York: Oxford University Press, 1963), p. 16.
4. Frank H. Underhill, *In Search of Canadian Liberalism* (Toronto: Macmillan, 1960), pp. 21–42, 164–66. Also see Escott M. Reid, "The Rise of National Parties in Canada," Canadian Political Science Association, *Papers and Proceedings* 4 (1932): 187–200. However, note the argument that there was a party system by 1837 in Charles H. A. Mair, "The Development of Canadian Parties to 1864" (Master's thesis, University of Saskatchewan, 1931), esp. "Conclusion," pp. 150–54.

tive government in the eighteenth century, they were not organically joined to a greater Canada until Confederation. In other words, the context in America provided continuity for party-system maturation. In Canada, frequent shifts in the governmental ground rules inhibited party development. Much of the organized political controversy until the 1820s was, in fact, over remedies for shortcomings in the governmental system, rather than over a range of public policy issues as such.

We also look to more subtle qualitative features of the two national experiences. One perspective is developmental. Louis Hartz, for instance, has argued that, because American society lacked a feudal component, a revolutionary tradition based on fundamental social collision did not develop. As a result, there was no counterimpulse of reaction.[5] Organized politics could take deeper root in a composed environment, where secular and participant political culture traits were already evident. Hence Samuel Huntington's conclusion that "American parties . . . directly reflect the nature of political modernization in America. They were created in the United States before they appeared elsewhere as a response to the earlier expansion of political participation there."[6] Analogously, William Chambers has shown that viable party life in late-eighteenth-century America sprang up first where (as in Pennsylvania) there was the highest degree of differentiation in the interplay of interests, and the fewest traces of "old patterns of domination by great families and clique politics."[7]

In Canada, such predisposing factors were less pure or less abundant. The insertion of American loyalists, the entrenchment of powerful family compact oligarchies, the restraints imposed by

5. Louis Hartz, *The Liberal Tradition in America: An Interpretation of American Political Thought Since the Revolution* (New York: Harcourt, Brace and World, 1955), and Louis Hartz, *The Founding of New Societies: Studies in the History of the United States, Latin America, South Africa, Canada, and Australia* (New York: Harcourt, Brace and World, 1964), esp. pp. 69–122.

6. Samuel P. Huntington, *Political Order in Changing Societies* (New Haven: Yale University Press, 1968), p. 131.

7. William N. Chambers, "Parties and Nation-Building in America," in La Palombara and Weiner, *Political Parties*, p. 83. Also see the conclusions of Richard Buel, Jr., *Securing the Revolutionary Ideology in American Politics, 1789–1815* (Ithaca: Cornell University Press, 1972), summation on pp. 1–7.

a British imperial presence, helped to induce a touch of tory qualities of limitation and hierarchy. More of this later. We should also be mindful that Canada has always been a plural and sectionalized society and that its French population for a long period reflected stratified and indeed quasi-feudal tendencies. These factors, all evolutionary in nature, depressed the rapid development of a confident, congealed party system.

One way or another, both English and French elements came to accept a more precautionary social order than had emerged in postrevolutionary America. Kenneth McRae has suggested that the loyalists' liberal orientations were diverted through acquiescence in oligarchic government, to avoid the risk of mob rule in the perceived American style. On their part, the French Canadians closed ranks against alien ways after the Conquest, thereby weakening the impulse of popular institutions and of competitive politics.[8]

These American-Canadian contrasts were themselves affected by the presence or absence of a revolutionary tradition in the two communities. The American Revolution, while not launched as a socially reordering event, served as a touchstone for legitimizing democratic ideals. It thereby helped to mobilize support and to energize party life, relative to overcoming remnants of oligarchic tendencies. Very shortly after the Revolution, at federal and state levels, a powerful wave of libertarian, reformist change took place in landholding, ecclesiastical status, suffrage, and decriminalization. Such developments were in turn a natural goad on behalf of more popularly constituent politics and thereby on behalf of party-system building.[9]

8. Kenneth D. McRae, "The Structure of Canadian History," in Hartz, *Founding of New Societies*, pp. 219–74. See Gad Horowitz's examination of these and other Hartzian interpretations in "Conservatism, Liberalism, and Socialism in Canada: An Interpretation," *Canadian Journal of Economics and Political Science* 32 (1966): 143–71, and his *Canadian Labour in Politics* (Toronto: University of Toronto Press, 1968), esp. pp. 3–57. For an old but still useful commentary on French-Canadian outlooks in the late eighteenth century, see Victor Coffin, *The Province of Quebec and the Early American Revolution: A Study in English-American Colonial History* (Madison: University of Wisconsin Press, 1896).

9. See especially J. Franklin Jameson, *The American Revolution Considered as a Social Movement* (Princeton: Princeton University Press, 1926).

Canada lacked this kind of trigger. Its political development was not only evolutionary, but came to include the memory of the defeated 1837 risings. It is true that the events of 1837 eventually speeded up the goal of responsible government. They also helped to accent the impulses behind the Rouges and the Clear Grits in the 1850s and a shift from oligarchic to more democratic values. But it should also be remembered that, in the aftermath of the American Revolution, the British reasoning that found its way into the Constitutional Act of 1791 was that the Revolution had occurred because of too much, rather than too little, democracy.[10] When responsible government came, it was not as a glamorous revamping of the machinery of government, but rather as an adjustment in its uses. Both responsible government and Confederation were as much results of British convenience as of a ground swell of Canadian pressure. A Canadian liberal ethic was of course not out of view up to the middle of the nineteenth century. The pre-1837 reform groups in both the upper and the lower provinces had a share in this spirit. There was a Jeffersonian-Jacksonian impulse behind the Mackenzie and the Papineau rebellions, and it is wrong to assume that, by 1837, the French-Canadian public as a whole was indifferent toward socioeconomic reform or toward organizing for political action.[11]

Still, as we have suggested, the liberal impulse was weaker than in America, and the flowering of a party system was accordingly inhibited. The trend was reinforced early in Canada by "anti-party" sentiments as such; it had a brief vogue in America, but then passed. The essential point about Canada is that after

10. In this vein, see A. R. M. Lower, *Colony to Nation: A History of Canada* (Toronto: Longmans, 1946), esp. pp. 124–26.

11. For suggestive assessments, see Fernand Ouellet, "Le Nationalisme canadien-français: De ses origens à l'insurrection de 1837," in *Constitutionalism in Lower Canada*, ed. Ramsay Cook (Toronto: University of Toronto Press, 1969), pp. 1–16, and Fernand Dumont, "Idéologie et conscience historique dans la société canadienne-française du XIXe siècle," in *Les idéologies québécoises au 19e siècle*, ed. Jean-Paul Bernard (Montréal: Les Éditions du Boréal Express, 1973), pp. 61–82. For English expressions, see Richard J. Ossenberg, "The Conquest Revisited: Another Look at Canadian Dualism," *Canadian Review of Sociology and Anthropology* 4 (1967): 201–18, and S. D. Clark's observations in his *Movements of Political Protest in Canada 1640–1840* (Toronto: University of Toronto Press, 1959), pp. 100–102.

the Revolution and the creation of a new government in America, tory elements and the British authorities cultivated the impression that democracy was synonymous with maddening factionalism, republicanism, and even annexation. Parties, especially since they came to be identified with "reform" prior to the rebellions, were thereby portrayed as mischievous, not "natural." It was harder for parties to crystallize, to legitimize themselves, when moving under a cloud of disloyalty. Indeed, what one author has described as Upper Canada's first party (1805), lent itself to this impression in that it was dominated by Irishmen who drew on Ireland's unhappy conflict with Britain and bitterness toward it.[12] With Lord Elgin's acquiescence in the Rebellion Losses Bill and other factors, the stigma of party illegitimacy was removed by the 1850s, and even old tories came to appreciate the need for a *public* political appeal. But the impulse of a suspect *popular* democracy kept its hold for some time; witness the very leisurely pace, even after Confederation, at which universal manhood suffrage was extended, and the propertied, appointive character of the Canadian Senate.

America had begun its experience on an anti-party note. The tone of opinion in prerevolutionary America was that a well-ordered polity was free of party spirit; the representational good lay in the comprehension of interests, not in adversarial groups. Madison, Washington, and others who defended the new constitutional document conceived of party in the older, loose, factional/divisive sense. They did not comprehend a modern party system. The Revolution and the new national experience seemed to call for men of good will, not of party (faction). While Madison's tenth Federalist paper acknowledged that "faction" could not be stifled, faction should and could be contained. The checks and balances of the Constitution were in part designed to frustrate domination by faction. This reasoning, as E. E. Schattschneider noticed, left a great "blank spot" between "the sovereign people and the government which [became] the habitat of

12. Harry H. Guest, "Upper Canada's First Political Party," *Ontario History* 54 (1962): 275–96.

parties."[13] Anti-party sentiment was seemingly strengthened by the often vicious recriminations between Republicans and Federalists in the 1790s, each side accusing the other of subverting the new, fragile republic.[14]

But perceived threats to the new republic weakened. The peaceful transfer of political power in the 1800 presidential election had a calming effect. Rapid organization for political purposes converted the older, notionally baneful parties into something more acceptable, more in accord with ascendant libertarian values and the spread of antiprivilege legislation, and construed as instruments for securing checks in the system. Party growth and the popularization of an already generous suffrage, the extension of elective offices and such measures as de facto popular presidential elections, reinforced one another. In America, popular government became the norm. In Canada, America's popular style was often portrayed as and believed to be unpalatable. One result was delayed legitimization of popular party life.

When Canadian party life had become legitimized, Canadian-American distinctions in public perceptions and expectations of organized politics remained. Writing well into the twentieth century, Lord Bryce saw Americans as almost superstitiously devoted to popular sovereignty. The people's power was just as effective in Canada, but there "neither the idea in theory nor its application in the incessant exercise of voting power has possessed any special fascination."[15] Important, mid-nineteenth-century events in both countries are in this regard worth recounting. Before the American Civil War, some who feared for the South's interests reexamined the Jeffersonian view that the majoritarian principle had become a desirable part of the party system ethos.

13. E. E. Schattschneider, *Party Government* (New York: Rinehart, 1942), p. 15. On views of precolonial factions, see George A. Dargo, *Roots of the Republic: A New Perspective on Early American Constitutionalism* (New York: Praeger, 1974), esp. pp. 146–53.

14. See John R. Howe, Jr., "Republican Thought and Political Violence of the 1790s," *American Quarterly* 19 (Summer 1967): 147–65.

15. James Bryce, *Modern Democracies*, rev. ed. (New York: Macmillan, 1924), 1:495.

In this sense, Calhoun's spokesmanship was anti-party and dualist rather than pluralist in temper. Depreciations of true liberty, engendered by a numerical (rather than concurrent majority) principle, were exacerbated "by the violent party struggles incident to them."[16] But the American pre–Civil War debate was conducted within the ambit of differing interpretations of the Constitution as a given. After the Civil War, nullification was laid to rest. The liberal-democratic assumptions of organized politics—themselves an outgrowth of the revolutionary tradition—were restored as an operative principle of party life.

The appearance of Confederation at this time was not associated with either any widening of self-government or an alteration of Canada's continued, nonsovereign status. Confederation was an evolutionary, very nearly administrative step. The moving forces behind Confederation centered on Macdonald and the Conservatives, who became the new dominion's first ruling party. Macdonald did not share Hamilton's disdain for the common people, but he was Hamiltonian in his political conceptions. In the post-1867 context, this meant that "party," while an appropriate and necessary thing, was as much guide and teacher as an emanation of some popular will. The Liberals were more Jeffersonian in their outlook, drawing on their Parti Rouge and Clear Grit ancestry. But, as seen, they did not establish themselves as a major party force until well after Confederation, after the political tone had been set by the Conservatives. Moreover, a major thrust of Confederation was the promise of securing certain *group*, rather than individual, rights. As such, this did not impugn the salience, or importance, of Canadian parties, but it did suggest a variation on the view of party that was found in the more popular and individualistic American culture. Among the Québécois, the element most eager to protect group rights, Confederation was very carefully weighed. There was apprehension that even under

16. John C. Calhoun, *A Disquisition on Government and Selections from the Discourse*, ed. C. Gordon Post (New York: Liberal Arts Press, 1953), p. 46. Also, see the interpretation in Richard Hofstadter, *The Idea of a Party System: The Rise of Legitimate Opposition in the United States, 1780–1840* (Berkeley: University of California Press, 1969), pp. 252–56.

a federal arrangement electoral politics could produce majorities in Ottawa hostile to French group interests. Cartier turned the party argument around, noting that "there would always be French Canadians in the cabinet and they would be backed by a phalanx of sixty-five French-Canadian votes in the House of Commons."[17] Partially as a reflection of their attraction to group/ parochial rather than popular/universalistic outlooks, it is the Québécois who among present-day Canadians hold the lowest sense of interparty difference and have the highest proportion of nonparty identifiers.

Consonant with Bryce's characterization, the Confederation process was also suggestive of the lower key, almost *counter-revolutionary* political temper exhibited by Canada in its party life and otherwise. Negotiations over a suitable governmental instrument were capped by a *British* Act, and not in the aftermath of a popular, revolutionary stroke. An important incentive for Confederation was fear of being absorbed by or at least being excessive hostage to the United States. The Civil War was thought to have been made possible by a combination of weak central authority and boisterous party politics. Confederation was not popularly ratified by the Canadian people, and no libertarian charter such as a bill of rights was written. Such steps would have been un-British (and therefore to an extent un-Canadian), and no compelling popular ethos demanded them. What there had been of a "system of parties" prior to Confederation had not been informed by such an ethos, and party development after the British North America Act did not draw upon any powerful impulse of this kind.

Both Canada and the United States have known "anti-party" movements during the past century. These movements have had features in common, but their nuances suggest something about the standing of parties generally and of their cultural and historical inheritances in the two countries. In both places, by the late nineteenth and early twentieth centuries there were allegations

17. Ramsay Cook, "Quebec and Confederation Past and Present," *Queen's Quarterly* 71 (Winter 1964): 471.

of party unresponsiveness and corruption, and remedies were urged. But the American reform movement *accomplished* more than its Canadian counterpart in such forms as initiative and referendum, recall, American party primaries and the popular election of the United States Senate. Also, the American populist/ progressive era impulse was somewhat more comprehensive than its equivalent in Canada, where the phenomenon was very largely Western and agrarian. America's popular ethos was stronger than Canada's, and the culture was more participatory and less impressed by the symbolic authority represented by organized parties and their elites. Prairie discontent critical of established parties spilled out in part because the region was new to Canada and different in composition, not part of the founding core. It did not share the more limitational, cautious inheritance of the central and Maritime provinces, their more settled and charter-group populations, or familiar routines of the Conservative-Liberal dialogue. The Canadian Nonpartisan League was less effective than its American namesake, which it sought to emulate. Movements that began as hostile to the idea of a party role even for themselves, as in Alberta under Henry Wise Wood, were very soon, for all practical purposes, transformed into parties.[18]

Party-System Roles

The nature of nonparty group inputs is itself a scale on which to assess party-system roles. In both Canada and the United States, group interests are significant, as would be expected in modern, open societies. But a few special notes are in order, especially about Canada. Robert Presthus, for instance, has drawn attention to the relatively low decision-making autonomy of the

18. On these phenomena, see, for instance, Paul F. Sharp, *The Agrarian Revolt in Western Canada: A Survey Showing American Parallels* (Minneapolis: University of Minnesota Press, 1948); Austin Ranney, *Curing the Mischiefs of Faction: Party Reform in America* (Berkeley: University of California Press, 1975), and Ranney's earlier *The Doctrine of Responsible Party Government*, 2nd ed. (Urbana: University of Illinois Press, 1964). A brief, but forceful, comparative statement on the American populist roots as derivative from revolutionary experience is found in John L. Finlay, *Canada in the North Atlantic Triangle: Two Centuries of Social Change* (Toronto: Oxford University Press, 1975), pp. 226–37.

Canadian cabinet (a *party*-dominated body), because of the lace-work of accommodative transactions among legislative, bureau-cratic, and interest-group elites. Among contributing reasons, he identified Canada's historically counterrevolutionary, ascriptive strain.[19] Also to be reckoned with are influential structures that have weakened pride of place for parties—for instance, until recently the Roman Catholic church in Quebec. It is also worth considering Seymour Martin Lipset's view that particularistic, third-party manifestations across Canada have been "consistent with the assumption that Canada is more particularistic (group attitude conscious) than the seemingly more universalistic United States."[20] In both nations, the role of "party" in any unified and comprehensive sense has been further reduced by federalism, which has fostered distinctive state/provincial or sectional party-system qualities. For various reasons, in Canada public-policy decisions are more conspicuously the result of provincial-federal bargaining (i.e., outside conventional party sites) than is found in state-federal bargaining in the United States.[21] A good recent example is the negotiating over the amendment and repatriation of the British North America Act. Despite differences among provincial and federal spokesmen as to terms, there has been general agreement that an election fought on the issue would be uncalled for and divisive. Kenneth McNaught reminds us, how-ever, of the relative weakness of the Canadian judiciary as a posi-tive social instrument, certainly as compared with the United States. For McNaught, a corollary of this in Canada is suspi-cion of politics outside their proper, party-parliamentary sphere. Mainly responsible is the familiar refrain of ascriptiveness in the culture. "We have certainly shown deference to the concept of

---

19. Robert Presthus, *Elite Accommodation in Canadian Politics* (London: Cambridge University Press, 1973), p. 62. The elite symbiosis is also a dominant theme in John Porter, *The Vertical Mosaic: An Analysis of Social Class and Power in Canada* (Toronto: University of Toronto Press, 1965).
20. Seymour Martin Lipset, "Revolution and Counter-Revolution—The United States and Canada," in *The Revolutionary Theme in Contemporary America,* ed. Thomas R. Ford (Lexington: University of Kentucky Press, 1965), p. 38.
21. A key study is Richard Simeon, *Federal-Provincial Diplomacy: The Making of Recent Policy in Canada* (Toronto: University of Toronto Press, 1972).

established authority and procedures and even to the legal idea that valid authority flows downward from the crown."[22]

The roles of party systems can, moreover, be viewed from the perspective of load burdens. Both party systems carry socio-economic management roles. Everett Ladd's description is that in America, "the party system was never asked to *effect* sweeping social change," and has been well suited to a national political system "in which the principal impetus for modernization comes from outside government, in which conflict over social change is minimal."[23] The same is essentially true for Canada, although there the party system from 1867 shouldered a burden of nation building not duplicated in the United States. Canada after 1867 still had to develop a sense of community and of national identification and to engage itself self-defensively in a program of economic growth that was unnecessary during the early, post-revolutionary years in America. Canada had to work this out in an environment less congenial than the American, taking stock of an ambiguous destiny rather than of the confident sense of "mission" that has colored American thought.[24]

The American party system has had to deal with crises of systemic legitimacy. Up to the Civil War, however, resistance movements generally operated within accepted authority structures or (as in Shay's Rebellion) were generally condemned. The Civil War was an acute example of party-system failure to accommodate. But even that conflict's prologue was bruited about in terms of how to steer an existing constitutional order, and systemic continuity was reinforced in the Civil War's aftermath.[25]

22. Kenneth McNaught, "Political Trials and the Canadian Political Tradition," in *Courts and Trials: A Multidisciplinary Approach,* ed. Martin L. Friedland (Toronto: University of Toronto Press, 1975), p. 138.

23. Everett C. Ladd, Jr., *American Political Parties: Social Change and Political Response* (New York: Norton, 1970), p. 45.

24. The destiny-versus-mission distinction is from W. L. Morton, *The Canadian Identity* (Toronto: University of Toronto Press, 1965), p. 86.

25. On crises and conflicts, see Paul Goodman, "The First American Party System," in *The American Party Systems: Stages of Political Development,* 2nd ed., ed. William N. Chambers and Walter D. Burnham (New York: Oxford University Press, 1975), pp. 58–65; Daniel Boorstin, *The Genius of American Politics* (Chicago: University of Chicago Press, 1953), esp. pp. 99–132; Robert A. Dahl, *Pluralist Democracy in the United States: Conflict and Consensus* (Chicago: Rand McNally, 1967), pp. 282–301.

The United States has not had to face a genuine systemic crisis in the past century. In Canada, parties have had to cope with potential systemic crises on and off throughout the post-1867 period. Confederation began amidst Nova Scotian and New Brunswick misgivings over whether these provinces should participate at all. For a time there was preoccupation about annexation, and there has been recent feeling in the Prairies about leaving Canada. French Canada has had abiding worry, with such crises as the two conscription controversies and current separatism.

In this sense, the Canadian party system has had to carry a heavier burden, at times approaching overload. Yet John Meisel has pleaded that the parties must persevere. Since the country lacks a strong *national* culture, parties must be agents for creating viable national symbols. "An absolutely critical latent function of the party system in Canada is . . . the role it plays in the development and fostering of a national political culture; it must play a vital role, in fact, generating support for the regime. So few other institutions do so and . . . few are as well suited for this task as the parties."[26]

Party-System Styles and Appeals

By comparative standards, the party systems of both Canada and the United States are widely regarded as stylistically accommodationist and pragmatic. Various mechanical and structural factors work in this direction. Among them are first the postelectoral procedures, federalism, and the institution of the American presidency. Also, in Maurice Duverger's meaning, there is the fact that both party systems originated and were molded as art-of-the-possible, "parliamentary" groups, rather than as extraparliamentary movements attempting to wedge their way into entrenched regime politics.[27] Our focus, however, remains on cultural/historical constraints.

26. John Meisel, "Recent Changes in Canadian Parties," in *Party Politics in Canada*, 2nd ed., ed. Hugh G. Thorburn (Scarborough: Prentice-Hall, 1971), p. 34.

27. See Maurice Duverger, *Political Parties: Their Organization and Activity in the Modern State* (London: Methuen, 1954), esp. pp. xxiii–xxxvii.

With hindsight, we can suggest that the accommodationist tone in both party systems was influenced by patterns of who governed at key developmental stages. After the American Revolution and the adoption of the Constitution, it probably was helpful that the Federalists, with their emphasis on national consolidation, had a turn in office. It was also helpful that their tenure was relatively brief and was followed by a lengthy period of government under the Republicans, who were more supportive of dominant, universalistic outlooks among the populace, yet who drew on some Federalist precedents in nation building. The principal sponsors and principal early rulers of a confederated Canada were the Conservatives. They were guided by a nation-building impulse. They mixed French and English clienteles and combined the liberal and the tory streaks that had entered Canada's political culture. We have seen that their opposition, the Liberals, became a fully competitive national party only after Laurier had neutralized the more "radical" (i.e., less centrist and less accommodationist) Rouges and Clear Grit elements in the party. The accommodationist style was also implanted into Canada's post-Confederation party system because the early ranking party leaders, especially from Quebec, were "national patriots." Later they became more narrow "nationalists."[28]

Looking at the two political leadership traditions at large, it would seem that Canada is more hospitable to a low-key, mannered, accommodationist style than is the United States. The American popular ethos has been suspicious of "men on horseback," and has taken up the myth of government under law rather than of men. But it has not repudiated charismatic personalities. The Canadian style is more comfortable with leaders than with passionate, popular politics. But it has been more comfortable with group, collective "heroes" such as the Hudson's Bay Company, the Royal Canadian Mounted Police, grain growers' associations, etc., than with individual heroes, since its "environment

---

28. This point is especially made by George Heiman, "The 19th Century Legacy: Nationalism or Patriotism?" in *Nationalism in Canada*, ed. Peter Russell (Toronto: McGraw-Hill, 1966), p. 338.

was to be mastered more by organization than by men."[29] Even more directly pertinent to the theme of this paper, Roger Graham has argued that Canada has lacked charismatic leaders (Aberhart perhaps being the chief exception) because it has lacked a revolutionary movement or a major socioeconomic transformation and because its consistently ambiguous identity has affected political confidence.[30] A collateral sign of accommodationist politics in the two nations is the relative frequency with which ranking politicians have shifted from one party to another. The phenomenon has been especially striking in Canada. Two of the leading candidates at the 1976 Progressive-Conservative convention, Hellyer and Wagner, were former Liberals of high standing.

In both countries, though in somewhat different configurations, crosscutting cleavages have encouraged adjustive, accommodationist politics. In America, in the first half of the nineteenth century, politics were constrained by the broadly gauged spirit of public confidence and nation building and by the absence of an autocratic tradition, or reaction to autocracy. In Canada, where gradualism and a tory touch were featured, concrete concerns such as responsible government, sectional accommodation, and national unity were addressed, as opposed to abstractions.

We now need to identify some of the concerns that in both societies may have helped to induce a pragmatic and incremental political style. The systemic consequences of such politics we defer until later.

The sectional diversity of both nations, while imposing strains, has also fostered bargaining values. In the years immediately preceding the Civil War, American politics became severely sectionalized and remained so for generations. The South stood out, owing to its relatively agrarian, submodern, and racially grounded

29. Robin Winks, *The Myth of the American Frontier: Its Relevance to America, Canada and Australia,* Sir George Watson Lecture (Leicester: Leicester University Press, 1971), p. 26.

30. Roger Graham, "Charisma and Canadian Politics," in *Character and Circumstance: Essays in Honour of Donald Grant Creighton,* ed. John S. Moir (Toronto: Macmillan, 1970), pp. 22–36. Comparatively, see Dennis H. Wrong, *American and Canadian Viewpoints* (Washington, D.C.: American Council on Education, 1955), pp. 31–34.

characteristics.[31] But until the 1850s American politics were not markedly sectional, and there was broad party-political accommodation to the mainsprings of the revolutionary-constitutional legacy. While accommodation between the South and the rest of the country remained weak after the Civil War, it was at least tolerable, because the party system could operate in highly decentralized fashion apart from the quadrennial presidential elections. In Canada, even allowing for federalism, national politics under cabinet government required more attention to cohesive party effort. Cultural/historical forces produced a more complex system of sectionally identifiable cultural values in Canada than within the more emphatically American "mosaic." From the early stages of Canada's organized political experience, before Confederation, Union demanded close French-English cooperation, as, for instance, in the resort to the "double majorities" of the time. The most successful Anglophone Canadian prime ministers have been the ones with the closest attunement to Quebec, partially reflected in their employment of effective Quebec lieutenants such as Cartier, Lapointe, and St. Laurent. The object was to do more than maximize electoral gain. At a formative party stage, as George Grant has written, "the inherited desire not to become Americans allowed [the Canadian English] to come to modus vivendi with the more defined desires of the French."[32] There also was and continues to be the drive for national unity, based both on sectional accommodation and on national growth. John Porter, among others, has concluded that Canada's absence of a unifying myth, of clearly articulated major goals and values that might otherwise stem from some charter instrument of progress and equality, has left a special mark on politics. The party system's style has become dominantly accommodationist, since polarization and dogmatism would disrupt Canada's overriding national goal.[33]

31. See, in general, V. O. Key, Jr., *Southern Politics in State and Nation* (New York: Knopf, 1949).

32. George Grant, *Lament for a Nation: The Defeat of Canadian Nationalism* (Toronto: McClelland and Stewart, 1965), p. 70.

33. Porter, *Vertical Mosaic*, p. 369. Also see Ramsay Cook's comment in *The Maple Leaf Forever: Essays on Nationalism and Politics in Canada* (Toronto: Macmillan, 1971), p. 200.

If impulses for sectional accommodation have tended to strengthen the brokerage value among American and Canadian parties, what of socioeconomic concerns? We will comment on relations with the business community, on the uses of the state as a socioeconomic regulator, and on the collectivist/socialist dimension.

The hallmarks of American and Canadian main-party relations with business interests are traceable to cultural and historical influences, which have encouraged nondoctrinaire politics, although perhaps more clearly in Canada than in the United States. Prior to the American Civil War, parties were strongly affected by the liberal inheritance of the negative state—that progress could occur through largely uninhibited, individual effort. After the Civil War, with a quantum jump in economic and entrepreneurial activity, "[i]t was possible to complete the immense task of industrialization . . . with a minimum of state direction and intervention in part because the culture was so strongly supportive. The 'captains of industry' of the post–Civil War period were not unnatural heroes for Americans. In their commitment to hard work, thrift and industry, and the use of technology in the building of a richer and more prosperous society, they spoke to values broadly disseminated."[34] In a way, at least to the point of an industrially mature America, the party system was not invaded by serious dissonances between the requirements of capitalism and of the norms of democracy.

We have seen that Canada developed in a far more hostile natural environment and with a smaller resource base and less pronounced acquisitive values. The Revolution had released America from the British mercantile system, and it gave root to entrepreneurial initiative long before the release took place in Canada. Traditions of authority, of the crown, and of reliance on group/organizational rather than on individual effort encouraged a more natural liaison between parties and business. The Canadian middle-class businessman became a bureaucratic man.[35] First the Conservatives and then the Liberals developed close links

---

34. Ladd, *American Political Parties*, p. 119.
35. See S. D. Clark, *The Developing Canadian Community*, 2nd ed. (Toronto: University of Toronto Press, 1968), esp. pp. 227–28, 243–52.

with the business community and have retained them. In fact, these parties became major electoral forces in part because of their willingness to accede to business claims for sympathetic assistance. Yet this development did not happen without at least implicit popular approval. Meisel's summary is pertinent to this theme. He argues that Canada's absorption of doses of both statism and individualism, although not through dogmatic inspiration, has created an ambivalence of values of an "almost ideal environment for the flourishing of non-doctrinaire political parties susceptible to business and other influence. When conditions have required it, they have facilitated an easy pragmatic interaction between the private and public sectors of the economy."[36]

Canada's mixed tradition of statism and individualism also stimulated a pragmatic party approach to planning, to socioeconomic reform, and to cross-class appeals. Its major parties are not readily classifiable as "liberal" or "conservative," or as skewed to the "Left" or to the "Right." This became less true for American Democrats and Republicans. As we saw, for a long time the individualistic, antistatist strain was dominant. Toward the close of the nineteenth century, A. Lawrence Lowell could write that the prime object of American government was seen as negative at bottom. The majority's will over minorities and individuals was to be prevented, except within definite limits when a popular majority feeling was plain. Weak parties and conciliating politicians served this purpose well.[37] After a mass industrial society had appeared, the American political mood developed more sharply delineated branches or interpretations, and the effect on parties was especially visible from the New Deal onward. A brokerage quality remained, but by American *socioeconomic* standards Republicans became "conservatives" and Democrats "liberals." The former party stressed the simpler version of individualism (or "liberalism" in the Continental European sense),

36. John Meisel, "Canadian Parties and Politics," in *Contemporary Canada*, ed. Richard H. Leach (Durham: Duke University Press, 1967), p. 132.

37. A. Lawrence Lowell, *Essays on Government* (Boston: Houghton Mifflin, 1889), pp. 22, 106–8. Also see the commentary in Austin Ranney, "Toward a More Responsible Two-Party System: A Commentary," *American Political Science Review* 45 (1951): 495–98.

whereas what the Democrats borrowed from that tangent of individualism, taken from the revolutionary tradition and universalist values, was transposable into a form of egalitarianism. This was not an entirely newly "discovered" version of social purpose and change; it was only more explicit. Lipset has seen a common germ in a tradition extending through Jackson, Bryan, Wilson, the New Deal, the New Frontier, and the Great Society. The absence of such a tradition in Canada he ascribes to a society originating in a defeated democratic revolution and defeated reformist movements, joined to an absence of egalitarian-universalist historical referents.[38] American parties, such as the contemporary Republican, have adjusted to social claims and to mixed-economy principles. American Democrats have studiously avoided associating themselves with socialism, which Americans still think of as a tainted doctrine threatening individual values. In this sense the American party system has remained largely pragmatic and accommodative. But it has manifested more interparty cleavage than arose between the two major Canadian parties. After the Depression, both the Liberals and the Conservatives remained basically centrist parties, while Roosevelt, proclaiming the need to *save* capitalism, turned sharply left. Mackenzie King abhorred class politics, typifying the historical Canadian preoccupation with national unity, which in itself represented a doctrinally neutralizing or pragmatizing influence upon Canada's party system. His reforms, like those attempted by the Conservative Bennett before him, were an expression of an established "tory radical" statist tradition that sought a norm of balance. Still it is contemporary Canadian Liberals, more than the Progressive-Conservative party, who through their style of reformism and opportunism, through their effort (in Mackenzie King's phrase) to portray socialist parties as "liberals in a hurry," have become competitive with the CCF/NDP.[39]

38. Lipset, "Revolution and Counter-Revolution," pp. 43–44. Also see his *The First New Nation: The United States in Historical and Comparative Perspective* (New York: Basic Books, 1963), pp. 85–90.

39. See William Christian and Colin Campbell, *Political Parties and Ideologies in Canada: Liberals, Conservatives, Socialists, Nationalists* (Toronto: McGraw-Hill Ryerson, 1974), pp. 123–24.

What of the socialist political style itself in the two nations, and what of the style of challenging, "third" parties? Socialism has been only a secondary political force in both the United States and Canada, although more persistent in the latter. In both places, moreover, it has tended to work within the system rather than confronting it. The stylistic mildness of socialism/social democracy has been somewhat more evident in Canada than in America, even allowing for the Norman Thomas brand of American socialism and for features of early socialism in British Columbia. The American Socialist party reached its electoral crest by World War I, and by now is a trivial force. In Canada, the most electorally serious social democratic party, first in the form of the CCF and later the NDP, did not get under way until the 1930s. The current NDP collects about 16 to 18 percent of the popular vote at national elections and, apart from Alberta, enjoys marked provincial political strength in the West and to an extent in Ontario.

Socialist party strength has been relatively weak and basically nondoctrinal in style and emphasis, partly because of cultural features distinctive of both nations. Hartz has asserted that it is "not accidental that America which has uniquely lacked a feudal tradition has uniquely lacked also a socialist tradition."[40] A similar, but less strong, case can be made for English Canada. French-Canadian feudal remnants could over time be regarded as peculiarly resistant to collectivist appeals when perceived as threats to jealously guarded cultural and linguistic inheritances. Underhill, however, traced the Canadian Left's relative weakness not so much to any prominent liberal ethos as to the country's lack of successful revolutionary, universalist traditions from which a forceful gospel of social change could spread.[41] Lipset's summary of the assessment of socialists themselves about America is that "socialism as a political movement is weak in the United States because the ideological content of Americanism is highly similar

40. Hartz, *Liberal Tradition in America*, p. 6.
41. Underhill, *In Search of Canadian Liberalism*, p. 12. Also see the review in Martin Robin, "Determinants of Radical Labour and Socialist Politics in English-Speaking Canada between 1880 and 1930," *Journal of Canadian Studies* 2 (1967): 27–39.

to socialism and that Americans believe they already have most of what it promises."[42]

The origins of American socialism were mainly based on Continental Europe. This helped to give it a somewhat alien reputation among a public that by the end of the nineteenth century lived within a strongly congealed, liberal-American milieu. Canadian socialism was more British-based and inspired. This made it relatively acceptable, since British examples were not alien and because Canadian popular culture had not at that time congealed as firmly as in America. Party-political Canadian socialism also became relatively acceptable and generally lacked stylistically doctrinaire overtones, because the British version from which it largely borrowed was philosophically equable. Also, the major, nonsocialist parties had generally found a statist, "tory socialist" approach programmatically convenient and culturally comfortable.[43] The language of the CCF's Winnipeg Declaration of 1956 is a better guide to Canadian socialism's stylistic temper than its predecessor, the Regina Manifesto of 1933; David Lewis and Ed Broadbent are better guides than is the Waffle movement.

Third-party movements, Left/socialist or otherwise, have nonetheless cropped up in both countries. American third-party movements have, overall, proved more ephemeral and less influential than the Canadian. Our primary concern is with cultural/historical variables. We do, however, need to remind ourselves that the Canadian parliamentary/cabinet government system, federally and provincially, is considerably more susceptible to third-party penetration than is the American presidential/gubernatorial arrangement. In the past half century or so, American national third parties have concentrated on the presidency and, of course, have not even succeeded in throwing an election into the House of

42. Seymour Martin Lipset, "Radicalism in North America: A Comparative View of the Party Systems in Canada and the United States," Royal Society of Canada/American Academy of Arts and Sciences Conference Paper, Quebec City, 1976, p. 20. For a good summary of noncultural as well as cultural inhibitions on American socialism, see Leon D. Epstein, *Political Parties in Western Democracies* (New York: Praeger, 1967), pp. 138–45.

43. See especially the discussion in Horowitz, *Canadian Labour in Politics*, pp. 24–29.

Representatives. Their supporters have tended to reassimilate into the major parties. Canadian third parties have pursued goals of parliamentary representation and—when we apply Maurice Pinard's thesis—have surged electorally when there has been a combination of one-party dominance plus social strain.[44]

We are not immediately concerned with the nature of strains that may have caused third-party manifestations in the two countries. In both, however, third-party strength has tended to be sectionally or ethnically rather than randomly distributed. Part of this relates to what might very broadly be regarded as an imperfectly homogenized value system. But this has been a more prominent factor in Canada than in America, with the main historical exception of the South, from which have come the Dixiecrats and much of the enthusiasm for the American Independent party. Quebec is a good example of a subculture that has produced movements peculiarly its own, such as the Bloc Populaire, the Union Nationale, and the Parti Québécois. But perhaps even more instructive is the example of the Maritimes. There, despite persistent economic deprivation and a sense of regional identity, third parties have scored very few inroads against the two major parties. Among the reasons, combined with Maritime dependence upon Ottawa, has been the deep strength of traditional, cautious, quasi-tory values—more than in Ontario and considerably more than in the West. The principal exception to Maritime main-party allegiance has been on Nova Scotia's Cape Breton, where there was a considerable influx of migrants after the more traditional political culture had seeped in throughout the region. Indeed, while cultural diversity and sectionalism generally have improved chances for Canadian parties to make an impact in a number of locations, these have also been among the most powerful deterrents to third-party achievement of genuinely nationwide follow-

44. Maurice Pinard, *The Rise of a Third Party: A Study in Crisis Politics* (Englewood Cliffs, N.J.: Prentice-Hall, 1971). Pinard concentrates on Quebec. For a comparable judgment on British Columbia, see Martin Robin, "The Social Basis of Party Politics in British Columbia," *Queen's Quarterly* 72 (Winter 1965): 675–90. For a summary of conditions under which challenging parties have arisen in America, see V. O. Key, Jr., *Politics, Parties and Pressure Groups*, 5th ed. (New York: Crowell, 1964), pp. 254–81.

ings. When third parties (including those in the United States) have tried to move beyond regional bases, the usual results have been a tempering of their doctrines and a more accommodationist style.

Overall, of course, third parties in both countries have tended to be more zealous in their advocacy of claims than have the older, more widely reaching, mainline parties. All the same, even the populist temper, insofar as it favored technical approaches as well as popular accountability, was not divorced from pragmatism. Then too, age and governmental experience, including that on a localized scale, have tended to dilute doctrine and rhetoric. British Columbia has a reputation for hot politics. But, as its new Social Credit premier William Bennett expressed it, "We are a populist party slightly to the right of centre. The NDP is a populist party slightly to the left. The mistake of . . . [his father, W. A. C. Bennett] is that he allowed the party to get too far to the right."[45]

Parties and Systemic Outcomes

We might for a moment turn the theme around. Frederick Engelmann and Mildred Schwartz have suggested that "the presence of ideological minor parties in Canada has in turn drained ideology from the major ones, which thus have shown even less class-based ideology than the major parties in the United States."[46] One of our following concerns will be with how the dominant party orientations in the two nations have affected policy outputs and particular outcomes bearing on systemic viability.

We proceed to assess party-system performance by repeating that parties are not the only agents that mediate between publics

45. Cited in Allan Fortheringham, "Bennett the Second," *Toronto Globe and Mail Weekend Magazine*, 21 Feb. 1976. For a comment on Canadian third-party style, see J. R. Mallory, "The Structure of Canadian Politics," in Thorburn, *Party Politics in Canada*, pp. 26–27.

46. Frederick C. Engelmann and Mildred A. Schwartz, *Canadian Political Parties: Origin, Character, Impact* (Scarborough: Prentice-Hall, 1975), p. 216.

and authority structures and that they are not the only agents responsible for shaping policy decisions. Nor are they solely responsible for shaping the feedbacks within the cycle of the political process, feedbacks that variously recondition cultural norm patterns and the mix of new demand and support inputs. Moreover, the very question of whether a party system adequately satisfies demands and contributes to systemic integration very much depends for answers on the normative perspectives of whoever is asking. The standard of "effectiveness" is bound up with presuppositions as to what are desirable outputs and systemic outcomes. One approach will be to outline some of the major doubts that have been cast on the effectiveness of the two-party systems and then to suggest countervailing or modifying interpretations.

A general and commonly heard criticism of both the Canadian and the American party systems is that they have carried brokerage too far. Their quest for electoral advantage is said to have resulted in an opportunism that has blurred issues and choice and has fostered a misplaced incrementalism that has blunted creative responses to national problems. The main parties especially are accused of having borne out all too conclusively the Downsian model of party rationality—i.e., that parties formulate policies to win elections, rather than fighting elections to formulate policies.[47]

Various evidence has been offered to suggest that main party styles and programmatic outputs have fallen short of community desires and requirements. One line of argument has been that, on an *intra*party basis, the main parties have basically failed to resolve what they themselves stand for. If they do stand for something distinctive, they are inhibited from reliably translating positions into firm policy by their very diffuseness and range of clientelistic interests. Hence the argument in the American context that the Civil War's promise of black liberation was for a

47. See Anthony Downs, *An Economic Theory of Democracy* (New York: Harper and Row, 1957). On Canada, see for instance, Presthus, *Elite Accommodation in Canadian Politics*, pp. 351–53, and Porter, *Vertical Mosaic*, pp. 368–69, 377. On the United States, see the much-discussed report of the American Political Science Association's Committee on Political Parties, *Toward a More Responsible Two-Party System* (New York: Rinehart, 1950), esp. pp. 15–36, 91–96.

century de facto frustrated because the great parties were neither willing nor, given their structure and composition, able to insist that such social change be fulfilled. Or, in James MacGregor Burns's formulation, a deadlock of democracy was brought about. Flexibility, accessibility and representativeness had been gained at the expense of vigor, speed, and comprehensive national action. The Madisonian view of countervailing power had been effected. The Civil War and other reordering episodes had brought about a host of tendencies within each party. One result has been a four-party system of congressional Democrats, congressional Republicans, presidential Democrats, and presidential Republicans.[48]

In Canada, it is often pointed out, each major party contains important elements of elites and supporters who persistently weaken and embarrass the production of clear-cut positions. Among these elements one could count Western conservatives within the PC party and French members within the Liberal caucus. Stanfield could not hold his party together on the Official Languages Bill vote. Trudeau faced dissent among Quebec members and lost a minister over concessions promised to English-speaking air controllers. Party discipline has tended to break down over major English-French issues, such as the two conscription crises. On some tender English-French issues, such as the adoption of a national flag and language usage among air controllers, governments have allegedly abrogated responsibility by promising free votes in the House of Commons. Diefenbaker failed to make much headway with his vision of a new Canadian national identity because, in part, his post-1958 Commons majority was too large and diverse, rather than compact.

It has also been claimed that, on an *inter*party basis, the main parties in the two systems have been overly timid and accommodationist. One illustration is said to lie in the persistent appearance of third-party movements and, especially in Canada, in their durability. Another indication is said to be found in swelling public disenchantment over conventional politics and parties as they are, whether or not third-party surges result. In Canada,

48. James MacGregor Burns, *The Deadlock of Democracy: Four-Party Politics in America* (Englewood Cliffs, N.J.: Prentice-Hall, 1963). See the summary on pp. 265–67.

some of the most compelling evidence is identified as the continuing estrangement of the West and of Quebec, the strong separatist momentum in Quebec, and the failure of the major parties to alleviate pungent French-English suspicions. Such suspicions are aggravated by a tendency in various quarters to magnify or to distort events as a function of existing prejudices. Many Anglophones feel that the Liberals are trying to shove the French language down their throats. Many people in Quebec were convinced that Liberal losses outside Quebec in the 1972 federal election were simply the manifestation of a powerful, anti-French backlash, and some felt that Joseph Clark's selection as PC leader in 1976 was a repudiation of leadership candidates from Quebec.

Particular interpretation has been placed on the absence of any measurable Canadian major-party polarization on socioeconomic issues. Such polarization might, for instance, help to weaken Canada's ethnic/sectional cleavages, with which the parties have struggled with indifferent success. A weakening of these cleavages would be a great stride toward national unity. Some writers, although not necessarily arguing in a strong, party-critical spirit, have offered data to show that Canada's relative classlessness is associated with the failure of conventional parties to mobilize publics among whom sentiment for change exists and is potentially mobilizable.[49]

Malaise in America is said to be less sectionalized than in Canada, but perhaps even more indicative of party distrust. Sorauf writes that the "new politics" has brought about broader and deeper conflict. "The old politics of consensus and compromise appears to have passed. Whether it was based on a genuine social consensus or was the product of suppressed differences . . . it is less pervasive, at least for now."[50] The argument is said to be underwritten by recent survey and electoral data, such as have

49. In this context see Pinard, Rise of a Third Party and his "Working Class Politics: An Interpretation of the Quebec Case," Canadian Review of Sociology and Anthropology 7 (1970): 87–107, and Rick Ogmundson, "Mass-Elite Linkages and Class Issues in Canada," Canadian Review of Sociology and Anthropology 13 (1976): 1–12.

50. Frank J. Sorauf, Party Politics in America, 3rd ed. (Boston: Little, Brown, 1976), p. 419.

been assembled in *The Changing American Voter*. The American electorate's partisan identifications have softened; issues rather than parties enjoy increased focus as standards of evaluation. The center of politics has been losing ground to both left and right orientations. Trust and confidence in government, and in parties, have declined.[51]

It is not our purpose to deal in detail with these and other indictments of Canadian and American party-system performance. It is, however, helpful to consider some of the ways in which the party systems, especially because of the historical/cultural legacies held by them and by the publics they serve, can be regarded as making reasonable contributions to processing claims and contributing to systemic integrity. While our emphasis is new, we draw substantially on our previous analysis.

We turn first to socioeconomic outputs. Canada was "light" on such outputs until World War II, and did not emulate Wilsonian reforms or the New Deal in America. Continuity rather than brisk change was stressed by Mackenzie King. In his study of the CCF, Walter Young saw this as consistent with dominant Canadian values, even working-class values, wherein "[t]hose who were victims of capitalism often viewed their misfortune as simply the luck of the game." While objectively a working class existed, "the members of that class did not, for the most part, accept their position as such. Their aspirations and attitudes were middle class."[52] Wartime and postwar Liberal governments did, however, undertake various reforms. The CCF scored well during the war but then receded, with the Liberals "drawing socialism's

51. Norman H. Nie, Sidney Verba, and John R. Petrocik, *The Changing American Voter* (Cambridge: Harvard University Press, 1976). Also, for instance, see Walter D. Burnham, "The United States: The Politics of Heterogeneity," in *Electoral Behavior: A Comparative Handbook*, ed. Richard Rose (New York: Free Press, 1974), esp. pp. 719–20. Canadian data for the 1960s showed less mistrust-cynicism than in the United States at that time. See Mildred A. Schwartz, *Politics and Territory: The Sociology of Regional Persistence in Canada* (Montréal: McGill-Queen's University Press, 1974), pp. 185–239.

52. Walter D. Young, *The Anatomy of a Party: The National CCF 1932–61* (Toronto: University of Toronto Press, 1969), p. 289. Also see William J. McAndrew, "'Weighing a Wild-Cat on the Kitchen Scales': Canadians Evaluate the New Deal," *American Review of Canadian Studies* 4 (Autumn 1974): 23–45.

sharpest teeth." The Liberals did so as a centrist party. They have continued to avert being squeezed out by public flight to either right- or left-party alternatives.[53] The Liberals were borrowers, but borrowers from both a democratic socialist movement and a conservative tradition in which government intervention was neither unknown nor despised. We recall that, unlike in the United States, there has not been a serious tradition in Canada of "the best government is government that governs least," in part because corporate values have weakened the individualistic ethic. Liberal and Conservative party socioeconomic programs and policies have not been substantially different. While this can be interpreted as a restriction on choice for voters interested in either more radical or more regressive orientations, it also means that the major parties have hardly been indistinguishable because they were both so *un*reformist.[54]

By 1976, Canada had adopted a wide range of social reforms, among them medical care and old age security, in which it was ahead of the United States. Total Canadian government spending as a proportion of the gross national product stood at 43 percent, while it was only 35 percent in the United States. Two special developments occurred in postwar Canada, both bearing on cultural adaptations and to which the parties have at least in part adjusted. For one, as S. D. Clark suggests in a provocative piece, World War II and the major governmental efforts associated with it released in Canada a more modern, opportunity-seeking ethos, a kind of "breakout of the middle class," of individual aspiration. What this meant was not an embrace of laissez-faire, but a whole new set of demands for both qualitative and quantitative advancement, and it carried redistributive connotations.[55] By general, historically/culturally induced disposition, the major parties

53. See Horowitz, *Canadian Labour in Politics*, p. 40.
54. On major-party similarities, see especially Howard A. Scarrow, "Distinguishing Between Political Parties—The Case of Canada," *Midwest Journal of Political Science* 9 (1965): 61–76, and the interesting report in Paul M. Sniderman H. D. Forbes, and Ian Melzer, "Party Loyalty and Electoral Volatility: A Study of the Canadian Party System," *Canadian Journal of Political Science* 7 (1974): 268–88.
55. S. D. Clark, "The Post Second World War Canadian Society," *Canadian Review of Sociology and Anthropology* 12 (1975), esp. pp. 27–29.

were not averse to acceding. At first, national governmental activism was sharply rebuked by Quebec, where Duplessis ruled. Duplessis demurred when offered participation in various socioeconomic programs because he alleged that centralization would mean suffocation for French Canadians and their institutions.[56] On the other hand, the Quiet Revolution that followed in Quebec was in part a revolt against the regressiveness and parochialism of the Duplessis system. In one sense, collectivism as represented by centralizing, English-dominated parties remained suspect in Quebec. But Quebec's heritage, we recall, included a collectivist/corporate strain based on the governance of old France, the seigneurial system, the pervasive social as well as pastoral role of the Church, and so on. Quebec's *provincially* directed movement toward social reform has been swift, and has included a popular, social democratic component within the Parti Québécois (PQ), its separatist position aside. It has even been asked whether Quebec is experiencing a tardy liberal "revolution" or whether it is moving almost directly from a relatively authoritarian to some form of a postliberal, socialist stage.[57] Canada's national parties are not socialist, but, as suggested, their stances are not regressive. Their acquiescence in the David Lewis portrayal of institutionalized corporate rip-off has another face, which does not frown upon social change.

In America, the individualistic ethic has a deep historical base. Some critics have argued that Americans hold only a very ambiguous commitment to egalitarianism at the operational level, that they are libertarians who easily tolerate and even encourage inequalities of all kinds.[58] In his in-depth study of ordinary Americans, Robert Lane did indeed find them more supportive of individual opportunity than of economic equality.[59] Some of our

56. The phenomenon is treated in Donald V. Smiley, *The Canadian Political Nationality* (Toronto: Methuen, 1967), esp. pp. 51–55.
57. McRae, "Structure of Canadian History," p. 273.
58. For instance, see H. Mark Roelofs, *Ideology and Myth in American Politics: A Critique of a National Political Mind* (Boston: Little, Brown, 1976), pp. 137–49.
59. Robert E. Lane, *Political Ideology: Why the American Common Man Believes What He Does* (New York: Free Press, 1962), esp. pp. 57–81.

earlier discussion, however, suggested America's ability to evolve an egalitarian strain from its individualistic and feudal-free background. In party terms, as we have seen, there have been a number of reformist stages, clustered in the period of the New Deal and onward. The New Deal was not socialist, but it went farther, and more boldly, than Canada did at that time. This egalitarian streak, to the extent that it has been part of the American makeup, has helped to promote a sharper left-right cleavage than Canada has faced in its main-party competition. Neither major American party has taken a polar position. When in recent years there seemed to be a significant drift, the drifting party has paid the electoral bill, as the Republicans did in 1964 and the Democrats did in 1972. Both parties continue to engage in accommodation and in brokerage, as electorally they feel they must. Nominal Democrats are far more numerous than nominal Republicans, but Republicans are more firmly anchored. Still, the Democratic party remains as the party most often in office, and, comparatively, it is the party of socioeconomic progressivism. The most progressive civil rights legislation was sponsored by a Democratic president from Texas with a wheeler-dealer reputation. In 1976 the party nominated a Deep South Georgian, a person who was both highly adept at brokerage politics and sternly antiracist, and whose socioeconomic views divulged a populist streak. Thus, while Canada's main parties offer less explicit "choice" than do America's, one of America's main parties offers at least as much, if not more, reformism as do Canada's Liberals and Conservatives.

The South has historically been held up as America's foremost example of sectional politics, to an extent of national disunity. Although the North won the Civil War, southern politics for a considerable time upheld an older, less nationally integrated value system. But it is misleading to consider the South as having been America's Quebec. Regime values have essentially not been challenged by the South over the past century; but they have been challenged in Quebec. Systemically centrifugal tendencies in the two nations have not been equally severe in part because the relative strength of nationalism has been different. "The

United States, with even more cultural diversities than Canada —even more local autonomy, many more political units smaller than the nation, greater size, a similar 'dissident' region in the South—can maintain unity because of a national identity, well defined by its Revolution and firmly established by its Civil War."[60]

In recent times, significant changes have taken place both in the South and in Quebec. But while the South has become more melded into the American mainstream, Quebec's politics have assumed a more questioning, self-assertive tone and have produced a serious separatist movement. The American South essentially had to come to terms with itself, while Quebec's special cultural and political qualities have been systemically disconcerting because Quebec has been in clash with the rest of Canada as well as with the burden of its own traditions. Canada's weak national identity can thereby once again be seen as a liability and a handicap to accommodation within the sphere of conventional organized politics. We are reminded of Trudeau's own plaintive conclusion of twenty years ago that "[h]istorically, French Canadians have not really believed in democracy for themselves, and English Canadians have not really wanted it for others. Such are the foundations upon which our two ethnic groups have absurdly pretended to be building democratic forms of government. No wonder the ensuing structure has turned out to be rather flimsy."[61]

Ironically, it is the PQ, a separatist party, that may have done something to animate liberal values in Quebec. By sedulously fostering democratic norms and procedures and by renouncing terrorist separatism, it has probably fortified the community's liberal-democratic ethic. It also has probably channeled toward democratic action energies that otherwise might have leaned toward disgust or even outbreaks of anarchy and has provided one kind of vehicle for political and social renewalists. In this

60. Robert R. Alford, *Party and Society: The Anglo-American Democracies* (Chicago: Rand McNally, 1963), p. 256.
61. Pierre E. Trudeau, "Some Obstacles to Democracy in Quebec," *Canadian Journal of Economics and Political Science* 24 (1958): 297.

sense, it may be construed as catalytically constructive rather than, through its separatist platform and otherwise high-demand content, as simply systemically disruptive.[62]

The national unity load, especially as it has related to Quebec, has been a heavy one for Canada's parties to shoulder. It is easy enough to claim that the Conservatives have a poor record of accommodating French Canada or even that the federal Liberals, in part because of their disproportionately strong Quebec base, have lacked credit in sections of English Canada. But the burden of fault probably lies more in the nation's culturally mixed and often historically ambiguous identity than in party-system inability to handle ethnic and sectional stress. There is evidence that the accommodationist strain in party politics has at various times been helpful in the quest for a higher, better-resolved national identity. Examples would include the Conservatives' application of the National Policy and Mackenzie King's extraordinary political footwork in dealing with conscription during World War II. While the early nationalist impulses came mostly from the Conservatives, nationalism's most declaratory expressions are presently found on the Left, both in and outside the New Democratic Party. We previously noted the argument that a more class-based politics might serve a nationally integrating objective. Yet the nationalist spirit is no one's monopoly. Conservatism, liberalism, or socialism have all become engaged. It has been suggested that it is Canadian nationalism's very weakness, its need for allies, that "has probably widened its influence, for through alliances it has been able to appeal in one way or another across the whole ideological spectrum in Canada," and nationalism "can with justice claim the ideological leadership of the 1970s."[63] And, as in the past, Canadian nationalism takes much of its incentive from a wish to disengage from American influence and from some of the

---

62. See the present author's comments in his "Quebec and Canadian Unity," *Current History* 66 (1974): 160, and more broadly in his *Canadian and Australian Politics in Comparative Perspective* (New York: Oxford University Press, 1973), esp. pp. 141–44.

63. Christian and Campbell, *Political Parties and Ideologies in Canada*, p. 196. See their general discussion of nationalism in Canadian politics on pp. 158–98.

styles and mores that America's peculiar historical experience have evolved.

The United States and Canada have not been fully successful in processing demands and in achieving fully scaled systemic integration. It is difficult to attribute this lack to the party systems as such, as opposed to factors exogenous to the party systems. In both societies, nevertheless, the party systems have not been unresilient. There have been major realigning elections in both countries, which in a way have served as surrogates for social upheaval or despair. Even within the compass of the major parties, it has been shown that poor stress management by incumbents will bring defeat. Reconsideration of appeals and programs is thereby stimulated among losers, who themselves are part of a flexible, adaptive party tradition.

Third-party appearances in both nations should not be written off as signs that organized politics, in their party form, have lost their capacity to mediate and to process demands. An uninterrupted, overlapping two-party-system model is probably inadequate to handle new patterns of public socialization and demands. "Consensus" can be overstressed and pressed to the point of dysfunctionality. As David Easton has remarked, "What may be 'inadequate' socialization for maintaining existing political structures may be highly 'appropriate' for bringing into being new structures [such as new parties] based upon new ideals and new kinds of political accommodations among members of the system."[64]

Third-party movements, even apart from circumstances when they have actually governed at some political level, have had stimulating effects upon the politics of both countries. In America, it may be that they are "deviations from the norm of . . . two-party politics whose chief function apparently is to preserve the norm."[65] But that "norm" includes major-party adaptation and

64. David Easton, "The Theoretical Relevance of Political Socialization," *Canadian Journal of Political Science* 1 (1968): 146. In a larger framework, see his *A Systems Analysis of Political Life* (New York: Wiley, 1965).

65. Clinton Rossiter, *Parties and Politics in America* (Ithaca: Cornell University Press, 1960), p. 7.

often presages major-party acquisition of new programs and increased efforts to attract clienteles flirting with third parties. This, for instance, was the effect upon the Democratic party, first by the Populists and later by the La Follette Progressives. It also was the effect of Western Canadian protest movements upon Laurier's position on reciprocity in 1911, of the Progressives in the 1920s, and of the new CCF in the 1930s upon Mackenzie King's programs. Also, the presence of a third-party movement of "regressive" outlook need not similarly taint major parties. In 1948 the Truman-led Democrats were able to champion a more pronounced civil rights position because, in part, they essentially had to write off much of the South to the Dixiecrats.

Various factors have accounted for the greater success of third parties in Canada than in the United States. These Canadian parties have served as sounding boards for grievances, have contributed to adjustments within the major parties, and have often refocused the direction of public debate. Their public acceptance as fairly normal features of the political scene in part relates to the way in which Canadian values, including the absence of a keen sense of popular nationalist feeling, have accommodated political diversity. From Tocqueville onward, observers of the United States have noticed a strain of glorified majoritarian will.[66] Reactions to such incidents as the Winnipeg General Strike and the Front de Libération du Québec in Quebec notwithstanding, Canada—and Canadian parties—have taken diversity rather better in stride than generally has the United States, and the tone of politics has been less zealous. In a way, the absence of a mythologized "Canadian way of life" has made reconfiguration of the party system more possible. Plurality has been in one sense a bane for Canada and for its organized politics and in another sense an outlet for tolerance.

It may be arguable that America's more integrated, more universalistically minded society can better afford suspicion of heterodoxy and more easily afford idealistic traits both among the public and within the parties. But nativist, hyperpatriotic,

66. See Alexis de Tocqueville, *Democracy in America*, ed. J. P. Mayer and Max Lerner (New York: Harper and Row, 1966), esp. pp. 227–54.

and globally reformist exclamations by parties and their leaders can lead to distortions of both personal and national interests, producing Palmer raids, McCarthyism, and swift oscillations between enthusiastically idealistic intervention abroad and withdrawal. The impact of zeal of destiny and of self-assertion was for generations directed against Canada and in turn helped to produce a more cautious quality in Canada's political culture. It also helped to produce a greater Canadian acceptance of authority, and of regulation, than evolved out of America's own individualism. In part, therefore, Canada's national parties have needed to make fewer apologies than their American counterparts for being associated with the "Ottawa scene." Quebec and Western suspicions of Ottawa have historically not so much been a reaction against authority per se, as against those who have used that authority, and how—"the Eastern establishment," or "les Anglais," or whatever.

The American public's individualism, together with tendencies toward idealism and leeriness of government, combine to exaggerate popular disappointment in government performance and in the party system. This has been made more conspicuous in the aftermath of Vietnam and of Watergate, by failed social programs and by perceptions of decay in order and in social behavior. The more conventional distrust of "big government" is in part being replaced by a more subtle outlook, in which government is being queried for its errors, not just for being an encroacher upon individualism. We have noticed trends toward an erosion in trust of government and toward confidence in parties. Some observers have been pessimistic about the resiliency of the existing party system. Apparently, however, there is a considerable reservoir of public attachment to procedural consensus in America, to the rules of the game.[67] The survey data reflect various signs of public

67. For examples of the general argument, see Donald J. Devine, *The Political Culture of the United States: The Influence of Member Values on Regime Maintenance* (Boston: Little, Brown, 1972), and the shorter summary in Walter A. Rosenbaum, *Political Culture* (New York: Praeger, 1975), pp. 75–89. For older but still suggestive primary data, see Lane, *Political Ideology,* pp. 82–112, and Gabriel A. Almond and Sidney Verba, *The Civic Culture. Political Attitudes and Democracy in Five Nations* (Boston: Little, Brown, 1965).

discouragement, but they also suggest that a remarkably high 90 percent of the public remains convinced that the system can be made to work.[68] One British observer has noticed historically/culturally conditioned buffers at work. The popular reaction against the shortcomings of organized politics is being channeled by an instinct "not to demand more of the same medicine but rather to hibernate for a while in the warmth of their own wayward [Revolution-inspired] individualism."[69]

Americans continue to have historically conditioned values on which to lean and agree, from which the party system is not exempt. The development of Canada's political culture and party character has taken place under somewhat different conditions. The Canadian party system has been forced to operate under more severe community cleavages and often less accessible material and symbolic resources. But it has not been bereft of valuable supports in the service of reasonably distributive and systemically integrative outcomes. The American revolutionary experience has produced a more florid, perhaps pretentious political climate than in Canada. But the Canadian accomplishment has been noteworthy. It is not with excessive sentimentality or hyperbole that H. A. Morton has written that Canada, founded in *defiance* of the ideals of the American Revolution, "has expanded across a continent, changed its international status, reformed its social order, developed its economy, secured to its variety of nationals their individual rights and liberties, all without a revolution or a Civil War."[70]

68. See a review of recent survey data on Jon Nordheimer, *New York Times,* 5 July 1976.
69. Peter Jenkins in *Guardian Weekly* [London], 2 May 1976.
70. H. A. Morton, "The American Revolution: A View from the North," *Journal of Canadian Studies* 7 (1972): 49–50.

6

Evolution and Canadian Political Culture:
The Politics of Accommodation

Robert Presthus

At a rather abstract level, the critical aspect of evolutionary versus revolutionary paths of national development is the extent to which they facilitate or inhibit social change. I shall argue that the Canadian evolutionary experience has included certain dysfunctional consequences that have aggravated the problem of accommodating change. This condition, in turn, reflects the extent to which an evolutionary ethos in Canada has insured, in contrast to the revolutionary experience of the United States, the persistence of traditional values. A major political consequence of the historical interplay between such values and the unique character of Canadian national development has been a style of governance that may be called "elite accommodation." Some evidence exists, however, that an alternative style of class politics may be emerging, built in part upon traditional values but mainly reflecting post–World War II conditions of technology, urbanization, multiculturalism, industrialization, and democratic ideals of participation.

As the emerging field of biopolitics suggests, biology and ecology are intimately related to politics. The social environment makes possible both the satisfaction of basic human needs and the practice of politics.[1] A major consequence of natural selection among living creatures is to perpetuate those characteristics that enhance the survival probabilities of man in society. The linkage

1. Glendon Schubert, "Biopolitical Behavioral Theory," *Political Science Reviewer*, 5 (1975): 403–28.

is sharply apparent in the physiological alterations that prepare the organism for adaptation to environmental changes that induce stress. Similarly functional adaptations are evident in sociopolitical activity. As Konrad Lorenz shows, warning signals among ape bands are selectively differentiated by members of the band, with the effect that only those expressed by senior oligarchs become stimuli for protective action.[2] Thus hierarchy, emerging essentially from congenital traces of dominance, sex, and aggression, becomes vital for group survival.

It seems, however, that the consequences of evolution in the social sphere are sometimes less felicitous than those found in biology. Holding human needs constant, the interplay between cultural values and institutions may result in protracted stress rather than the nice balance that often seems to occur in nature. Moreover, while the social environment is obviously essential for the sustenance of human life and political development, it may in certain contexts provide objective conditions that make adaptation painfully difficult. Crystallizations of social class, political and economic structures, and their attending patterns of ideological and behavioral socialization may prove resistant or even impervious to ordered change in the liberal tradition. In some cases, as is well known, the accumulated weight of traditional institutions and values can be displaced only by revolutionary change,[3] which I shall define here as *violent* change. It thus differs from the gradualism that has characterized Canadian sociopolitical development since Confederation, and in contrast it characterizes that of the United States.

Regarding comparative political cultures, a striking difference between the two systems is that the United States has experienced armed revolution and the ultimate tragedy of civil war. In contrast to the Canadian milieu, in which incrementalism and traditionalism sometimes provided psychic and institutional bar-

2. Konrad Lorenz, *On Aggression* (New York: Harcourt Brace, 1967), pp. 40–45. See also Edward O. Wilson, *Sociobiology: The New Synthesis* (Cambridge, Mass.: Harvard University Press, 1975).
3. Cf. Barrington Moore, *Social Origins of Dictatorship and Democracy* (Boston: Beacon Press, 1966).

riers to innovation, this revolutionary experience tended on the whole to encourage experimentation and modernity. Each orientation encouraged its own kind of substantive modes of change. A striking example exists regarding equal protection and equality before the law in the two societies. The cross-national difference is nicely symbolized by the fact that, whereas the American Bill of Rights was incorporated into the Constitution and the original intent of the Fourteenth Amendment was greatly expanded by judicial interpretation, in Canada a Bill of Rights did not emerge until 1960 and then only in a statutory form that weakened its judicial influence. Observers often attribute this contrasting experience to the Canadian antirevolutionary tradition and a generalized rejection of egalitarianism. As Frank Underhill wrote in the 1946 Canadian Historical Association *Report,* "In Canada we have no revolutionary tradition; and our historians, political scientists and philosophers have . . . tried to educate us to be proud of this fact."

From a broader perspective, it seems that the rupture of the British connection had its greatest impact in the American economic arena. A new liberating conception of class relationships and social mobility transformed individual aspirations, releasing a great deal of human energy, which was quickly put to the service of a vigorous industrial capitalism. Here, the revolutionary experience had perhaps its primal influence by encouraging the most pervasive rationalization of economic techniques and attitudes yet seen.[4] Virtually every human impulse was harnessed to the dominant pecuniary impulse, as seen, for example, in the scientific management movement. Despite mixed human consequences, foreseen by Max Weber in his gloomy visage of the "iron cage" of history, the competitive ethos and its institutional apparatus created a wealth-producing system of unprecedented scale. Rejecting, at least in its early stages, the British legacy of protectionism, combination, and mercantilism, which became

4. On rationalization as a dominant force in history, see Max Weber, *The Protestant Ethic and the Spirit of Capitalism,* trans. T. Parsons (New York: Charles Scribner's Sons, 1958).

evident in Canada from Confederation onward, this new industrial system honored competition and entrepreneurship.

The rationalization of individual and collective effort was carried to its ultimate in huge bureaucratic organizations, which appeared in virtually every sector, including putatively noneconomic areas such as mass communications, entertainment, and higher education.[5] The absence of an aristocratic tradition, which might have inhibited rationalization by its commitment to "being" as opposed to the dominant norm of "function," had been insured by the break with Old World traditions. Such inapposite values were restricted to the literati and probably remained unknown, and surely unacceptable, to the vast majority of Americans inspired by a pragmatic ethic. Their preference was validated moreover by both the ideal and the reality of upward mobility, usually achieved in an intergenerational time frame.

Some Conditions of Canadian Evolutionary Development

Any broad perspective of Canadian political history must begin with the fact that the nation has always been divided by the two "solitudes"—French and English Canada. The two cultures have been typically regarded as completely distinct, so that Quebec is often treated as the great exception to generalizations about Canada. I would like to suggest, however, that these two charter groups can be defined as being quite similar along many politically relevant dimensions. Their ethnic and religious differences are obvious, as is the psychological distance between a victorious and a conquered society. But in social and economic spheres, certain critical continuities seem to occur and may make it possible to treat them commonly. Both cultures share European heritages from which many of their early formative institutions and values were transmuted. Class lines have been rather sharply etched and reinforced by elitist attitudes toward higher learning. Traditional spheres of emphasis have in turn limited the capacity

5. Cf. Robert Presthus, *The Organizational Society*, 2d ed. (New York: St. Martin's Press, 1978).

of each culture to accommodate itself to the skill needs of industrial society. In English Canada the partial vacuum has often been filled by immigration, while among French Canadians, following upon decades of inability to qualify for managerial roles in industry and commerce, change began to occur mainly during the Quiet Revolution inspired by the Lesage government in the 1960s. Economic dependence upon exogenous sources of entrepreneurship and capital, mainly the United States and Britain, provides another common dimension. A secular emigration as a result of greater economic opportunities to the south also characterizes both societies.

The political-cultural effects of these several conditions include a precarious level of national political integration, limited rank-and-file participation in the political system, a tendency for party organization and politics to be dominated by notables, and a reliance upon elite accommodation as a generally successful mechanism for achieving democratic stability. Given these rough continuities it may be possible to make limited generalizations about political culture across the English-French spectrum.

A review of Canadian history leaves the foreign observer with conflicting impressions, perhaps especially when he brings to it the assumptions of American ideals and experience.* At many critical points, it seems, the nation has found itself in situations where its alternatives were sharply limited. A forced reaction to events was sometimes more common than the opportunity to shape them into a more plastic mold. The sense of being controlled by exogenous events and forces seems to run through the national consciousness. The pervasiveness of *survival* as a literary theme has been cited as an index of this somewhat negative perspective of individual and collective experience.

In English Canada, the dominant values and institutions are part of the British legacy, brought to Canada initially by the Empire Loyalists, some forty thousand of whom emigrated from the United States during the Revolutionary War period. The Empire

---

* I shall use the terms "American" and "Canadian" to characterize the two societies, even though members of both nations may be called "Americans."

Loyalist influence seems to me critical for Canadian political culture, insuring, as it did, the survival of conservative British social values in North America. As A. R. M. Lower concludes, "Needless to say, a change of residence did not work a change of philosophy. In its new wilderness home, and its new aspect of British North Americanism, colonial Toryism made its second attempt to erect on American soil a copy of the British social edifice. From one point of view this is the most significant thing about the Loyalist movement: it withdrew a class concept of life from the south, moved it up north and gave it a second chance."[6] Here again, regarding the possibility that Quebec need not be excluded from certain generalizations about Canadian political culture, it may be said that British values and institutions had a critical impact within Quebec through the dominance of its financial and economic life by English Canadians and the vital socializing role of McGill University.

Unlike most immigrant groups, the Empire Loyalists brought a formative set of normative and institutional preferences to English Canada, the residues of which remain visible in contemporary Canadian institutions and behavior. The decisive weight of the British tradition is dramatically apparent in the extent to which it effectively shaped the values and institutions of Canada, despite the existential fact that Canada shared with the United States a variety of economic, demographic, and geographical conditions that might have seemed to make the United States a more logical model for her national development. Both societies were "new"; both shared the problem of settling a vast frontier, which provided the foundation for a large middle class based on individual ownership of land; both attracted an ethnically heterogeneous people. The critical difference was that in the Canadian case an Old-World set of ideals and institutions, rejected in America, was superimposed upon a somewhat inapposite physical and demographic environment.

This essentially British legacy had mixed consequences. Among

6. *Colony to Nation:* A. R. M. Lower, *A History of Canada* (Toronto: Longmans, 1946), p. 118.

its positive ones is surely a pervasive respect for law and order, which on the whole insured more social stability than found in the United States. Reinforcing this advantage is an organic political philosophy, manifest in a collectivist attitude toward society, contrasting sharply with the competitive individualism of American life. This philosophical drift, however, was challenged incessantly by the English-French dualism. Subsequent waves of immigrants from diversified cultures further aggravated the problem of achieving Canadian identity and political consensus. The tolerance of minorities, as seen in the religious and linguistic rights granted French Canadians after the Conquest and in the "mosaic" philosophy of ethnic acculturation, provides another impressive example of the British legacy.

In a more strictly political context, one must also salute the evolution of a generally successful "elite accommodation" style of national politics, which brought political stability, despite serious ethnic, linguistic, regional, religious, and class cleavages in Canadian society.[7] In terms of political analysis, this condition provides an alternative to the conventional explanation that democratic stability is usually attributed to two-party political structures, crosscutting group memberships, and a widely shared popular consensus on the political "rules of the game." Canada has sustained Confederation for over a century, despite a political culture in which these attributes are either absent or precarious.

The evolutionary drift of Canadian development has had a decisive effect upon national political integration and identity. It is often said that Confederation, essentially an economic union, could hardly hope to achieve the sense of national identity and structural integration instilled, in some other national contexts, by revolutionary or civil conflict. Such integrative symbols as conflict, defeat, victory, national heroes, and evocative nationalistic ideals were thus less available than in the United States. Data sustaining this generalization are limited, although surveys pro-

---

7. For analyses that develop this theme, emphasizing interaction and ideological cohesion between Canadian political elites and interest group elites, see my *Elite Accommodation in Canadian Politics* and *Elites in the Policy Process* (New York and London: Cambridge University Press, 1973, 1974).

vide some useful information. Studies, for example, indicate considerable antinational bias among Canadian youth, including
some fairly unrealistic beliefs that government is less effective
and trustworthy in Ottawa, compared with the provinces.[8]

Tensions also appear regarding symbols and institutions that
affect national over against British loyalties. Such tensions are
symbolized by policy differences between the two major parties.
In rough contrast to the Liberals, Progressive Conservatives tend
to favor a strong imperial, monarchical posture, attended by an
anticontinental disposition and somewhat less sensitivity to the
claims of Quebec for special status. In terms of such ideological
preferences as welfare capitalism, defined as a preference for "big
government," Conservatives rank significantly higher.[9]

As John Porter has shown, the shifting tides of immigration and
emigration that have characterized the Canadian experience have
also inhibited political integration.[10] Demographic instability, in
effect, is not conducive to the inculcation of common national
values. Some unknown measure of demographic stability is probably required to develop political identity. In addition, had immigrants found themselves in a culture with a sharply defined,
evocative set of political symbols, integration might have been
easier to achieve.

Such political consequences of Canada's evolutionary separation from Britain, again contrasting sharply with the surgical
detachment characteristic of the United States, are seen in the
continuing tendency to conceptualize Canada as a *bicultural*
society. This assumption will probably generate tension in the
future, as so-called new Canadians become more fully accultur-
ated and demand greater participation in the political system.
Here, ironically, the "mosaic" pattern of acculturation may inhibit political integration as "new Canadians" find it difficult to

8. See, for example, A. B. Hodgetts, *What Heritage? What Culture? A Study of
Civic Education in Canada* (Toronto: Ontario Institute for Studies in Education,
1968), pp. 79–80.

9. Robert Presthus, "Variations in Social Class and Ideology: American and Canadian Legislators," special issue, *Cross-National Perspectives: United States and
Canada*, ed. Presthus, special issue, *International Journal of Comparative Sociology* 28 (March–June 1977).

10. See, for example, John Porter, "Canadian National Character," *Cultural
Affairs* 5 (1969): 46–50.

reconcile the possibly contradictory role of perpetuating their indigenous cultural heritage while at the same time becoming Canadians. Regardless of the outcome, the difficulty of achieving an overarching Canadianism, given the absence of a patent set of integrative symbols and experience, is a salient condition of Canadian political culture. In the present context, it may be regarded as one of the costs of Canada's evolutionary pattern of political development.

Contrasting Effects of the American Revolutionary Experience

Canada's evolutionary experience meant above all, as noted, the perpetuation in North America of British values and institutions. The influence of continental French culture upon Quebec has been less sustained, asserted perhaps mainly through the Church. To some extent, Quebec was abandoned by the mother country, and the great liberalizing influence of the Enlightenment is sometimes said to have had little impact upon Quebec. In both societies, however, it seems that the transition from traditional and charismatic bases of authority to those resting, in Weber's phrase, upon legal-rational norms has been complicated by their European legacy.

In the United States, the Revolution insured a dramatic break with European traditions. By turning their backs upon Europe, so to speak, Americans were able to escape the cramping effects of a feudal-born class system and any attending social dysfunctions. In the process, a great reservoir of human energy was released. However often honored in the breach, the ideals of upward mobility, of recruitment based upon achievement, of the attainment of great rewards for great individual effort—these provided a system of widely dispersed incentives often unknown in tradition-bound European societies. As Blau and Duncan have shown in their sophisticated analysis of occupational mobility in America, the reality as well as the myth of upward mobility has been widely realized in the United States.[11] Moreover, status

11. Peter Blau and O. D. Duncan, *The American Occupational Structure* (New York: Wiley, 1967), pp. 432–41.

distinctions based essentially upon potentially temporary variations in material possessions were less invidious than those predi-
cated upon immutable ascriptive criteria, as often seen in Britain
and Western Europe.

The most vital product of this revolutionary concept was the
achievement of democratic political integration in the United
States, despite its ethnic, religious, and regional diversity. The
viability of the concept is clear in the extent to which it was able
to bind together such disparate elements. The synthesis of the
democratic ideal of upward mobility and the empirical reality of
occupational progress, symbolized in equality based upon personal achievement rather than upon static ascriptive criteria, was
uniquely suited to the American milieu. It provided a system of
ideological rationalization and empirical effects that generally,
and with many exceptions, may have been as effective as is possible in an imperfect world.

Canada's evolutionary absorption of European class values may
also have had an inhibiting effect upon national economic development. The impact of educational policies provides one example. A persistent problem in Canada has been low productivity
in industry. As one Canadian economist concludes, "the level of
real output per employed person in Canadian manufacturing is
about 35 to 40 per cent lower than in the same sector of the
American economy." Comparison of quantitative data on sex, age,
hours worked, level of capital facilities, cross-national flow of
technical information, and machinery and equipment per em-
ployee "leads to the conclusion that most of the differences are
small . . . only educational differences are important with the
general level of education in Canada, and particularly business
and technical education, being substantially lower than in the
United States."[12]

12. D. J. Daly, "Manufacturing Productivity in Canada," *Cost and Management*
44 (1970): 2. See also D. J. Daly and S. Globerman, *Tariff and Science Policies:
Application of a Model of Nationalism* (Toronto: University of Toronto Press,
1976), which documents the costs of tariff policy in terms of low productivity,
high costs for consumer products, and relatively slow adoption of technological
innovations; and E. F. Denison with J-P. Pouiller, *Why Growth Rates Differ:
Postwar Experience in Nine Western Countries* (Washington, D.C.: Brookings
Institution, 1967).

Perhaps this secular condition reflects in part the absence of the kinds of incentives made possible by the American break with British traditions. The Gray Report on industrial strategy for Canada (1972) includes the following conclusions about the sources of uncertain domestic industrial growth in Canada:

i. Canada's colonial history may have led to a mentality of looking elsewhere for the new and the better in goods and services.
ii. The Canadian educational system, especially in Quebec, was more heavily geared to a classical curriculum than the United States and it did not turn out the engineers and business graduates needed to lead the development of an entrepreneurial and innovative society.
iii. Entry to financial institutions and, to some extent, to other large business tended in the past to be restricted to individuals having the right social connections. This lack of social mobility in Canadian society may have played a part in repressing the growth of indigenous innovation and entrepreneurship.[13]

The consequent historical dependence upon external sources for technical and entrepreneurial skills and investment capital has had decisive political consequences. Most obvious is a pervasive reliance upon government, federal and provincial, for support in private institutional sectors. Compared with the United States, which has of course had a laissez-faire rationale, ideological support for this condition is dramatically higher among Canadian political elites. The following evidence (see Table 1) is based upon my own research (1968–72) covering the responses of Canadian and American legislators to an index of "economic liberalism," defined as a positive acceptance of government intervention in the private economy. Clearly, Canadian legislators rank dramatically higher on this "big government" dimension, with over half of the sample at the "high" level, compared with one-quarter of their American counterparts. Within each system, the differences between federal and state/provincial members are not significant, suggesting that the often-cited regionalism of Canadian politics does not include this salient dimension.

The relatively strong Canadian preference for government

13. Herbert E. Gray, *Foreign Direct Investment in Canada*, (Ottawa: Information Canada, 1972), p. 40.

intervention is probably associated with a traditional policy of mercantilism, symbolized by a protective tariff policy that, despite its advantages, proved dysfunctional in some respects. As the economist Harry G. Johnson said, "There are strong domestic reasons for reducing Canada's trade barriers. These reasons are inherent in the economic waste and damage imposed on the Canadian public by the existing tariff."[14]

Table 1. *Economic Liberalism, United States v. Canadian Legislators, in percentages*

Economic Liberalism*	United States		Canada	
	Federal	State	Federal	Provincial
High	21	25	56	63
Medium	55	53	43	37
Low	24	22	—	—
	(90)	(147)	(122)	(117)

Federal = state: X^2 = .68741 with 2 d.f. = .1030
  Gamma = .03790
Federal = provincial: X^2 = .85141 with 1 d.f. = .1397
  Gamma = −.13863
Federal = federal: X^2 = 45.70766 with d.f. = .0000
  Gamma = .71306
State = provincial: X^2 = 50.44708 with 2 d.f. = .0000
  Gamma = .70495
* "Economic liberalism" is defined here by the following items: "That government which governs least governs best" (reverse scored); "Economic security for every man, woman and child is worth striving for, even if it means socialism"; "If unemployment is high, the government should spend money to create jobs"; "A national medicare plan is necessary to ensure that everyone receives adequate health care"; and "More federal aid to education is desirable if we are going to adequately meet present and future educational needs in this country."

Relatively low industrial productivity is allied with the Canadian policy of protective tariffs. One consequence is a high-cost economy, the principal burden of which is borne by urban wage earners, in lower wages and higher costs of living. Meanwhile, a small managerial class enjoys incomes that are perhaps higher than they deserve, a condition aggravated by nationalism. As

14. Harry G. Johnson, *The Canadian Quandary* (Toronto: McClelland and Stewart, 1977), p. 96.

Albert Breton concludes, "some people will be paid more than they are worth because they are of the 'proper' national origin and/or more people will be employed than is economically optimal."[15] The persistence of the protective tariff policy, despite its untoward effects upon a majority of the public, may suggest certain limitations upon effective popular participation in the political system.

Some Dysfunctional Consequences of Educational Elitism

As often noted, a major spur for both political and industrial development and high productivity is a highly educated society. Here again, the American and Canadian experiences are inapposite. Whereas education became a hallowed instrument of individual mobility in the United States, in Canada the British elitist tradition inhibited the development of a similar ethos, especially at the university level. And, once again, Canada's control of the resources and institutions required for sustained political and industrial growth was weakened by the resultant need to rely heavily upon immigration for the talents required to man its socioeconomic system.

The impact of the tendency toward elitism insofar as higher education is concerned may be seen in the following conditions. Despite a sustained and generous effort since World War II to expand educational opportunity at the university level, the proportion of Canadian youth aged eighteen to twenty-four in universities increased only from 5 percent in 1945 to about 15 percent in 1975.[16] In the United States the comparative proportion at the latter period was over 40 percent. Moreover, as is true to some degree in all Western countries, higher education in Canada is strongly and positively associated with class status. As Wallace Clement showed in 1972, less than 10 percent of Canadians have

15. Albert Breton, "The Economics of Nationalism," *Journal of Political Economy* 72 (1964): 376–86.

16. Dominion Bureau of Statistics. See also the first report of the Commission on Canadian Studies, Association of Canadian Universities and College, 1976.

attended university, compared with over 80 percent of the same age groups among elites in the mass media, over 60 percent of whom enjoyed upper-class status.[17]

The operational effects of class-based conceptions of society are again evident in labor-management relations in Canada. Here again, one must generalize at a very broad level, but the essential fact remains that union leaders in Canada often bring to the bargaining table the stale adversary attitudes and rhetoric that have traditionally characterized union-management interactions in Britain. Moreover, these residues (unlike those in some other sectors) seem to be growing in intensity, as seen in the emergence of a class politics in Quebec, led by a Common Front of blue- and white-collar unions. Sympathy for the generalized postmeritoc-racy orientation of the union movement seems to be widely ap-parent among university students and professors, further en-couraging the influence of collectivist definitions of social policy, often made good by an appeal to government.

The consequences of elitism include considerable dependence upon immigration for skilled workers and professionals required to staff Canadian industry and higher education. As John Porter has shown, this condition is of long standing and it has been ag-gravated by a secular "brain drain," whereby highly educated Canadians have often moved south to take advantage of some-what more favorable levels of income and somewhat lower costs of living.[18] A significant normative corollary is the dampening effect upon upward social mobility. Widely available higher edu-cation, of course, has been among the most salient avenues of mobility in Western society. More important for the present analysis, its absence symbolizes the existence of a tradition-oriented culture. As Ralf Dahrendorf writes, "Autonomous equal-ity of opportunity for all men . . . epitomizes modernity."[19]

17. Wallace Clement, *The Canadian Corporate Elite* (Toronto: McClelland and Stewart, 1975), p. 338.

18. John Porter, *The Vertical Mosaic* (Toronto: University of Toronto Press, 1965), pp. 240–41.

19. Ralf Dahrendorf, *Society and Democracy in Germany* (New York: Double-day, 1967), p. 402.

In terms of political effects, educational elitism results in considerable strain upon a thin stratum of highly educated men and women. Among the consequences is a tendency for federal and provincial governments to compete strongly with the universities for talented people. Pushed in part by inflation and pulled by substantially higher incomes, some university faculty members move into governmental hierarchies. Others take leaves of varying lengths to serve government. In both cases, one consequence is to weaken occupational commitment to higher education and to disrupt the continuity of university programs.

Despite some positive benefits, a related effect may be to reduce popular control of government by further strengthening the bureaucracy vis-à-vis legislators. Some observers maintain that the federal bureaucracy is the lodestar of the policymaking process, given its tendency to monopolize substantive knowledge and information. Evidence suggests, moreover, that while the major interaction in Canadian government occurs between interest-group leaders and senior civil servants, in the United States it occurs between such groups and legislators or legislative committees; i.e., between elected rather than appointed members of the political apparatus.[20] Such variations obviously reflect differences in the locus of power in parliamentary and presidential systems, but the implications for democratic control remain suggestive.

Further implications for popular control arise when participation is defined as penetration of the political system through interest groups, which provide the major practical avenue for citizen participation. Participation is in part a consequence of educational levels, in that group membership rises with education. But, despite the fact that levels of group membership are very similar in the two societies, the extent of interest-group penetration of the political system is sharply lower in Canada. As my research indicates, 42 percent of a random sample ($N =$ 1,414) of Canadian interest-group leaders, compared with 70 percent of their American counterparts, interact "frequently" with

20. Cf Presthus, *Elites in the Policy Process*, pp. 258, 269, 301, 315.

legislators and bureaucrats.[21] This finding is probably influenced by the relatively "closed" nature of the parliamentary system, which in itself tends to limit interest-group participation.

Meanwhile, some evidence suggests that low educational levels and popular cynicism tend to restrict *individual* participation in politics. A national election survey (1965), for example, indicated that only 4 percent of the Canadian sample participated at a "high" level.[22] Information from the 1974 national election reveals a similar pattern. Voting remains high at 85 percent, but other forms of participation engage only a small proportion of citizens. At the "frequently" level, 30 percent of respondents ($N = 1,201$) discussed politics with neighbors and friends; 10 percent attempted to convince a friend to vote for a given party; 5 percent attended political meetings; and only 4 percent were directly engaged in campaign activity.[23] Meanwhile, national surveys during 1965 and 1968 found that 83 and 90 percent, respectively, of Canadian adults agreed that "the government is pretty much run by a few big interests looking out for themselves." More detailed information on participation and trust will be presented below, including an important qualification of the strong positive relationship usually found between educational level and political involvement.

Problems of Political Integration

Any analysis of Canadian political integration must include the question of Quebec and separatism. Personal identification with Canada as a national state is vitally affected by the French fact. When a national survey (1968) asked, "How do you think of yourself?" about 60 percent of English Canadians and other ethnic groups replied, "Simply as a Canadian." This compares

21. Ibid., p. 178.
22. R. Van Loon, "Political Participation in Canada: The 1965 Election," *Canadian Journal of Political Science* 3 (1970): 384, 4.
23. H. Clarke, J. Jenson, L. Leduc, and J. Pammett, *The 1974 Canadian Election Study* (made available by the Institute for Behavioral Research, York University, Toronto, 1976). Interpretations of these data are the responsibility of the author.

with only one-third of French Canadians who gave the same answer.[24] The persistence of British traditions has probably aggravated the English-French duality by making it more difficult for the English-Canadian majority to abandon institutions, rituals, and symbols that at times appear simply provocative to some segments of Quebec society.

French and English Canadians have been sharply divided regarding such political conditions as the monarchy, bilingualism in government communications, ethnic proportionality in appointments to the federal system, and, perhaps, regarding the legitimacy of Confederation itself. The resistance of French Canadians to conscription during the world wars provides another critical example.

The resultant politics of *ressentiment* are apparent in recent Quebec political history. Revolutionary groups such as the Quebec Liberation Front received considerable popular support, for their objectives but not their methods. More recently, the separatist Parti Québécois appeared. Since new parties appear in bewildering succession in Quebec, it was easy to overemphasize the significance of the Parti Québécois as the official opposition party, based upon the some 30 percent of the popular vote it received in the 1974 election. However, riding upon the decline of popular support for the Bourassa Liberal government, especially during 1975–76, the party assumed power in Quebec in November 1976, on a platform including separation from Confederation and further nationalization. Regardless of party fortunes and the resolution of the separatist issue, the underlying reality of Quebec nationalism and cultural particularism continues to make Canadian integration precarious and provides the most critical cleavage in Canadian politics.

Deferential Patterns of Authority, Political Efficacy, and Participation

Another element in the colonial mold that seems to affect Canadian political culture and participation is hierarchically based

24. John Meisel, national election survey, 1968, unpublished data.

conceptions of authority and leadership. Such tend to take prece-
dence over authority based upon expertise. Here again, the British
cultural heritage seems to have direct implications for political
styles and participation. Deferential patterns of authority, sometimes characterized as the "Old Tory theory of leadership"[25] and
institutionalized in the highly centralized parliamentary system
with its strong party discipline, may inhibit participation and
feelings of efficacy, among both elected officials and unorganized
publics. Regarding back-benchers, it may be relevant that only 38
percent rank high on a political efficacy scale. Not unexpectedly,
cabinet members rank substantially higher at 55 percent.[26] Given
their advantaged educational and occupational status,[27] it is unexpected that back-benchers rank this low. The explanation lies
in part in their relatively jejune role in the parliamentary system,
where power and influence rest mainly in the prime minister,
cabinet, and senior officials.

Among ordinary citizens, deferential patterns of authority are
reinforced by socialization, educational elitism, the rankings symbolized by such institutions as the monarchy, nice bureaucratic
distinctions of authority and status, and the hierarchy characteristic of religious and corporate orders. Typically, mass media
tend to legitimate such distinctions, encouraging a popular climate of deference. As Arthur Stinchcombe writes, "such a feeling
of awe, wonder, and worship toward powerful people—tsars, mil-
lionaires, geniuses, stars, or bosses—tends to make them into
models or ego-ideals which children, adolescents, and schizo-
phrenics model themselves after. . . . Power makes a man extraordinary and people imitate extraordinary men, thus regenerat-
ing institutions over the generations. By selection, socialization,

25. Harry Eckstein, *Pressure Group Politics* (London: Allen and Unwin, 1960),
pp. 24–25.
26. Presthus, *Elite Accommodation in Canadian Politics*, p. 292.
27. In 1970, for example, 71 percent of legislators in Ottawa and three provinces
(N = 269) ranked in the two highest categories of the Hollingshead SES scale;
ibid., p. 341. For the extent to which political efficacy and participation tend to
be monopolized by those of advantaged class status, see Sidney Verba and
Norman Nie, *Participation in America* (New York: Harper and Row, 1972), pp.
82–93, 95–101.

controlling conditions of incumbency, and hero worship, succeeding generations of power-holders tend to regenerate the same institutions."[28]

The political consequences of such patterns of socialization are likely to include relatively low levels of efficacy on the part of ordinary citizens. It is perhaps significant here that Canadian legislators themselves do not generally regard the political subsystem as being very "open" to penetration. Among federal and provincial-state respondents ($N = 518$), for example, 43 percent of Canadian members of Parliament, compared with 62 percent of American legislators, ranked "high" on perceived "openness of the political system."[29]

If legislators have somewhat restricted perceptions of their own opportunities for group participation, we should expect to find citizens themselves expressing similar reservations about political efficacy. Some evidence regarding this dimension among rank-and file members of North American society is shown in Table 2.

Table 2. *Comparative Levels of Citizen Political Efficacy, United States and Canada, in percentages*

	Percentage Agreeing	
	United States[a]	Canadian[b]
"Voting is the only way people like me can have a say about how the government runs things."	68	76
"Sometimes politics and government seem so complicated that a person like me can't really understand what is going on."	69	69
"People like me don't have any say about what the government does."	34	49
	(1,571)	(2,721)

[a] American data from 1966 Election Study, Survey Research Center, University of Michigan.
[b] Canadian data from John Meisel, national election survey of 1965 (unpublished data). The last item was phrased slightly different in this survey, i.e., "I don't think the government cares what people like me think."

28. Arthur Stinchcombe, *Constructing Social Theories* (New York: Harcourt, Brace and World, 1968), p. 111.
29. Presthus, *Elites in the Policy Process*, p. 391.

Such comparative data suggest that feelings of efficacy are not very highly developed in either Canada or the United States, but that the former ranks significantly lower on the last item. A national survey (1965) provides additional comparative evidence regarding rank-and-file "alienation"[30] from government.[31] When asked, "Do you feel that people high in government give everyone a fair break or that some pay more attention to what the big interests want?" 83 percent of Canadians maintained that "big interests" received favored treatment, compared with 39 percent of a national American sample. By 1968, the comparative rates were 90 and 44 percent.

Not surprisingly, such perceptions of efficacy and participation vary over time. Given recent American experience with Vietnam and Watergate, one would assume that political cynicism in the United States had increased and that feelings of efficacy and participation would have declined. Evidence from the 1972 (United States) and 1974 (Canadian) national elections generally suggests that such is the case and that earlier variations found between Canada and the United States have decreased. Participation rates, for example, have apparently become somewhat higher in Canada, as shown in Table 3.[32]

Clearly, voting turnout has been consistently higher in Canada during the period measured. Although not shown here, there are no significant regional or language variations. More interesting is the fact that education plays a much stronger part in participation in the United States, compared with Canada. For example, in their "low" category of education (1–8 years), Beck and Pierce find that fully one-fifth of Canadians have participated in campaign or party work or have attended a political meeting, com-

---

30. "Alienation" is a multidimensional concept, defined here simply as a feeling of disenchantment regarding government and politics, sometimes attended by withdrawal from or lack of support of the political system. For one detailed analysis, see Ada Finifter, "Dimensions of Political Alienation," *American Political Science Review* 64 (June 1970), pp. 389–410.
    31. John Meisel, national election survey, 1965 (unpublished data).
    32. Revised from Nathaniel Beck and John Pierce, "Political Involvement and Party Allegiance in Canada and the United States," in *Cross-National Perspectives* ed. Presthus.

Table 3. *Political Participation, Efficacy, and Trust in the United States and Canada, in percentages*

	United States			Canada		
	1972	1968	1964	1974	1968	1965
Political Activity[a]						
Read newspapers often	37	49	47	43	—	—
Tried to convince others	32	32	31	23–34		23
Attended rally, meeting	9	9	9	19–32	—	15
Did party work	5	5	5	11–17	—	5
Displayed sticker	14	15	16	16–21	—	—
Voted	75	76	78	85	86	86
Political efficacy (% efficacious)[b]						
Leaders soon lose touch	32	44	—	35	39	40
Government complicated	29	28	32	35	28	29
Government doesn't care	50	56	63	42	54	52
People like me have no say	64	59	70	45	51	49
Political trust (% cynical)						
Government wastes money	68	61	48	—	46	38
People in government crooked	38	20	30	—	27	27
Government by big interests	59	44	30	—	90	83
People in government smart	42	39	28	—	49	57
Trust government to do right	46	37	22	—	39	39
Average	51	40	32	—	50	49

[a] The entry in each cell is the percentage of the sample in that year reporting that they engaged in that political activity. On these activities, questions in the two countries were asked differently. In the Canadian study, individuals were given the opportunity to indicate the *frequency* with which they participated in the activity, while in the American the alternatives were simply yes or no. The first figure in the Canadian percentages excludes respondents saying they "seldom" or "never" participated in the activity. The second figure excludes only those individuals who said they "never" participated in the activity.

[b] For the political efficacy questions, the entry in each cell is the percentage giving an *efficacious* response. For the political trust questions, the entry in each cell is the percentage giving a *cynical* response. No political trust questions were asked in the 1974 Canadian study.

pared with only 4 percent of Americans. At the "medium" level (9–13) the corresponding rates are 23 and 10 percent, while among those with university experience the variation falls to 25 versus 19 percent. Overall, it seems that the present generalization is that Canadians participate more but have less trust in politics, compared with Americans.

The main variations regarding efficacy appear on the two items that tap political responsiveness rather directly. Americans are more likely to state that officials do not care what "people like me think," but also they are less likely to agree that they "don't have any say about what government does." As Beck and Pierce conclude, although the American responses vary considerably across items, they rank positively on the latter item, which most directly confronts the meaning of the concept of efficacy—the individual's perception of an ability to impact government."[33] The cross-national comparison is clouded by the fact that the Canadian survey of 1974 did not include items regarding political trust. In the American case, as suggested, there has been a dramatic increase in cynicism. Earlier bases of cynicism, however, vary. In the Canadian case, citizens most often feel that government is unresponsive, while American ambivalence is based upon government's alleged inefficiency.

The British legacy shapes Canadian political culture and occupational recruitment in yet another salient way. If one thinks in sociological terms of recruitment criteria ranging from ascription to achievement, Canada and the United States seem to occupy different points along the continuum. As several observers have concluded,[34] Canadian norms tend to be somewhat more ascriptive and particularistic, reflecting the survival of British class influences. Such residues, set down initially in Loyalist institutions such as the Family Compact, 1790–1841, remain salient. As Wallace Clement says, in an analysis that concludes that entry to high-level economic posts is more restricted today than in earlier periods:

The ruling classes of Upper and Lower Canada formed a tight set of family relations and were firmly based on a union of interlocking interests. Alliance was formed through political, religious and financial control which united them into a single social class active as an "elite of office" and represented in the inner circles of the Executive Council by a "power elite." Their power was political as much as economic and they enjoyed the advantages of both through land grants and access to capital but they were not engaged in industrial

33. Ibid.
34. See, for example, Wallace Clement, *The Canadian Corporate Elite* (Toronto: McClelland and Stewart, 1975) and Porter, *Vertical Mosaic*. For evidence concerning Quebec, see Norman Taylor, "The French-Canadian Entrepreneur and his Social Environment," in *French-Canadian Society*, ed. M. Rioux and Y. Martin (Toronto: McClelland and Stewart, 1969), pp. 271–95.

pursuits, choosing rather to build on merchant capital. . . . Initially, each filled a "political vacuum" but by accumulating advantages evolved into a rigid structure commanding political and economic power which remained dominant for some fifty years.[35]

Here again, perhaps, the evolutionary pattern of Canadian social development seems to have insured the survival of residues of such historical experience.

The early synthesis of economic, familial, and political power was reinforced by such instruments of socialization as private schools that emulate British public schools, the classical colleges in Quebec, elite clubs, the use of military titles associated with venerable regiments, educational and cultural ties with the imperial British tradition, and the use of the British model in political affairs. Such influences lie behind any "generalist," ascriptive assumptions that tend to characterize political and bureaucratic recruitment in contemporary Canada.

The historical strength of financial-commercial structures and the bureaucratic ethos[36] in Canadian life may also have provided a powerful conservative socializing force to the extent that the "security" orientation of such institutions contrasts sharply with an entrepreneurial ethos. The attending political effects are perhaps apparent in the extent to which party organization and politics in Canada remain influenced by "notables,"[37] in the tendency for parliamentary office to be an interlude in a career devoted to some nonpolitical activity, in the 40 percent rate of turnover among members of each national parliament, and in the policy of rotation in cabinet posts and the higher bureaucracy.

The Politics of Accommodation

As suggested earlier, centrifugal forces in the Canadian environment have been successfully contained by a political mecha-

---

35. Clement, *Canadian Corporate Elite*, p. 50.
36. S. D. Clark, *The Developing Canadian Community*, 2d ed. (Toronto: University of Toronto Press, 1968), p. 234.
37. Cf. Max Weber, "Politics as a Vocation," in *From Max Weber*, ed. H. Gerth and D. W. Mills (New York: Oxford University Press, 1946).

nism known as "elite accommodation."[38] Elite accommodation was initially advanced as an alternative explanation for democratic stability in certain Western political systems that did not exhibit the characteristics commonly held to insure stability. Briefly, such characteristics include a popular consensus regarding certain political "rules of the game," such as the belief that parties should voluntarily relinquish office when defeated. This consensus is said to rest, in turn, upon a "high" degree of national political integration. Other critical components include two-party systems, which are held to insure consensual politics and majority government, and the assumption that most individuals belong to groups with inapposite goals. Such "crosscutting" membership presumably has a moderating effect upon individual claims, similar to that of two-party systems.

Certain highly stable political systems such as the Netherlands, Belgium, Austria, Canada, and Switzerland, however, are characterized instead by deep-seated religious, ethnic, linguistic, and regional cleavages. Group membership, moreover, often tends to be reinforcing: a Catholic worker might belong to a Catholic trade union, read a Catholic paper, and belong to a Catholic political party. Intergroup contacts are minimal, since the various subcultural enclaves tend to remain isolated from each other. The question then arises, how is stability maintained in such political settings?

The theory of elite accommodation answers this question by assuming, in effect, that policymaking and political leadership are delegated to elites representing the major subcultural groups in society. They reconcile divisive issues and determine major policies in concert, isolated from their various subcultural constituencies. Such elites must, in turn, possess certain psychological characteristics. They must understand that cleavages exist; they must be capable of acting in ways that overcome the disintegrating effects of such cleavages; they must have a "nation-saving" purpose.

Such "consociational" systems usually possess certain other

38. See Presthus, *Elite Accommodation in Canadian Politics.*

characteristics, including surplus wealth, which enables them to afford occasional symbolic, economically unjustifiable (or at least questionable) expenditures, which have an integrating effect. A relatively moderate "load" on government is often cited as a necessary condition, presumably because it permits such expenditures. Institutionally, such systems must possess deferential constituencies who will delegate considerable autonomy to their leaders. The existence of some fear of an external threat is another of the prescribed conditions, possibly because this might increase integration as well as the desire to find mutually acceptable solutions to national problems. Meanwhile, within each subculture a fairly high degree of cohesion and organization must exist. A corollary is that polarization among subcultures is useful, easing conflict and again encouraging the tendency to delegate political authority to elites and to accept their determinations.

Although space permits only a brief analysis, Canada seems to meet most of these conditions. The ancestral fear and ambivalence of Canadians toward the United States provides one such motivating incentive. French- and English-Canadian dualism is perhaps the most critical and well-known example. Moreover, within these isolated subcultures, one often finds a miniature system, as it were, of elite accommodation, which tends to contribute to the effectiveness of accommodation at the national level. As Jacques Dofny and Marcel Rioux say, regarding Quebec politics before 1948, "working-class conflicts tended to be settled between employers, politicians, and the High Clergy over the heads of the workers. Although the dominant ideology was nationalist, there was always collusion between, on the one hand, the politicians, the French-Canadian middle-class businessmen, and certain members of the High Clergy and, on the other, the non-French-Canadian middle-class businessmen and politicians. With the development of a more dynamic trade unionism, the workers' class consciousness became more and more assertive."[39] The inclusion of French-Canadian elites in successive Liberal cabinets

39. Jacques Dofny and Marcel Rioux, "Social Class in French Canada," cited in *French-Canadian Society*, ed. M. Rioux and Y. Martin, 1:311.

in Ottawa, ethnic proportionality in high bureaucratic and federal court appointments, protracted "nation-saving" concessions to Quebec, the reconciliation of federal-provincial issues by informal mechanisms such as federal-provincial conferences, the siting in Montreal of such symbolic events as Expo 67 and the 1976 Olympic games—these provide examples of accommodative mechanisms.

There is some evidence that the kind of bargaining that characterizes the process of elite accommodation has occurred throughout Canadian history since Confederation. The synthesis between economic and political leaders, nourished by the dependence of business and industry upon government subsidies and tariff protection, has been apparent since that time. Some observers believe that the apogee of business-politician partnership was reached in the Family Compact, but other evidence suggests that the nexus remained strong during the two great wars and down to the present time.[40]

The success of elite accommodation is clearly apparent in the century-long survival of Confederation, despite the strains and tensions provided by a difficult and challenging environment. Evidence is beginning to appear, however, perhaps most clearly in Quebec, that a new, more dynamic class basis for national politics may be emerging.[41]

Toward a Class Politics in Canada

Despite the cultural and economic factors that have shaped the accommodative style in Canadian politics, there are some indi-

40. Among others, see Frank Underhill, *In Search of Canadian Liberalism* (Toronto: Macmillan, 1960), p. 167; A. Siegfried, *The Race Question in Canada* (Toronto: McClelland and Stewart, 1966), p. 118; Clark, *Developing Canadian Community;* Clement, *Canadian Corporate Elite;* G. Myers, *History of Canadian Wealth* (New York: Argosy-Antiquarian, 1968); and R. N. Naylor, *The History of Canadian Business,* 2 vols. (Toronto: James Lorimer, 1975).

41. For analyses that challenge the conventional view that social class is tangential in Canadian political behavior, see Porter, *Vertical Mosaic;* and John Wilson, "Politics and Social Class in Canada: The Case of Waterloo South," *Canadian Journal of Political Science* 1 (1968): 288–309.

cations that a class style of politics is appearing. Here again, the class consciousness and sense of exploitation that inspire this movement are essentially of European origin. As is well known, American workers never accepted the Marxian interpretation of their relationship with industrial capitalism. Instead, as part of the generalized American rejection of class-based analysis (again reflecting the revolutionary experience), they internalized the values of individualistic capitalism and upward mobility. The presence of a viable socialist, labor-oriented party in Canada suggests the extent to which class analysis, however neglected, has been more relevant in Canadian society.

The most patent manifestation of class politics may be seen in French Canada where the historical dampening of class consciousness by religiosity, cultural nationalism and a quasi-participative political culture is being eroded. Labor unions are in the vanguard of this movement, but it is significant that in the early 1970s such white-collar groups as civil servants and teachers had also accepted working-class ideology and in some cases had combined with blue-collar workers in strike action. The long-standing assumption of Quebec political and economic elites that huge infusions of foreign capital would spark industrial development in the province, and thus insure some measure of economic equality, is probably no longer accepted by most Québécois. The political language of the mass of working men and women is increasingly spoken in a Marxian dialect.

The ideological factors underlying this emerging drift thus include the belief that industrial capitalism can no longer provide the secular growth upon which its earlier success has been built. Socialism is regarded as the antidote. Such problems as the long-run impact of higher energy costs upon living standards in Canada are aggravated by the fact that the gross national product slowed virtually to a halt in Canada in 1973 and 1974. This condition may be temporary, but in addition to the problems of scarce energy and the capacity of major oil-producing countries to form cartels (following the classical Western model), pervasive psychological changes in North American society regarding work and accumulation will probably intensify the problem of increasing the size of the gross national product in both Canada and the United States.

The decline of the Protestant Ethic is, I submit, quite clearly apparent in both English Canada and the United States. Canada's historic dependence upon government to cushion the risks of the marketplace and its bureaucratic ethos may aggravate the decline. The consequences may include what is often regarded as a saner, more mature life-style, but its by-products will almost surely include some decline in the productivity upon which national wealth and cultural growth ultimately depend.

When the net social product levels off, while inflation continues, reconciliation of the claims of great social interests tends to become a zero-sum game in which the gains of one group are obtained at the expense of other, perhaps less well-organized, groups. This dialectic encourages class tensions that will, it seems, manifest themselves in a challenge to traditional "brokerage" politics and welfare capitalism in Canada. The resultant collectively based ideologies will tend, over time, to replace the individualistic, competitive values that have often been vital socializing instruments in North American society. Since such values have been somewhat more precarious in Canada, their decline may also occur more rapidly. Meanwhile, the generalized erosion of public confidence in government following Vietnam and Watergate, the decline of electoral support for the Trudeau Liberal government, the victory of the Parti Québécois in 1976, and the resentment of many Canadians at Ottawa's apparent inability to deflect inflation or curb unemployment are undercutting traditional deferential patterns of authority, with attending effects upon the legitimacy of political elites and their capacity to govern in the traditional style.

The emergence of a class politics may also be encouraged by another environmental condition, Canadian multiculturalism. As noted, the persistence of evolutionary patterns of thought is perhaps evident in the extent to which Canadian society continues to be perceived by the two charter groups as bicultural. About a third of Canadians, however, are now members of other subcultures. Many are from European societies in which the language of social class and socialism is common. As these "new Canadians" become more closely welded into the national mosaic, as their children experience social mobility through higher education, prevailing allocations of power and influence, and conventional French- and English-Canadian values and institutions will undergo change. The traditional, essentially reactive, "brokerage" role of Canadian parties seems less likely to prove acceptable. For some unknown period, it may be that the institutions will change less than the individuals who man them, but it seems reasonable to assume that "new Canadians," for whom some charter-group values are probably tangential, will press for modified social and political structures that will more closely reflect their own needs and preferences.

In summary, it seems that the effects of the Canadian evolutionary path of national development contrast sharply with the revolutionary tradition of the United States and that the Canadian experience may at times have inhibited the capacity of the nation to incorporate social change with reasonable ease and dispatch. Certain judicial, economic, and educational policies provide illustrations with decisive political consequences. A very slow development in the area of such civil rights as equal protection of the law provides an example. The survival of a protectionist tariff policy, with attending untoward effects upon productivity, inflation, the implementation of technical innovation, and a broader sharing of national income suggests that political participation has been insufficient to overcome certain inequalities of the distributive system.

More recently, pervasive political and cultural nationalism has probably aggravated to some unknown extent any tendencies toward ascriptive recruitment in educational and corporate structures. As Gunnar Myrdal has written, while nationalism among developing nations is perfectly understandable, it is often a costly anachronism among rich Western societies.[42] Meanwhile, educa-

42. Gunnar Myrdal, *Beyond the Welfare State* (New Haven: Yale University Press, 1960), pp. 206–9; 286–87.

tional elitism has undercut the capacity of Canadian society to meet the skill needs of a modern industrial state. Finally, the transmutation of British class values has almost certainly had a significantly negative influence upon labor-management relations in Canada, which continue to be characterized by class antagonisms. To some considerable extent, the perpetuation of such traditional values and their institutional crystallization is a function of the unique Canadian evolutionary experience.

The contrasting American experience has enabled that country to escape some of these dilemmas, but as recent history suggests, its own experience includes other persistent problems of social and ethnic equality, the pervasive rationalization of life in the service of economic goals, and the ultimate disenchantment of materialistic indulgence.

7

The Implications of an Evolutionary Tradition for the Structure and Functioning of Canada's Economic Development

André Raynauld

"Unquestionably the economic interpretation illuminates much history," observe Will and Ariel Durant in their book, *The Lessons of History.*

The money of the Delian Confederacy built the Parthenon; the treasury of Cleopatra's Egypt revitalized the exhausted Italy of Augustus, gave Virgil an annuity, and Horace a farm. The Crusades, like the wars of Rome with Persia, were attempts of the West to capture trade routes to the East; the discovery of America was the result of the failure of the Crusades. The banking house of the Medici financed the Florentine Renaissance; the trade and industry of Nuremberg made Dürer possible. The French Revolution came not because Voltaire wrote brilliant satires and Rousseau sentimental romances, but because the middle classes had risen to economic leadership, needed legislative freedom for their enterprise and trade, and itched for social acceptance and political power.[1]

Indeed, economic factors explain much of the chronicle of mankind, and we cannot hope to understand the differences between Canada and the United States or to learn from these differences without an examination of the economic forces that have shaped the two societies. We all know the importance of economic considerations in the events that led to the American Revolution and thus created the United States. The economic elements in the mix of concerns that kept British North America

1. Will and Ariel Durant, *The Lessons of History* (New York: Simon and Schuster, 1968), pp. 52–53.

loyal to the Crown are perhaps less clear; but that "forced marriage" between French-Canadian *habitants* and English Tories that formed the basis of modern Canada certainly had many economic aspects. The French Canadians were anxious to maintain their own style of landholding and agriculture, as well as to continue the profitable fur-trading activities across the northern half of the continent, which the British conquest of Quebec fifteen years before the American Revolution had not interrupted. On the other hand, the Loyalist refugees from the English colonies were motivated in significant degree by the desire to preserve their prosperous bourgeois status. "Nearly all the important property owners of the province of New York were Tories," according to the American historians Nevins and Commager.[2] Undoubtedly, they intended to reestablish their privileged situation, threatened by the populist tendencies associated with the Revolution, under the protection of the British imperial authority in Canada.

However, all this was a long time ago. Since then, the integrating influences of a common North American experience, in which each country moved from its agrarian origins to become a part of the industrial civilization that dominates modern life, have greatly narrowed the distinctions that characterized their early economic orientation. Today the casual visitor to Montreal, Toronto, Winnipeg, or Vancouver may be aware that he is in a separate political and cultural milieu from New York, Chicago, or Los Angeles, but he will not perceive much difference between the economic basis of affairs in Canadian cities and in the comparable places south of the border. He could be excused for believing that the years had virtually expunged all the peculiarities that at one time clearly distinguished one economy from the other.

But that conclusion would be wrong, as anyone knows who has had the opportunity to penetrate at all below the superficial similarities. The structure of Canadian industry is different from that of American—more heavily concentrated in primary products

2. Allan Nevins and Henry Steele Commager, *History of the United States* (New York: Pocket Books, 1951), p. 102.

and with a greater dependence on foreign trade. Although capital flows strongly between the two countries (Canadians indeed investing, in per capita terms, somewhat more in the United States than Americans invest in Canada), the forms in which this capital moves are usually very different in the one direction than in the other. Related to this factor, much of Canadian economic activity is owned or controlled by United States interests, whereas Canadian money in the United States tends to be part of an equity portfolio rather than a direct investment in productive facilities. Government involvement in the economy is appreciably more apparent in Canada than it is in this country. The extent of publicly funded social welfare arrangements is also, as a general rule, somewhat greater in Canada than here.

More Fundamental Factors

The trouble, for present purposes, is to know how much of these differences arises from the evolutionary as against the revolutionary tradition—the subject of this conference—compared with the fundamental factors of Canadian geography and climate as they contrast with the American. Because, of course, the map of North America, which shows your country and mine as having a roughly similar overall area, provides no indicator at all of the respective economic potential of the two territories. Quite apart from the cold, which renders the greater part of Canada extremely inhospitable for perhaps four months of each year in the southern regions and seven or eight months in the far North, there is the effect that past ice ages have had on the geological characteristics of the country. Vast glacial movements denuded three-quarters or more of the Canadian land area of all surface rock strata, leaving behind a barren wilderness that is rich in minerals but virtually useless for agriculture. As a consequence, Canada is, for most practical purposes, a narrow strip just above the United States frontier capable of sustaining only a fraction of the population that the generally congenial environment to the south is able to support.

It is this much smaller carrying capacity, and all the relative disadvantages it entails of inferior scale and possibilities for industrial specialization, that is at the root of Canada's economic weakness vis-à-vis the United States. One cannot imagine for a moment that the situation would be otherwise if there had been a Canadian revolution too, paralleling the American—assuming that the two countries had remained separate. Henry Fairlie, the British writer who has made his home in the United States for a number of years, showed a woeful misunderstanding of these elementary facts when he observed recently in the magazine *Encounter*, "The mystery of Canada's backwardness—and it *is* backward when contrasted with its neighbour—is something that the Englishman in North America is bound to contemplate. It cannot be explained only in terms of resources; and as the Englishman puts his question to the Canadians whom he meets, he cannot ignore how often they reach in the end the same answer: Because we have had a monarchy all this time."[3] To my mind this is just nonsense; it is degrees of latitude, rather than imperial and regal connections, that must bear the overwhelming responsibility for making Canada economically smaller and poorer than the Republic.

Nevertheless, the longer colonial experience north of the border doubtless has had some influence on the nature of that society, including its economic situation and past performance, so let us try to see what the lessons of history may teach us in this respect.

The Importance of Trade

As everyone knows, one of the peculiarities of colonial economies tends to be their integration into a transnational system of trade and factor movements that is focused on the imperial metropolis. All the North American colonies were naturally in this position

3. Henry Fairlie, "Transatlantic Letter to England," *Encounter,* January 1976, p. 11.

in the seventeenth and eighteenth centuries, and both the United States and Canada became steadily less dependent as time went on. Do the data on this relationship, imperfect as they are for the early periods, tell us anything about the differences between the two countries after 1776?

So far as trade is concerned, the striking factor is perhaps the extent of United States reliance on the British market, and to a smaller degree on British sources of supply, up to comparatively recent times. Close to half of all American exports went to the United Kingdom throughout the nineteenth century, and the proportion then weakened only very gradually to a third until World War I and the Great Depression radically changed trade patterns. For imports, the British share of the United States market fluctuated between a third and a half until around 1880, when it started to fall, going down to about one-sixth in the early 1900s. Today Britain accounts for a mere 5 or 6 percent of exports from and imports to the United States.

In Canada's case, surprisingly, the importance of Britain as market and source of supply was almost exactly comparable to the United States experience—that is, a third to a half of all trade was with the United Kingdom—throughout the nineteenth and early twentieth centuries. However, the proportion of total shipments in either direction held up substantially better in Canada than here during the interwar years. It was only after World War II that Canadian exports to Britain dropped from their previous one-third or more to one-fifth and then eventually to one-tenth and even less. Imports from Britain also maintained a fairly good level as a share of the total—about one-sixth to one-quarter—until World War II, when they too began to decline rapidly, reaching one-tenth in the 1950s and not much more than one-twentieth today.

What does this tell us of revolutionary and evolutionary paths to economic development? Well, the paths are not very different, since the experience over at least 125 years after 1776 was so similar in the two cases and is similar again now. Admittedly, an imperial factor had its effect in the period between the two world wars, maintaining Canada's British trade link while it declined in the case of the United States. This was the so-called British preference system of import-tariff arrangements among Commonwealth countries, which was reinforced in the depression in response to the ferocious increases in United States duties embodied in the Smoot-Hawley tariff. However, its effects have rapidly eroded with the general decrease in international trade barriers since World War II, and now Canada's dependence on commerce with Britain is again only slightly greater than that of the United States. In other words, the only significant difference between the two countries on this score occurred over a span of some thirty years out of the two hundred.

Note, though, that this reference to degrees of dependence on trade with Britain is related only to total trade, not to total economic output. That is to say, Canadian reliance on the British market for exports and on British sources of imports may not have been, most of the time, much more pronounced in terms of Canada's overall foreign trade than the minor United States involvement in commercial relations with the United Kingdom. But Canada was and is still a far more trade-oriented country than America. Indeed, today some 20 percent of Canadian national production is accounted for by foreign trade, as compared with no more than 5 percent or so in the American case. In other words, the trade of the two countries with the outside world—including Britain—is very different in proportion to the absolute size of their economies, looming far larger for Canada. And this characteristic has been apparent, to varying degrees, throughout the whole span of the past two hundred years. Does that bespeak a greater influence of colonial or neocolonial economic factors on Canada than on the United States?

I would argue otherwise, suggesting that this is the effect of the smaller size of the Canadian economy, plus a concentration on the output of certain staple commodities like industrial raw materials and a few agricultural commodities, which derive, once more, from the accidents of geology and geography. To show a colonial effect, it would be necessary that the trade was disproportionately with the imperial center—and we have already seen that this is not so.

The Investment Link

Another essential feature of colonial development patterns is the investment link between the metropolis and the colony, which involves not just the mechanism for transferring capital but a whole system of financial organization for the mobilization of creative resources. The data on this aspect of British and North American ties are extremely thin, so one is obliged to base any view of the matter largely on qualitative assessment. We know that the United States continued long after the Revolution to draw much of its capital from London for the buildup of agriculture and industry, as well as of what we would now call "infrastructure"—canals, railways, and so forth. The British went on investing very heavily in the United States economy virtually until World War I, and the main thing that changed the picture then was the liquidation of holdings in this country to pay debts incurred by the United Kingdom as a result of its commitments to the conflict. At the same time, the economic strength of the United States increased enormously and with it the capacity to finance needed developments from internal sources. By World War II Britain had a relatively minor importance in the provision of capital for United States economic activity.

In Canada, it appears, the role of Britain was proportionately rather greater during the early years than in the United States, but not so much greater than might be expected given the different size and strength of the two economies and the inevitable tendency of the smaller and weaker one to rely more extensively on outside sources of capital. It is true that in the period between the two world wars British investors were far more active on the Canadian scene, and the London financial market was more fully utilized by Canadian borrowers, than was the case south of the border. But this is explicable, again, mainly in terms of the phenomenon to which I have just referred—the liquidation of British holdings in the United States. America was infinitely more important as a creditor and more hardheaded as a bargainer than Canada at that time. The relative significance of British investment in the Canadian economy began to decline after World

War II, and by now its position as a capital source in Canada is not too much different, proportionately, from the comparable situation in the United States.

Does this tell us anything about the effects of revolution as compared to evolution in the development of economic affairs on this continent? Again, no real difference. The interwar period saw a marked divergence in investment relationships as between Canadian and American ties with the motherland, just as it had for trade. But this era is so short, in terms of the two centuries of history that have unrolled since the formal severing of the political connection between Britain and the United States, that one really doubts its importance.

Even so, I must recall that, with investment as with trade, Canada is a very much more dependent economy overall than is the United States, so that outside capital generally plays a more substantial role there than in the self-reliant and largely autonomous United States economic giant. That may ultimately be the crucial factor in Canada's peculiarities.

Four Revolutions, Not One

Let me try to pursue the question from a rather different angle. In a thought-provoking article in the *Washington Post* last July, Theodore Wertime made the following observation on the revolutionary experience of the United States: "The American experiment was born in four revolutions of the 17th and 18th centuries, not one. They were the revolution against colonialism [American], the revolution against medievalism and traditionalism [English and French], the revolution of modern technology [British Industrial], and the Scientific Revolution."[4]

I like this view of things, because it helps to put the United States political revolution in the context of a much wider and more fundamental renaissance that has reshaped our world—

4. Theodore A. Wertime, "The New American Revolution," *The Guardian* (London), 18 July 1976, p. 17 (extracted from the *Washington Post*).

particularly with respect to economic development. To my mind, although the American struggle for escape from the British Empire had all sorts of enormously influential consequences for mankind, most of the characteristics of present-day economic life are to be explained in terms of the scope and incidence of the three other revolutions mentioned by Wertime. And in respect to those revolutions, Canadian and United States history does not divide nearly as neatly as the organizers of the sessions of this conference sought to suggest.

What I am trying to say may perhaps best be highlighted by reference to some countries elsewhere in the world that have had revolutions against colonialism and some that have not. Can one really say that the republics of South America are revolutionary societies, whereas Australia and New Zealand—and Canada—are not? I hardly think so. In most of the Latin American nations, despite successful revolutions against Spanish and Portuguese colonialism, to say nothing of other political upheavals, there has been only a partial revolution against medievalism and traditionalism. Conservative forces have continued to prevent the emergence of the dynamic social behavior that is the source of most of our economic wealth in contemporary North America, as well as in such places as Western Europe and Japan. By contrast, Australia and New Zealand, like Canada, while never having experienced political revolution, have certainly known most, if not all, of the effects of the revolution against tradition, and that difference goes a long way to explain their relative advancement and prosperity by comparison with the Latin American republics.

Wertime ascribes the revolution against medievalism and traditionalism to English and French origins, by which he doubtless means that it was the great English social transformations and the French Revolution that sparked this wide-ranging revitalization of human affairs. Certainly it was in the heartland of Europe most influenced by events in France and England, as well as in the predominantly English-speaking and even ethnically British countries of recent settlement overseas, that the modernizing trend was most pronounced. In this connection I might add the footnote that Canada, of course, was always a mixture of

English and French, which in some ways gave it a special advantage. However, the vast majority of my French ancestors arrived in the New World prior to the French Revolution in Europe, and being dominated by state and church and confined largely to agriculture they were only partly affected by the revolution. That sequence of events helps to explain the slower emergence of Quebec from the thrall of tradition, an interesting and significant phenomenon that nevertheless must be left for fuller discussion at another time.

The point here is that continued political and other links with Britain or France, which can be seen as a negative factor in terms of the colonial revolution, are presumably positive with respect to the revolution against medievalism and traditionalism, whose roots are so largely to be found in Europe. That point is arguable, since such influences are transmitted between countries through the whole set of ideas and values incorporated in what we call culture, the most powerful vehicle for which is language. The common languages, English or French, may thus have exceeded in importance in this regard any more formal political ties, in which case there would be no particular edge for Canada as compared with the United States. But the colonial relationship can hardly have been a disadvantage in this connection.

The Revolution of Modern Technology

Much the same can be said of the third species of revolutions—the revolution of modern technology, which began with the industrial revolution in Britain. It is very obvious that the effects of this development were immediately and strongly felt in Britain's colonies, as well as in those countries such as the United States that were receptive to British influences. Whether colonial status was likely to produce a more active determination to emulate the British example is a moot question. However, it would be difficult to show that Canadians knew and understood less than Americans what was happening in the motherland or that they were less attracted by the rewards that the new industrial economy was capable of producing.

One could suggest, on the other hand, that British colonial policy might have prevented Canada from establishing industry —and that would be a normal expectation, given the usual tendency of imperial powers to arrange that the home country becomes a workshop while the colonies supply needed raw materials and foodstuffs. The data certainly support the notion of some retardation of industrial growth in Canada by comparison with the United States, since serious development of manufacturing activity commenced in the Canadian economy only in the latter part of the nineteenth century, at which time United States industrial strength was already impressive. By 1890 the United States was producing more steel than Britain, whereas Canada was a good deal less developed, relatively speaking, in terms of output of manufactured goods. Statistically, the difference does not seem all that great; for example, by 1900 the proportions of the United States and Canadian labor forces that were engaged in manufacturing were just over 20 percent and a little more than 15 percent, respectively. Nevertheless, a gap exists, and it is reflected in the dates for economic takeoff given by W. W. Rostow in his famous thesis on this topic—for the United States, 1843 to 1860; for Canada, 1896 to 1914.[5]

No doubt the later emergence of Canada as an industrial power can be explained in some measure by the very determined use of tariff protection by the United States government during a crucial period. Economists are divided regarding the virtues of tariff protection as a means of forcing industrial growth. However, most would agree that, while it can seriously distort the allocation of resources and thus impair long-term efficiency, protection is certainly capable of fostering the manufacturing sector and thus for a time of pulling labor out of low-productivity into higher-

5. W. W. Rostow, "The Take-Off into Self-Sustained Growth," *The Economic Journal*, March 1956, reprinted in A. N. Agarwala and S. P. Singh, eds., *The Economics of Underdevelopment* (London: Oxford University Press, 1970), pp. 154 ff.

productivity employment. As a consequence, there may be substantial short-run gains, even if the longer-term effects are decidedly adverse, and in this limited sense the early introduction of tariffs can accelerate the industrialization process.

Perhaps there is here an implication of the revolutionary versus evolutionary experience for the differing economic development in the two countries. Can we explain these trends in terms of a resort to import protection by the independent United States as compared with a position of imposed preferential trade access to encourage imperial commerce in the case of colonial Canada? It is true that the United States tariff was raised to fairly significant levels in 1816, although it did not become really entrenched until the start of the Civil War in 1861. According to one American writer, "In 1865 the average duty on dutiable imports [equivalent ad valorem rate] was 48 per cent. Between that date and 1935 the average rate never fell below 39 per cent except in the period when the Underwood Law was in effect [1914–1921], the average rate of which was 27 per cent."[6] By comparison, Canada's rates were relatively low; they ranged from about 15 percent to 25 percent (computed on the same basis) during the 1860s and 1870s and only occasionally topped 30 percent from the introduction of the National Policy in 1879 right through to the start of World War II in 1939.

In fact, though, when we examine the evolution of the Canadian tariff in greater detail, it does not square with an attempt by London to restrain industrialization in Canada. The old preferential trading arrangements between Britain and its colonies were ended in the 1840s, when the British government embraced a policy of universal free trade, and no amount of pleading by colonial legislatures would induce Britain to restore those arrangements over the next fifty years. Accordingly, the Province of Canada repealed the differential rates afforded British products in 1847 (as it had been empowered to do under the British Possessions Act) and instituted a common tariff against all countries.

6. D. D. Humphrey, *American Imports* (New York: Twentieth Century Fund, 1955), cited in Irving Brecher and S. S. Reisman, *Canada-United States Economic Relations* (Ottawa: The Queen's Printer, 1957), p. 170.

But the Canadian colonies also began to approach the United States for a reciprocity treaty—still without producing any reconsideration by London—and from 1854 to 1866 actually achieved a fairly wide-ranging bilateral free-trade agreement, covering close to 30 percent of all imports by the Province of Canada during those years. Finally, with Confederation in 1867 the new government, having tried and failed again to revive preferences, determined to "go it alone." In 1879 the National Policy effectively consolidated trade protection for the whole dominion on the basis of a single-column tariff. This was to remain the position until the preference for British products was reinstituted in 1897.

Since it is generally accepted that by 1897 the United States had established a fully developed industrial economy, whereas Canada's manufacturing sector was just beginning to emerge, we need not be concerned for this purpose with what happened from then on. The delay in Canadian industrialization, relative to the United States, occurred during the crucial second half of the nineteenth century. And we see that, although Canadian tariff protection was quite a bit less stringent than American over that period, the difference can in no way be ascribed to colonialism.

Science and Society: The New Dynamic

This brings me to the last of Wertime's four revolutions—the scientific revolution. I take this to mean the emergence, over comparatively recent times, of a capacity to harness scientific discovery to the economic process in ways that yield a constant proliferation of entirely new products, new industrial systems, new technologies, even new ways of looking at the world around us. The whole fields of synthetic materials, of wonder drugs, of aerospace activity, of computers, of atomic energy, and of a dozen other realms of pioneering industrial application owe their origins to the scientific revolution. In a sense it is a straight continuation of the industrial revolution before it. But the difference is that now the application of systematic and highly sophisticated effort to the challenges of economic man—whether as producer or consumer—gives rise not just to fresh techniques by which familiar objectives might be attained but to hitherto unimagined means for the achievement of goals previously barely dreamed of.

In my view, this revolution is at the very heart of the problem of economic development as we will be facing it henceforward. To quote that most perceptive analyst of the contemporary scene, Peter Drucker:

> Technologically, the established "modern" industries may still enjoy a long period of growth and advance. Financially—that is, as investment channels—they may be highly attractive and offer rich returns. . . . But in their ability to provide the thrust for further substantial growth of the developed economies, they are mature, if not stagnant. . . . They will increasingly be unable to provide economic dynamics for the developed countries.[7]

And he continues:

> The new emerging industries . . . embody a new economic reality: knowledge has become the central economic resource. The systematic acquisition of knowledge, that is, organized formal education, has replaced experience . . . as the foundation for productive capacity and performance. . . . [T]he new industries ahead represent a qualitative rather than a merely quantitative shift. They are different in their structure, in their knowledge foundations, and in their sociology. . . . They represent a discontinuity.[8]

Canada and a few other advanced countries are in a rather strange and interesting position with respect to this phenomenon. My thesis up to now has been that Canada's evolutionary tradition does not seem to have been a critical factor, so far as one can see, in determining its economic differences from the revolutionary society to the south. Those differences can be explained largely in terms of geography and climate (past and present) and what such fundamental characteristics have meant for the carrying capacity of the Canadian living space as compared with the

7. Peter F. Drucker, *The Age of Discontinuity: Guidelines to Our Changing Society* (New York: Harper & Row, 1969), p. 12.
8. Ibid., pp. 40 and 41

American. Canada has been condemned by these influences to the status of a medium-sized economic power, despite its vast territory, whereas the United States has assumed the scale and strength of a superpower; from this huge discrepancy derive all the other distinctions between the two economies. Even so, the differences would have been far greater had not Canada shared with the United States the heritage of British (and to some extent French) origins, kept alive through a common language and the cultural forces thus transmitted. It was because of our common background that we both enjoyed the benefits of the European revolution against medievalism and traditionalism and the British industrial revolution. However, I would now add that the scientific revolution *may* be introducing some elements into the situation that will cause our paths to diverge somewhat more than has been the case hitherto.

The reason that these scientific developments are so important from the present point of view is that, whereas both the revolution against traditionalism and the industrial revolution began in Western Europe—so that the United States and Canada were each at the receiving end of transatlantic influences, in the scientific revolution the impulse of the revolution is focused largely in one of our two countries while the other is the recipient. It is true that Europe and Japan are also centers of scientific innovation. But the United States has been and still is a major force—in many fields *the* major force—for the generation of scientific research and its application to industrial uses. Canada is at the periphery of this new revolution. Its position could thus perhaps be compared in certain respects to the one it occupied in regard to the American political revolution in 1776. Accordingly, one might certainly expect some kind of disjunction in the community of experience that has so largely offset our separate revolutionary/ evolutionary traditions over the past two centuries.

Perceptions of the implications of this phenomenon vary considerably, and the matter is becoming increasingly confused by polemics and ideology. I think it is necessary, if we are to understand what is happening in Canadian-American relations today, that the essential points at issue are kept clearly in view.

First of all, there is no argument about the dissemination of scientific knowledge. Canada has extensive economic and intellectual links with the United States—as well as with Europe and Japan—and there is no hindrance to the communication of scientific ideas across the frontiers and oceans of the world. Science is an international language; its comprehension requires only the relevant skills, and these we have. Insofar as the diffusion of applied scientific knowledge takes place through institutional mechanisms, be they professional associations or business corporations, Canada is as well integrated into the international network as any country on earth. Exclusion from scientific information and its practical results is clearly not our problem.

Where some people do perceive a problem is in the way science is giving rise to what might be called a new imperial system, in which the main benefits accrue to the center (or centers) while the "outlying" areas have a kind of colonial or satellite status. This is felt to be so primarily because the application of science to economic endeavor occurs in large measure through the medium of very big, integrated industrial and financial concerns of worldwide scope. The strength of these vast enterprises is their capacity to command the resources required to turn scientific initiative into operational business activity—that is, into viable products and processes meeting the specifications of a sophisticated market attuned to every competitive nuance. Given that advantages of scale and specialization, once again, have enabled United States corporations to achieve such successes far more frequently than Canadian companies, the major poles of scientific-industrial concentration in the United States have tended to become the centers of economic power for North America. Canada's economy, being dominated by the subsidiaries and branches of these transnational firms, is believed by many to yield only the rewards appropriate to its subordinate position and derivative industrial culture. Needless to say, there is also the argument that economic relationships are closely tied in with political power and that the Canadian position is therefore one of real national dependence on a foreign hegemony, new style.

Dependency and Underdevelopment

The case being advanced in many parts of the world against the so-called multinational corporation, which is castigated by its innumerable critics as an obstacle to true economic development, is that it promotes dependency and underdevelopment. I do not intend to pass judgment today one way or the other with respect to that controversy, which is far too complicated for even the most fleeting assessment in a half-hour talk.[9] What I want to suggest, however, is that the whole dependency/underdevelopment proposition is based on a static view of the world. Observation of growth processes based on the expansion of nuclei with intimate linkages to the periphery—something one can see in urban and regional development patterns, for example—seems to me to indicate a strong tendency for main centers to spawn subcenters, which in turn may ultimately become centers in their own right. That is, while the statics of the situation may appear to justify a dominance/dependency interpretation, its dynamics over time give this interpretation a much more positive twist. There is historical evidence for the belief that, unless such processes are actually suppressed, spin-off effects from the activity at the center will help to create new poles of growth and development in the hinterland.[10]

Is not this one of the lessons of the experience of empire, about which we are concerned in our deliberations? When Britain was an imperial power, there was no doubt that New York and Boston, Montreal and Toronto, Cape Town, Bombay, Singapore, Hong Kong, Sydney, and Wellington were all clearly outposts of an economic system dominated by London. Yet it is obvious that none of these places is any longer in any way subservient to the

9. An extremely well-reasoned discussion of this whole issue is contained in Benjamin J. Cohen, *The Question of Imperialism: The Political Economy of Dominance and Dependence* (New York: Basic Books, 1973), especially chaps. 5 and 6.

10. This approach is more fully developed in André Raynauld, "Thoughts on the New International Economic Order," speech to the Chicago Council on Foreign Relations, 24 February, 1976.

old metropolis. The United States, India, and some other former colonies revolted against the motherland and her political and economic suzerainty. But Canada, Australia, New Zealand, and many more simply won their independence through the evolution of events. Who would say in 1976 that Hong Kong and Singapore lack economic autonomy because they are on the edge of a system centered in London? Who would describe Toronto and Sydney as underdeveloped hinterlands peripheral to a commercial universe whose focal point is in the British Isles? And note that it is hardly the decline of Britain that makes these questions appear ridiculous today; the outposts of empire became subcenters and then centers by virtue of their own growth, started by impetus from the original metropolis but in due course becoming self-sustaining, and by their strengthening ties with other dominant countries in the world.

Harmony and peace will depend greatly on which interpretation of affairs—the static or the dynamic model—is most effective in influencing political opinion in Canada, as in other "nonmetropolitan" countries around the globe, with respect to the transnational consequences of the scientific revolution. If the view gains currency that dominance/dependence relationships are an intolerable and permanent feature of the world order, rather than a relatively short period in the history of a country, then efforts will be made increasingly to escape from such situations through governmental interventions in the economic process. Branches of foreign firms will be nationalized; huge programs of tax-subsidized research will be launched in order to create an indigenous scientific-industrial capability; and state-owned corporations will be created to compete with or replace the multinationals.

A Break in the Evolutionary Tradition?

This prospect is particularly fascinating in the context of the present conference, because it represents in some sense a full turn in the wheel of fortune—from American revolution against the old British Empire to possible Canadian resistance against the new American empire. Since I am one who believes that evolution is usually the best route to political advancement—as I am sure you will have guessed by now—my hope is that Canadians will obey their traditional instincts and recognize what are the real revolutionary forces shaping modern society, the true challenges to which we must respond if we are to fulfill our potential as a nation. We will be helped in so doing, undoubtedly, if we can have the sympathetic understanding of a neighbor against whom our complaints are certainly less specific, and about whom our feelings are perhaps even more equivocal, than were yours with respect to the British two hundred years ago.

What aspects of these complex matters are susceptible to analysis by the interested scholar? It seems to me that we need to know more about the institutional settings within which scientific innovations are carried out and located around the world and about the linkages between such innovations and economic and social progress. We need to understand the forces behind the shifts in relative importance of different regions, cities, and countries as growth points for scientific-industrial enterprise. We need to comprehend the nature of the networks that bring innovations to certain places at certain times and the reasons that those innovations do not generate the same growth and prosperity everywhere. In this context, it would be hard to conceive of a more important area of study, not just in terms of Canadian-American relations but with respect to the interplay of vital forces in the world at large.

8

Melting Pot or Mosaic: Revolution or Reversion?

John Porter

What is revolutionary about the idea of the melting pot? It is, perhaps, that beyond its crude and metallurgic metaphor it calls for a rejection of the past. It suggests that human beings can be culturally transformed and set on a path that leads to the creation of a new nation with a new national type, a new modal character. Such, of course, are the objectives of our latter-day revolutions, which seek to obliterate bourgeois or other traditional cultures and collective personalities and to replace them with those conforming to some preferred "socialist" ideal. The leaders of the revolutions of our epoch, in Cambodia, for example, seem really to believe that if they are thorough in the eradication of the former, the latter can be cultivated. What distinguished the American experience was that the process of cultural transformation, if such it was, was to come through free institutions and not through the force and oppression that contemporary revolutionaries, perhaps more realistically, employ.

However, it is doubtful that the leaders of the American Revolution, or their successors, ever held doctrines about the transformation of human beings of different cultures into a new cultural type. George Washington, who may not have been typical of the leaders, wrote in a letter to Gouverneur Morris in 1776, "I do most devoutly wish we had not a single foreigner among us except the Marquis de Lafayette who acts upon very different principles from those which govern the rest."[1] This feeling about

1. Quoted in Samuel S. Busey, *Immigration: Its Evils and Consequences* (New York, 1856; reprinted ed., New York: Arno Press, 1969).

outsiders, to be echoed long after by the American nativistic movement, was scarcely an anticipation at the time of the laying down of the American charter of the seemingly boundless immigration that was to come in the following century.

Cultural transformation—using the term *culture* in the broad, anthropological sense—of "huddled masses yearning to be free" through some sociological crucible was a vision of the late nineteenth century. It implied a universalism and a rejection of all ancestral past. Where one came from, one's descent group, one's color or paternal language should not be the basis for the distribution of social rights. All are welcomed by the "mighty woman with a torch," although the inscription on the Statue of Liberty does not suggest that cultural parricide was a condition of entry or a likely prospect. The welcome was primarily to those who were seeking freedom from autocratic social structures.

The rejection of the European father, a collective oedipal syndrome analogous to the rejection of the authoritarian father on the part of the individual in Freudian psychology, was, according to the British anthropologist Geoffrey Gorer, an essential element in the development of the American national character. Gorer quotes an order of the day issued by General Patton to American troops at the time of the invasion of Sicily in 1943, a statement that might be construed as the ultimate outcome of the American transformation of Europeans. The flamboyant general said, "When we land, we will meet German and Italian soldiers whom it is our honor and privilege to attack and destroy. Many of you have in your veins German and Italian blood, but remember that these ancestors of yours so loved freedom that they gave up home and country to cross the ocean in search of liberty. The ancestors of the people we shall kill lacked the courage to make such a sacrifice and continued as slaves."[2]

In cultural terms all this rejection of historical bonds is radical enough, but with the melting-pot theory, in one of its versions at least, there is the even more radical notion that the host society of old American descendants should combine itself with the

2. Geoffrey Gorer, *The Americans* (London: Cresset Press, 1948), p. 13.

elements it was transforming. There has been much confusion of terminology both in the popular mind and in serious writing of how immigrants should be incorporated into the receiving society. For some, the melting pot is just another expression for assimilation to the values of the host society; for others it means that host and newcomers all melt together into a new people. It is in the latter, more radical sense that I am using the term. Of course, the melting-pot vision did not appear until the new immigration; Zangwill's play, which is considered to be the origin of the term, was not written until 1909.[3]

The old immigration of English and Irish laborers, of Germans and Scandinavians, although it may have generated some romantic speculation about "racial" mixture, had brought people who had some cultural affinities with native-born Americans. They differed from native Americans in religious observances and they bore the marks of poverty, but they were, except those from the Celtic fringe of Britain, Protestant and redeemable within the framework of American cultural patterns.

In the postrevolutionary period, the founders of America continued to be Anglo-Saxon in culture and outlook, shaping their new society from a heritage they had brought with them. Northern Europeans were similar to Anglo-Saxons, and it was easy for all to be absorbed by the expanding frontier. The Revolution was political, in a minor way social, and probably not at all cultural in the sense of taking in the foreigners, whom Washington so strongly disliked, to create a new people. As revolutionary as it was, the most we could say is that the melting-pot idea, when it appeared, was consistent with some of the themes of universalism and equality and citizenship that were part of the Revolution. When the idea of "racial" intermixture did appear with the new immigration, it was met with such a degree of hostility on the part of large numbers of the host society that it is difficult to imagine that the radical melting pot, which would have included themselves, was a part of their values. It was too revolutionary for that.

3. Israel Zangwill, *The Melting Pot: Drama in four acts* (New York: Macmillan).

If the melting pot is revolutionary in its rejection of the ancestral past, the mosaic is, beyond its subtle and picturesque metaphor, a reversion to ancestral patterns because it implies, particularly as it is found in its recent expression in Canada, that ethnic origin and descent-group identification should be salient features of social structure. It emphasizes the particular rather than the universal and requires individuals to seek out some segment of historical humanity with which to associate and identify. It detracts from the unity of mankind and the fundamental equality of humans because of its concern for differences.

The justification for labeling the mosaic a reversion is that its ultimate logic requires the endogamous descent group to be the carrier of culture. If that logic is pursued, there is the danger of arriving at the point where cultural differences, which it is the duty of the descent group to embody, are attributed to genetic qualities and so we return to a social biology of race and ethnic differences. It was this social biology of the early part of the present century that supported nativistic movements in both the United States and Canada and that had its impact on the exclusiveness of immigration policy.

With the current development of "mosaics" around the world, from the tribalisms of new nations emerging from colonialism to the separatism, language rights, and regionalism in the most advanced nations of Europe, ethnic claims are among the major themes of contemporary politics. These movements emphasize claims of descent groups rather than individuals and hence diverge from the principle of universalism and the unity of mankind.

If it is difficult to find the melting-pot doctrine in the intellectual history of the United States until almost the present century, it is equally difficult to find the mosaic image in the history of Canadian thought and institutions, although that image with its emphasis on cultural traditions would seem to be more consistent with the conservative counterrevolutionary foundations of Canada.

Despite the apparent compatibility of the images of melting pot and mosaic with the dominant values of the two societies, both are rather romantic views of the development of the social life of the two countries and the incorporation of immigrants within them. Neither is a statement of the realities of immigration to the New World. There are probably more similarities than divergencies between the two countries in their reception of newcomers. Both came close to demanding assimilation to the culture of the host society, despite the contrary images evoked by the colorful metaphors with which we are familiar. Moreover, technological change was to make assimilation almost inevitable, if not to American or Canadian values, which are perhaps not as different as we would like to believe, then to the more general values of modernism.

It is important to remember that the two countries shared in the massive population movements that built them, and that in the process they thus exchanged with each other large numbers of their native-born, so creating the extensive ties of kinship that are an unusual feature of two neighboring states. In the 130 years between 1820 and 1950 an estimated 3.2 million Canadians (including Newfoundlanders) went to the United States. The peak year of the movement, to emphasize its recency, was 1924.[4] In fact, if Canadians were ever allowed to consider themselves as an ethnic group, they would perhaps have now displaced the Russians as the sixth largest national group to have gone to the United States. A good number of these were French from Quebec who moved in the last century to the New England textile and forest industries.

Reciprocally, there was the movement of Americans into the Canadian West when the expansion there in the early part of the present century coincided with the end of it in the American West. Then, "the Canadian West received a basic stock of experienced, resourceful, English-speaking North American farmers."[5] Over a million Americans came to Canada between 1897 and 1914—almost as many as from Great Britain and more than

4. Oscar Handlin, *Immigration as a Factor in American History* (Englewood Cliffs, N.J.: Prentice-Hall, 1959), p. 16.
5. J. B. Brebner, *North Atlantic Triangle* (Toronto: Ryerson Press, 1945), p. 227.

from other sources.[6] It is interesting to note that in the 1970s once again the United States has become a major source of immigrants to Canada. Now they are the highly skilled counterpart of the flow of American capital. Despite the clamor that is made about multiculturalism, neither Canadian officialdom nor the statistics it produces recognize a United States or an American ethnicity— a neighborly rejection of the melting-pot process caused by a blindness to the existence of a real American type or by a sharp perception that the melting has not taken place after all, and that non-North American ethnicities have survived.

As well as the exchange of their own native-born populations, Canada and the United States shared up until 1914 in the large-scale "new" immigration from Europe. Some of these were leap-froggers who thought less about where they wanted to go in the New World than about their determination to leave the old one. Although there can be no strict accounting of this movement, there is little doubt that the United States was the net beneficiary. However familiar one might become with the Canadian estimates, one is always struck with the observation that between 1850 and 1950 something like 7.1 million people came into Canada, but 6.6 million left the country, leaving net migration to contribute little to population growth.[7] With this great outflow— mostly, no doubt, to the United States—Canada lost large numbers of both native-born and foreign-born persons.

Given this confluence of population movements from abroad and between the two countries, it might well be expected that in the settlement and the incorporation of immigrants there would be as many parallels as divergencies and some convergence, in the face of tradition-destroying modernization, toward a modest cultural pluralism, an escape from the extremes of melting pot and mosaic. If I earlier presented melting pot and mosaic in extreme terms, as polar models of how people of different cultural groups can relate, the revolutionary and the regressive, it was for the purpose of demonstrating that, in reality, in North Amer-

6. Ibid.
7. The original estimates are those of Nathan Keyfitz. See the discussion in John Porter, *The Vertical Mosaic* (Toronto: Univ. of Toronto 1965), p. 29.

ica neither extreme approximates the truth. In practice, neither has been possible, and neither has been particularly valued by the respective societies, despite the rhetoric in prose and poetry that has been devoted to them. The reality, in both countries, lies somewhere between the two poles.

It is doubtful that the melting pot was ever descriptive of the history of intergroup relations in the United States. Even with the old immigration from Northern Europe of similar cultural elements, there were areas of group settlement where some of the important elements of culture, particularly religion and language, were retained. It is true that common exposure to frontier conditions may have led to similar patterns of response to the physical environment, thus creating something of a homogeneous technological or material culture and giving the impression of a frontier melting pot; but nonmaterial aspects of culture survived and still do. Moreover, the old immigration—excluding, of course, the Irish—made up the human element of the expanding frontier, and so its successive flows passed over the old colonial cultures or released native Americans to move further West,[8] thereby lessening the physical contacts under which intergroup conflict might have arisen or the first stirrings of the melting pot might have taken place. While many of the old immigration over the generations became assimilated—which is not the same as the melting pot—some retained some degree of ethnic identity through to the present, the Irish perhaps being the most obvious, but Germans and Scandinavians also in some regions of the country.[9]

It is with the new immigration, from Eastern and Southern Europe, very much a rural to urban movement as well as a transoceanic one, that the idea of a melting pot may have been appropriate. However, intergroup hostility and rivalry and even hatred became marked to the extent that it is unlikely that the

8. Marcus Lee Hansen, *The Immigrant in American History*, reprinted in Handlin, *Immigration*, pp. 43 ff.

9. See the discussion in Nathan Glazer, "Ethnic Groups in America," in *Freedom and Control in Modern Society*, Morroe Berger et al., (New York: Van Nostrand, 1954), p. 156.

host society was willing to merge with the newcomers to create a new American type. Racial as well as religious fuel, added by the Irish, helped to heat up the feelings of hostility that many native Americans felt toward the incoming groups. George Washington's feelings about "foreigners among us" were shared strongly on the part of some Americans a century later. There is something of a contradiction in the outbursts of American nativism against those who were the fearful embodiment of alien cultures (or as it was more crudely put in the biological theories of the time, inferior racial stock), but who, on the other hand, were an essential component to the expanding economy. In our day we find an analogous situation in the ambivalence felt in many European countries toward imported labor or guest workers who are essential, but less than welcome. It is a remarkable reflection of American ideals that the newcomers to America, despite the hostility expressed toward them, could acquire citizenship, a status most unwillingly granted by European nations of our epoch.

In the long run American nativism won out, with the immigration quotas specifically designed to maintain an Anglo-Saxon dominance. The new immigration laws of the 1920s, which put an end to the laissez-passer system, were the outcome, too, of theories of racial superiority articulated in Europe by Gobineau and Chamberlain, trumpeted by Richard Wagner, and echoed in the United States by such writers as Madison Grant. If a melting-pot process was taking place, if the "Great Alchemist . . . was fusing . . . with his purging flame," as Zangwill so graphically put it,[10] old Anglo-Saxon Americans were holding back and resisting being drawn into the crucible, to use yet another metaphor employed by romantics to describe what was happening to host and newcomers. Moreover, the block settlement of the frontier was being reproduced in the ghetto settlement of the cities leading not to the melting pot, but to two peculiar patterns of American intergroup relations, namely, to ecological invasion and succession, which were so extensively studied by Park and his as-

10. In *The Melting Pot,* quoted in Handlin, *Immigration,* p. 150.

sociates in Chicago; and to the entrenchment of ethnic realities in American city politics. The hostility shown to the foreigners of the new immigration and their languages, which is reflected today in the low level of foreign-language training in the United States, scarcely indicated a willingness to forge with them a new culture.

Two forces working against the melting pot were the superiority felt by the old Americans and the strong communal identities felt by "the unmeltable ethnics," to use Michael Novak's term. It has been pointed out[11] that much of the new immigration was from national ethnic groups whose cultures and primordial identities were suppressed by the great multinational empires of the times, the Russian and the Austro-Hungarian. Many of the immigrants hoped to save or revive their cultures in the New World. They may have chosen American freedom, seen not so much as the freedom of individual rights, but as collective rights for groups to be able to live their own cultural life-styles away from oppression. Even the settlement houses in American cities created by Americans to assist in immigrant adjustment became shelters for European folkways.[12] In American social structure, the myth of the melting pot is too revolutionary to be a statement of reality, however much it might express a universalistic millennium.

If not the melting pot, what does characterize the course of ethnic relations in the United States? The answer, as far as it is provided by American sociologists who have studied the matter, is two somewhat contrary processes. One is assimilation to the social life of the dominant old Americans, the process that Milton Gordon has called "Anglo-conformity,"[13] and the second is a modest form of cultural pluralism that attests to the strength of ethnic identities across the generations. Initially strong ethnic communal ties developed because of the need for collective self-help in American urban squalor in the heyday of social Darwinism and laissez-faire capitalism. Immigration was linked to labor-force needs developing an association between ethnic groups and

11. See, e.g., Glazer, "Ethnic Groups in America," pp. 167 ff.
12. John Higham, *Strangers in the Land: Patterns of American Nativism 1860–1925* (New York: Atheneum, 1969), p. 121.
13. Milton M. Gordon, *Assimilation in American Life* (New York: Oxford Univ. Press, 1964).

particular kinds of jobs, with the result that the ethnic group became the one that helped to provide protection against exploitation, poverty, and threats to occupational rights. While some of these associations have been retained to the present time, others have disappeared because the members of some groups have been occupationally mobile or because they have taken the assimilation option. In an analysis of the March 1971 Current Population Survey, in which respondents were asked what their origins or descents were and were provided a list from which to choose, such as British, Polish, Italian, and so on, over 30 percent of men between 18 and 65 classified themselves as "other" or "don't know."[14] The author of a report on the survey suggests that most of these people were mixtures of specified groups or "must have no ethnic identity at all and have forgotten their ancestry." On the other hand, one can find sufficient examples of how ethnic and occupational communities survive to belie the melting-pot thesis.

The cultural pluralism that has developed in the United States is a very muted one. It falls far short of language rights, political representation on an ethnic basis, and separately controlled educational systems. At least that was the case until recently, when American nonwhite ethnic groups, who were never seriously considered as elements in the melting pot, began to demand recognition and redress as members of groups, thus creating something of a group-rights movement in the United States quite different from the principles of individual rights, central to the revolutionary principles upon which it had been founded. The demand for community control over schools, for affirmative action in the work world, and—in the case of Chicanos, Puerto Ricans, and other Spanish Americans—language rights, were ethnic movements.[15] The repressed hostility of the descendants

14. Geoffrey Carliner, "Has The Melting Pot Worked?" mimeographed (Madison: Institute for Research in Poverty, University of Wisconsin, 1975).

15. In their forward to the revised edition of *Beyond The Melting Pot* (Cambridge, 1970), Nathan Glazer and Daniel P. Moynihan use the terms "ethnic group status" and "separatism" to describe the alternative possible developments of ethnic group relations in 1970 (p. xxiii). They seem convinced of a movement away from assimilation further in the direction of pluralism, less muted than now exists.

of the survivors of the aboriginal peoples of America would also burst out. If their story is left out of this account, it is not because it is any less significant in human terms, but rather because a comparison of Indian policies of the two countries deserves a paper in its own right.

The existence of nonwhite ethnic groups in the United States and their relative deprivation is the main reason for the renewed emphasis on the descent group as one of primal identity and as a protective device as had been earlier ethnic communal ties among immigrants. Their demands for recognition and redress —quite justified by any ethical standards, lest these remarks are misunderstood—have set a new value on ethnicity and mean a reversion in the sense of moving back from universalistic principles. If the demands of nonwhites were in ethnic terms, then so were the responses to them. Sometimes ethnic occupational interests were threatened—Jewish schoolteachers in New York, for example—bringing a response in the same key. If black was beautiful, so was Irish and Italian or other parentage. Both melting pot and assimilation were far from complete.

For many who cannot or will not respond to ethnic questions on surveys, the ancestral past has been obscured and assimilation to Anglo-conformity has been complete. The "brutal bargain" has been a part of "making it,"[16] of upward occupational mobility, and this occupational assimilation has been achieved at the price of cultural assimilation. Rather than the melting pot, it is these assimilative processes, involving the loss of ethnic identity on the one hand and the muted form of ethnic pluralism inherent in the present ethnic revival on the other, that are descriptive of the incorporation of immigrant nationalities in a predominantly "Anglo" America.

If the melting pot is descriptive of neither the attitudes towards, nor the reality of, immigrant absorption in the United States, the mosaic is equally faulty as an account of the same processes in Canada. One thing is clear: in Canada the phenome-

16. For an insightful account, see Norman A. Podhoretz, *Making It* (New York: Random House, 1967).

non of mass migration has not attracted the attention of historians as it has in the United States. We have no Marcus Lee Hansen, Oscar Handlin, or John Higham concerned to analyze these vast population movements within the framework of charter values and myths. One reason might be that we have few myths, revolutionary or evolutionary, against which to examine the unfolding of our story. Indeed, it is difficult to find any extensive discussion of immigrant adjustment in Canadian historical writing, let alone its analysis in terms of some desirable mosaic. If the task of historians is to produce myths and countermyths, they have been particularly silent on the Canadian mosaic. At the most, they give a few pages in their general histories. It is remarkable that in a volume of essays entitled *Historical Essays on the Prairie Provinces*[17] the only articles devoted to immigrants or the national origins of the people there were on the Mennonites and Hutterites. The story of the new immigration to Canada was as dramatic as it was in the United States, but to find it one must go back to contemporary accounts such as that by J. S. Woodsworth of Winnipeg in the first decade of the century in his *Strangers within Our Gates*,[18] or to ethnic histories themselves, such as Senator Paul Yuzyk's *The Ukrainian Peasants in Manitoba*.[19] Not only has the great migration of Europeans to Canada failed to inspire Canadian historians, but they have also failed to create or develop the mosaic concept as the trend in Canadian social development.

The expression *mosaic*, as far as one can tell, was first used with this connotation by an American about ten years after Zangwill created his melting-pot image about the many groups that were living together in the growing American cities. Victoria Hayward, in a book called *Romantic Canada*,[20] referred to the varieties of church architecture that grew with the block settlement of

17. Donald Swainson, *Historical Essays on the Prairie Provinces* (Toronto, 1970).
18. J. S. Woodsworth, *Strangers within Our Gates* (Missionary Society of the Methodist Church, 1909).
19. Paul Yuzyk, *The Ukrainian Peasants in Manitoba* (Toronto: University of Tor. Press, 1953).
20. Victoria Hayward, *Romantic Canada* (Toronto: Macmillan, 1922).

prairies as a "mosaic of vast dimensions and great breadth." As far as I can tell the book has not been among the spate of reprinted material that has come with the current wave of Canadian nationalism, perhaps because the author was American or perhaps because the book has no merit other than its metaphor.

The term was given further currency by John Murray Gibbon in his book published in 1938 entitled *Canadian Mosaic*,[21] with the subtitle *The Making of a Northern Nation*. Originally conceived as a radio program for the Canadian Broadcasting Corporation, the book is a catalog of the various national groups (they were not called ethnic then) that had come to Canada and of the contributions they had made and could make to Canadian society. As others that were to appear during the war a couple of years later, the book was aimed at racial (the word then in use) understanding. There is no consistency in the discussion about the incorporation of immigrants, since the assimilative implications of the Canadianization program of the Imperial Order of the Daughters of the Empire are reported without comment and the IODE is identified as one of the organizations cementing the mosaic to which the book is dedicated. The confusion about the integrative processes taking place is illustrated by the following quotation:

The Canadian race of the future is being superimposed on the original native Indian races and is being made up of over thirty European racial groups, each of which has its own history, customs and traditions. Some politicians want to see these merged as quickly as possible into one standard type, just as our neighbours in the United States are hurrying to make every citizen a 100 percent American. Others believe in trying to preserve for the future Canadian race the most worthwhile qualities and traditions that each racial group has brought with it.[22]

Here we have something of an anticipation of the federal government's multicultural program of the 1970s, and since the Gib-

---

21. John Murray Gibbon, *Canadian Mosaic: The Making of a Northern Nation* (Toronto: McClelland & Stewart, 1938). The term had also been used by Kate Foster in a YWCA publication in 1926.
22. Gibbon, *Canadian Mosaic*, p. vii.

bon book is largely a recording of folk arts and high culture and quite neglects culture in the wider anthropological sense, there is a further resemblance. Gibbon made no attempt to discover if the mosaic had any roots in Canadian history or whether there were ideas about incorporating immigrants that might distinguish Canada from the United States. It is unlikely that he would have found much, since the theme seems to have had little interest for Canadian historians, and his book less so. Perhaps his book has deserved its fate, for it also has not been reprinted.

And so the image of the mosaic is not at all prominent in social comment or historical writing in Canada. Ideas of the melting pot, or some version of it in the variety of metaphors (many of them biological) that the subject seems to have prompted, can be more easily found. Writing a piece of war propaganda prepared for radio, and like Gibbon's book concerned with inter-ethnic understanding at a time when some groups might be viewed with suspicion in 1941, Watson Kirkconnell spoke of "the varied human ingredients that history has poured into the huge mixing bowl of Canada's national life," and of the "richness of the national amalgam."[23] A decade later J. M. S. Careless suggested that, although the group settlement of foreign-born in the West had proved the most difficult to absorb, between 1901 and 1911 "Canada for the first time became what the United States long had been, a melting pot of peoples."[24]

A. R. M. Lower, who was not reluctant to express opinions on what he considered the evils of immigration, added to the imagery. "Ukrainians, Hungarians, Poles and Germans all had to be ground through the mill of the public school, taught English, and painfully and roughly trained in that English tradition of law and government which was not understood too well by the natives themselves. . . . [They were] by mid century neither 'British' nor 'foreign', simply Canadian."[25] While the observation could be

23. Watson Kirkconnell, *Canadians All,* (Ottawa: Directorate of Public Information, 1941), p. 7.

24. J. M. S. Careless, *Canada: A Story of Challenge* (Toronto: Macmillan, 1953), p. 304.

25. A. R. M. Lower, *Colony to Nation* (Toronto: Longman's, 1957).

construed as suggesting either the melting pot or the assimilation to Anglo-conformity, there is certainly nothing of the mosaic in it. It would seem that in Canada, as in the United States, public education was to be the major road to assimilation. "It was taken for granted," wrote W. L. Morton of European newcomers to Manitoba in the early part of the present century, "that they would be and should be assimilated, and it was to this end that the flag legislation of 1906 had been directed and that the agitation for compulsory school attendance was now being raised."[26] In his more recently published account of immigration and colonization in Canada to 1903,[27] Norman Macdonald has managed to confuse the two images in a chapter entitled "The Melting Pot Era: Group Settlement," which suggests at least that neither of them was particularly salient during the long period of immigration that he surveys.

If, as in the United States with the image of the melting pot, the image of the mosaic in Canada is difficult to locate in charter mythology or historical writing, one might look to immigration policy as it was formulated by governments and discussed by public commentators. If one wanted to locate the origin of the mosaic, it might be tempting to start with the reserve system of block land grants to national and religious groups in the early phase of prairie settlement in the 1870s. There was a kind of official desperation about the Canadian government's attempt to make Canada more attractive than the United States, which was getting the bulk of European immigration. To do this the government was prepared to reserve blocks of land for particular national groups, members of which might settle together and maintain their old national ways and even, as in the case of the Mennonites in Manitoba, be exempt from the provisions of the dominion land policy by securing common, rather than individual, ownership.[28] Blocks of land were set aside for Mennonites, Ger-

26. W. L. Morton, *Manitoba: A History* (Toronto: Univ. of Toronto Press, 1957), p. 297.
27. Norman Macdonald, *Canada: Immigration and Colonization* (Toronto: Macmillan, 1966).
28. Ibid., p. 201.

mans, Icelanders, Hungarians, and Doukhobors, some of it through group negotiation rather than by a flow of individuals. The Canadian Pacific Railway and the Canadian government, which at that time may have been considered identical, shared a desire to populate the newly opened spaces, hence the tendency to recognize collective rights over individual rights in matters like landholding and the schooling of children, questions that over time were to become greatly disputed. The United States government legislated against this practice, but the difference between the two governments was not so much because of differing views about whether they were creating melting pots or mosaics, as because of Canada's desire to get people to the west.

Block settlement in Canada, both negotiated and free, as a response to the need for settlers may have been initiated in a different fashion than in the United States, but the outcome in both countries was probably almost the same, since in the process of westward expansion national groups would naturally congregate. Perhaps the main difference was the far greater hardships suffered by the settlers in Canada than in the United States where in large measure land already opened was purchased from native Americans.[29] However, there is no reason to suppose that community life based on national origins would be more intense in Canada than in the United States. By this time in the United States hardship was worse in the cities and national communities were probably no less important in the role of overcoming it there than they were in rural Canada. It is difficult then really to differentiate the melting pot and mosaic in the processes of settlement of the two countries.

Another important parallel between the two countries can be found in the discussions about how much immigration and from where. In Canada, there was certainly little of the generosity toward other nations and other cultures that would have been necessary for the building of a cultural mosaic. The Canadian counterpart of American nativism, expressed by the group called

---

29. Marcus Lee Hansen, quoted in Handlin, *Immigration*, p. 45.

the Canadian imperialists by Carl Berger,[30] was aimed, as in the United States, against the new immigration from Eastern and Southern Europe. Canada, thought G. R. Parkin, was to belong to "the sturdy races of the North-Saxon and Celt, Scandinavian, Dane and Northern German."[31] Parkin and others believed that Canada had a purifying ally in its climate, and for that reason they felt that the disastrous effects of the new immigration in the United States could be avoided. While it could have been a matter of dispute whether natural selection would work better in the pure air of a harsh prairie winter or the overcrowded slums of American cities, Parkin thought the United States was welcome to Hungarians, Poles, and Italians. What Canada needed was "more of the hardy German and Norwegian races."[32]

In the early part of the present century Sir Clifford Sifton's[33] search for his stalwart peasants for prairie development gave rise to concern not only in Winnipeg, but also in Toronto and Montreal. No one was to be more persistently against non-British immigration throughout his life than Stephen Leacock. He stated that a small number of Eastern Europeans "like a minute dose of poison in a medicine,"[34] might be helpful. In an address to the Canadian Club of Ottawa in the first decade of this century, he said, "Poles, Hungarians, Bukowinians and any others . . . will come in to share the heritage which our fathers have won. Out of all these we are to make a kind of mixed race in which is to be the political wisdom of the British, the chivalry of the French, the gall of the Galician, the hungriness of the Hungarian and the dirtiness of the Doukobor."[35]

Many English-Canadian writers were caught up in the strident tones of the racial phobias of the time. One denounced the melting pot, saying that "instead of the pure race from which we have come, we shall have a mongrel race, and this mongrel race is mak-

---

30. Carl Berger, *The Sense of Power* (Toronto: Univ. of Toronto Press, 1970).
31. Ibid.
32. Ibid., p. 137.
33. The minister in the Laurier government responsible for immigration.
34. Stephen Leacock, *Economic Prosperity in the British Empire* (Toronto: Macmillan, 1930), p. 195.
35. Quoted in Berger, *Sense of Power*, p. 151.

ing itself known in Canada as a result of the immigration we have had.["36] That was in 1920. There was more of this unwanted immigration before it stopped almost entirely at the time of the Great Depression.

It is impossible to know whether these influential writers and men of affairs were reflecting or molding public opinion, but there is little in the sentiments they expressed to conclude that Canada was building a plural society. Although it might have been preferable in Canada's view to keep the foreigners out, once they were in the country the ideal method of their absorption was Anglo-conformity, or Anglo-Canadianization, and there was a general faith that Canadian-British education and institutions would do their work and that all these people and their descendants could be accommodated to the benefit of empire. Education was certainly to play a role. In *The Education of the New Canadian*, J. T. Anderson, a one-time premier of Saskatchewan, wrote in 1918, "No better material can be found among our newcomers from which to mould a strong type of Canadian citizen than is found among these Ruthenians."[37]

There is little, then, in Canadian history that suggests an image of the Canadian future as one of ethnic pluralism. The United States and Canada have been remarkably alike in attitudes toward immigration and desirable types of immigrants. Both, in time, became exclusive in immigration policy, the United States with its blunt instrument of quotas and Canada with its more subtle understandings of preferability. It may seem strange that the two countries with their different histories and their different archetypes and preferred fantasies—revolution and evolution, if those are the correct labels—should have run parallel with respect to immigrants and how they should be absorbed into the developing social structure. These parallels may seem surprising, since for several reasons it might be expected that the two countries might have taken different courses.

One reason is that Canada remained a British colony until

36. Ibid
37. Quoted in Gibbon, *Canadian Mosaic*, p. 301.

1867; after that British influences still remained strong, and not only in those areas where they retained some constitutional prerogatives. As we hear so often, there was no revolutionary rejection of the past aimed at creating free institutions. Rather, what was sought were new arrangements that might lead to better exploitation of a vast hinterland. Sir John A. Macdonald's desire to die a British subject was never seriously jeopardized, and the great heroes of Canadian railway building bought their way into, or were rewarded with, seats in the British House of Lords. Indeed, until the 1930s Canadians of distinction, dubious or merited, might legitimately aspire to be ennobled by the British monarch without losing their Canadian citizenship. Even that loss does not undermine the high status enjoyed by Canadian-born press peers in their country of origin. One had to wait until the present governor general for a head of state whose plain and austere tailoring is without monarchical trappings. These strong British links may have caused less tolerance toward non-British immigrants than in the United States, but Americans seemed no more tolerant than Canada toward those nationalities seen by American nativism as responsible for "the passing of the great race," that is, the Anglo-Saxon group.

Canada's links with Britain survived the ever-falling proportion of the population, 43 percent in 1971, represented by those who claimed British ethnic origin. That proportion still makes them a major minority and accounts for the continuing strong cultural linkages. Moreover, throughout its history Canada has always seen Britain as the major and preferred source of immigrants. Although they no longer make up a majority of newcomers, the British are still the largest of the incoming groups, which have varied greatly in size in recent years. Up to the present, the British have retained their special place in the elite structure of Canadian society.

A second reason for the expectation that Canada and the United States would develop differently in the way in which immigrants would be incorporated into society is the fact that Canada was a binational state from the beginning. The uneasy tolerance that French and English were to show toward each other was not extended to foreigners who resisted assimilation or were believed to be unassimilable. The French were no more willing to welcome outsiders than were the British, and their hostility to a pluralism beyond the historic dualism is still as strong as ever.

Among English Canadians at times even the binationalism of Canada was in question. Religion and racial conflict exemplified by the battle over bilingual schools in Ontario, Manitoba and the Northwest; Orangism and the British Empire orientations of the Toronto "imperialists" created ambivalence about the future of the French within Canadian society. There were even thoughts that ultimately the French would assimilate to Anglo-conformity, so taken would they be with British institutions, and indeed French-Canadian collaborating elites seemed to accept ennoblement by the British monarch as readily as their English-Canadian counterparts. The less ethnocentric of the articulate British in the early part of the century romanticized about the survival of French-Canadian culture but saw it as no threat because of what they hoped would be boundless British immigration. It is a remarkable fact of Canadian demographic history that, unlike the ever-diminishing proportion of British, the French have managed to retain their proportion of the population at around 30 percent through the present century with scarcely more than a trickle of immigrants.

The French always seem to have been conscious of the threat that immigration posed to them in terms of both cultural survival and economic development. Consequently, toward the end of the last century when the great waves of immigration were passing over them, Quebec officials looked for immigrants in France, Belgium, and Switzerland, and—more importantly, for they were seen as the most likely to respond—to the French Canadians in New England. Thus repatriation of their own rather than a search of the world for others was Quebec's response at the height of the human movement across the Atlantic. Neither the European Francophone nor the expatriate French Canadians responded with enthusiasm.[38]

Rather than foster a tolerance toward pluralism, Canada's fun-

38. Macdonald, *Canada*, pp. 99–100.

damental duality might well have worked against it. In Manitoba one of the reasons given for withdrawing the right of the French to French-speaking schools at the turn of the century was that all national groups that were being swept in by immigration would demand their own language rights and thereby hinder the process of assimilation. French rights were taken away in 1915.[39]

Although the French up to the period after World War II continued to express hostility toward immigration and its predominantly British character, they were able to do very little about it because English-Canadian politicians were skillful in countering Quebec's objections. The development of immigration policy rested primarily with the federal government and the implementation of it with the activities and location of its immigration offices abroad. The French were to become bitter critics of federal policy and of what they perceived as its discriminatory character until finally they set up their own immigration department in 1968.[40]

The French saw their own falling birth rates and the continuing Anglo-assimilation of non-English ethnic groups in Montreal as major threats to the survival of their culture. The act that set up the immigration department in Quebec in 1968 made some slight acknowledgment of pluralism by including among its responsibilities, in addition to all the usual tasks of an immigration department, the preservation of ethnic customs. But this was in the late 1960s when the revival of ethnicity had well begun and so is a reflection of contemporary events rather than of historical values. Moreover, Quebec was faced with the same conflict of interest as faced any other host society wanting to attract newcomers: on the one hand, the need to integrate them into Quebec society and to teach them French, and on the other the need to make the assimilative process more attractive by allowing the preservation of ethnic customs. It was a particular conflict for the

39. W. L. Morton, "Manitoba Schools and Canadian Nationality, 1890–1923," in *Minorities, Schools, and Politics,* Historical Readings no. 7. (Toronto: University of Toronto Press, 1969).

40. Freda Hawkins, *Canada and Immigration* (Montreal: McGill-Queen's University Press, 1972), p. 227.

French, who so intimately link language and culture. Their dilemma was nowhere more acute than in the Quebec reaction to the federal government's multicultural program in 1971. "You will have gathered," wrote Premier Bourassa to Prime Minister Trudeau shortly afterward, "that Quebec does not accept your government's approach to the principle of multiculturalism."[41] The position of the Quebec government and of Quebec intellectuals seemed to be that multiculturalism would detract from the essential Canada that was bilingual and bicultural, conditions that should prevail if Canada was to survive. "Je veux souligner que pour la communauté canadienne française, cette nouvelle politique multiculturelle représente un immense pas en arrière dont, je crois, les Canadiens français n'ont pas encore pris conscience."[42]

There is, however, one curious way in which Canada's duality might be a reason for the saliency of ethnicity that now exists and that has helped to keep national origin groups alive: the effect the duality has had on the Canadian census. Before Confederation in 1867 censuses classified the population as "French origin," "not of French origin," and "Indian." To account for the large and varied immigration, the complex classification that we know today has grown out of that simple and logical one.

Although there was some inconsistency in the censuses after Confederation, *origin* was generally defined as the birthplace of the individual or that of his paternal ancestor before coming to North America. Over time, as immigrants came increasingly from Europe and as international boundaries changed, the problem of an origin classification became more complicated. The matter was not helped by the fact that census administrators were never quite sure what they were doing.

The 1931 census provides a good illustration in the discussion of the origin question. Here I am following a lead given some time ago by Joel Smith, who suggested that an examination of how the two countries have treated ethnicity in their respective

---

41. Howard Palmer, ed., *Immigration and the Rise of Multiculturalism* (Vancouver: Copp Clark, 1975), p. 151.
42. Guy Rocher, "Les Ambiguitiés d'un Canada bilingue et multiculturel," *Le Québec en Mutation* (Montreal: Hurtubise, 1973).

censuses would be an indication of orientation to melting pot or mosaic.[43] Guidance for the 1931 census stated,

It is a well-known fact that there are "Austrian," "Swiss" and "Prussian" types of Germans, and if these regard themselves as belonging to separate races, it is a question whether this distinction should not be carried out in Census enumeration. If a distinction is made between Norwegian and Dane, it seems reasonable to distinguish between Austrian and Prussian. . . .
The question may arise as to whether a grouping of ten races, some of them differing widely, is of value, even though the grouping is done solely to effect an adequate comparison between censuses. The answer mainly depends upon the particular purpose for which the information is required. Such a grouping has little or no value for ethnical study, but it is doubtful that this has ever been the purpose of taking a census of races. When the races have fused and their differentiation is no longer important from a *social* point of view, a census of races will be unnecessary but, up to the present time, the races in Canada show several important points of differentiation which are of great social significance.[44]

One is left wondering what racial fusion might have meant in the minds of these officials, but the fact that they thought it might come is some further evidence that the mosaic is not firmly rooted in the Canadian past.

In the preparation for the 1961 census the Canadian government then led by John Diefenbaker, who felt very keenly that hyphenated Canadianism was undesirable, attempted to get rid of the ethnic question. Strong resistance came from the French, who might have been satisfied with a language question—say, language first learned in childhood—except that there would then be no way of measuring French descendants who had lost their language, and had thus been assimilated. It is only by measuring this phenomenon that the threat to French survival in Canada could be monitored. By the time of the preparation of the 1971 census, the ethnic revival was well begun, and the Royal

43. Joel Smith, "Melting Pot-Mosaic, Consideration for a Prognosis," in *Minorities North and South,* Proceedings of the Third Inter-Collegiate Conference on Canadian-American Relations, Michigan State University, 1968.
44. *Seventh Census of Canada,* 1931, vol. 1, p. 235.

Commission on Bilingualism and Biculturalism had exploited what it could of the ethnic data of the 1961 census. So it became increasingly difficult to abandon the ethnic question in the census.

One of the working documents in the preparation of the 1971 census deals with the ethnic question. "This question," it says, "has given rise in the past to emotional feelings on the part of respondents but while its inclusion is sometimes criticized, there is a heavier demand for data on ethnicity than on most other items."[45] The listing of pros and cons for including the ethnic question indicates the difficulties surrounding it. For example:

Great use is made of census data on ethnicity by national and cultural organizations who are anxious to retain their identity.

A cross-classification of ethnic groups with mother tongue or language now spoken provides a good measure of the degree of assimilation of different groups.

Collection of data on ethnic groups is viewed in some quarters as tending to perpetuate distinctions along ethnic lines to the detriment of Canadian society as a whole.

This question irritates some respondents who think of themselves as Canadian but are expected to report themselves as English, Irish, Norwegian or some other nationality with which they no longer associate themselves.[46]

If these officials were alert to public feelings on the issue, and they probably were since representations would have been made to them, it was clear that even at this late date there appeared to be no clear commitment to mosaic or melting pot for Canadian society.

With all its sociological absurdities, the ethnic question was included in the 1971 census. It has long been known that the query has provided a very unreliable picture of ethnic structure. Even in 1971 the census planners were saying, "There is a relatively high degree of reporting error, since respondents may not know their ethnic background."[47] The absurdity of the question

45. Census Division, Dominion Bureau of Statistics, "The 1971 Census of Population and Housing, Development of Subject Matter Content," mimeographed (Ottawa, 1969), p. 13.
46. Ibid.
47. Ibid.

lies in requiring the citizen to answer the question "To what ethnic or cultural group did you or your ancestor (on the male side) belong on coming to this continent?" The exclusive patrilineal descent ignores the important socializing and cultural role of the mother, particularly in language learning. Moreover, it does not allow for a Canadian or American ethnicity, except for native Indian and Eskimo. Census administrators, somewhat exasperated, have dealt with the few who insisted on reporting themselves as Canadian or American by classifying them under "other."

Thus the picture we have of the ethnic structure of Canada is an artifact of the census. It requires all Canadians to have an ethnicity whether they feel it or not. Unlike the Canadian, the American census, which has had only a birthplace question and not an ethnic origin one, has been clear throughout, as Joel Smith pointed out with this quotation from the American census of 1880:

The census statistics will often appear inadequate to the facts of population. Thus a visitor in Cincinnati is likely to be told that in that section of the city which is called "Over the Rhine" there are 90,000 Germans. In one sense of the word German this may be true. It is not incorrect to speak of a child of German parents, perhaps himself speaking the German language and living in a community almost exclusively of that nationality, as a German. But this is not the point of view of the census law. For the purposes of the tables immediately following, those only are Germans or Irish, or French, who were born in Germany, Ireland or France. Their children born on the soil of the United States are known and ranked as Americans.[48]

So a new nationality or ethnicity takes root—by law! The outcomes of the law are not, however, clear. Does the inability of at least 30 percent of men in a 1971 survey to give their ethnicity indicate a measure of success in creating a new nation by the assimilation of immigrants, or does the continued vitality of ethnic groups in American society suggest that the primordial links are more secure than supposed? There are some interesting parallel Canadian data on this matter of wanting to identify not

48. Quoted in Smith, "Melting Pot-Mosaic."

with the past but with the present. In a 1973 national survey involving a very large sample for the purpose of analyzing occupational mobility, respondents were asked the census question on ethnic origin in order to determine the effects of ethnicity on mobility. But they were also asked another question immediately following: "To which ethnic or cultural group do you feel that you now belong? As responses, "American" and "Canadian" were allowed as well as those that appeared in the census responses.

The results show strikingly that most Canadians identify more strongly with Canada than with their "origin" groups. Eighty-six percent chose Canadian as the cultural group to which they now felt they belonged. When the foreign-born are taken out, about nine-tenths of male respondents saw themselves as Canadian. Thus, while in the United States the objective of the census law to obliterate descent-group identification after the first generation has not been an unqualified success, neither has the Canadian census been wholly successful in providing a picture of Canadian ethnic structure that would correspond to a set of identities. It might be surmised that in the long and difficult history of migration to the New World, because of their aspirations if nothing else, migrants leaving their place of origin sought to identify themselves with their new country. However, the difficulties that they faced, two world wars and the recognition of old and new nationalities that followed the wars, and the resurgence of nationalism and of demands for self-determination, have had a countereffect for the descendants of these immigrants. In both the United States and Canada neither the metaphor of mosaic nor that of melting pot aptly describe what has taken place.

We have to look not to their histories or to their charter values of revolution and evolution—if these are not themselves questionable labels—but to the recent past and to the worldwide revival of ethnicity to understand why, in both countries, ethnicity has found new strengths, expressed in Canada by multiculturalism and in the United States by the return to the old idea of a nation of nations. Ethnicity became salient in both countries in response to similar internal and world conditions.

The revival of ethnicity after World War II, which brought into question the dominant trend to Anglo-conformity in both Canada and the United States, can be traced to several sources. There was first of all decolonization. European powers were forced to retreat from their former empires in the face of nationalist movements of liberation that, after initial success, in turn revived traditional tribal hostilities that found expression in forms ranging from separatism from the new nation to outright genocide. Often the European retreat was not accomplished without a bitter struggle that greatly heightened the sense of peoplehood on the part of those who had been colonized. The war in Vietnam was a different example because it appeared that the United States was assuming the role of white domination in the affairs of the world. There were also the émigrés from Eastern Europe who feared that the socialist revolutions were obliterating national cultures and that these had to be preserved by émigré communities. In Canada, postwar émigrés played an important part in strengthening the ethnic identities of earlier arrivals and of second and third generations. There was also reaction against the large centralized and powerful states where tensions between center and periphery, metropolis and hinterland, were ethnic tensions, for example in Britain with the Celtic fringe. Devolution, as it has developed in contemporary Britain, can be viewed in part as an accommodation to ethnic demands. In France, too, peripheral regions contained ethnic and linguistic groups that sought to free themselves.

Within North America, perhaps the most important forces in the revival of ethnicity were the existence in both Canada and the United States of large, deprived minorities whose positions, although very different in the two countries, called for redress. The civil rights movement in the United States, civil rights legislation, and the equal opportunity legislation had their counterparts in Canada with the extended proceedings of the Royal Commission on Bilingualism and Biculturalism and the subsequent legislation on language rights, bilingual districts, and French representation in the federal public service.

These developments, often because they had repercussions in the occupational structures, raised the consciousness of other minorities, and eventually of women. So we find ourselves in the decade of the organized minorities demanding rights as members of groups rather than as individuals, and making ethnic affiliation or descent-group identification an essential part of a person's selfhood. The revival, as shown by the extensive review in the book edited by Glazer and Moynihan,[49] is worldwide. Many view it with approval because they feel that these primordial havens provide a new stability amid the merging mass societies and the global villages. Thus Canada's mosaic, scarcely adumbrated in its historical development, took on its firm design in the postwar years at the same time as the fires were dampened under America's melting pot.

It is difficult to say what future course the modest cultural pluralism that has followed from these developments might take. Stronger ethnic-group identification, a more sharply delineated mosaic, could be viewed as a reversion to the saliency of endogamous descent groups as a principle of social organization, with all the dangers of invidious rankings and comparisons where such types of social organization have existed. A melting-pot course toward the development of a universalistic modern character and culture that emphasizes common human qualities and the unity of mankind and sheds the particularisms of history continues as the revolutionary option. In the revolution, human history and human cultures need not be forgotten or abandoned. They might simply be released from the custody of the descent group to the responsibility of all.[50] One might hazard a judgment that, despite the current revival of ethnicity, the United States veers more toward the revolution than does Canada.

49. Nathan Glazer and Daniel P. Moynihan, *Ethnicity: Theory and Experience* (Cambridge, Mass.: Harvard University Press, 1975).
50. I have dealt with this notion in greater length in "Ethnic Pluralism in Canadian Perspective," in Glazer and Moynihan, *Ethnicity*.

9

The Place of Learning and the Arts in Canadian Life

Claude Bissell

This paper is concerned with formal higher education and the literary arts—with the writers of poetry, prose fiction, and drama. This focus is a means of concentration, but it also has its own logic. The independent scholar has rarely existed in Canada, and learning has always been associated with the universities; the literary arts have been at the center of cultural life since the time of the earliest settlements. Moreover, this limitation will help to bring out similarities in the development of English and French Canada, although the similarities emerge only as broad generalities from sharply differentiated particulars. The similarities appear more clearly in the field of higher education. For many years now leaders in higher education from English and French universities have met regularly to discuss their problems; they enjoy an easy association and follow a common language of discussion. But no such entente, *cordiale* or otherwise, exists in the literary arts, and a scholar who sets out to familiarize himself with Canadian literature in both English and French must master two distinct disciplines, each with its own chronology and pattern of relationships and influences. In the first section I shall deal with both English and French Canada (with an admittedly English bias); in the second, which deals with the literary arts, I shall be drawing my examples from the literature in English, and most of my conclusions will be valid only in an English-Canadian setting.

I shall examine the following questions: What kind of higher education and literary activity have flourished in Canada? From what sources have they derived their strength and direction? To what extent have they occupied an influential place in Canadian life? To what extent do higher education and the literary arts in Canada follow an evolutionary development, and—what is, I think, more important—to what extent have they been shaped by or in response to ideas that stemmed from the American Revolution?

Canadian higher education was not, as one might expect, a late arrival on a scene given over for the first two centuries to the most elementary and exiguous demands of survival. The traditional beginning, as Robin Harris observes in his recent and authoritative study, *A History of Higher Education in Canada 1663–1960*, is 1635, "the year when the Jesuits established at Quebec a college which eventually offered the complete *cours classique* or classical college course that until the 1950's constituted the required course of study for the B.A. degree in the Canadian French-language universities."[1] This ancient institution, it could be argued, was a first version of the University of Laval, even though over two centuries elapsed before the university received its official charter. In English Canada, the period between the idea and its realization is unusually short, but it did not occur until the late eighteenth century. The Loyalists who came to the Maritimes and to Upper Canada in the last decade of the century brought with them the wilderness memories of Harvard, Yale, and Columbia, and visions of Oxford and Cambridge. King's College at Windsor, Nova Scotia (later to become part of Dalhousie University) and the University of New Brunswick at Fredericton (also at an early stage known as King's College) have engaged in friendly disputation from time to time as to which was the more ancient. But it is unquestionably true that for both institutions the first official steps had been taken in the penultimate decade of the century. In Upper Canada, the first official steps were not taken so quickly, but the idea for King's College,

1. Robin S. Harris, *A History of Higher Education in Canada 1663–1960* (Toronto: University of Toronto Press, 1976), p. 14.

which was to become the University of Toronto, was enunciated by the first lieutenant governor, John Graves Simcoe, shortly after he took office in 1791; and the setting aside of the crown lands that were to constitute the endowment of the college took place shortly after. If we move ahead a century to the first years of a new major phase of settlement—the opening up of the West—we find a similar priority and urgency in higher education. The bill creating the University of Manitoba was passed in 1877, seven years after the province was formed. British Columbia took similar action in 1890, although the bill remained a pious declaration of intent until 1915. But Alberta and Saskatchewan, without British Columbia's sense of identity, fused legal intent and action in an extraordinary way. The two provinces were created in 1905, carved out of the Northwest Territories. In 1906 Alberta passed a university act; in 1907, it had a president, H. M. Tory, who was to be a dominant figure in Canadian higher education for the next four decades; and in 1908 it had a habitation, five faculty, and forty-five students. Saskatchewan followed an identical sequence, one year behind at each stage, and it, too, chose a president, W. C. Murray, who was to give strong leadership both to his own university and to Canadian higher education.

The foundation of the early Canadian universities, especially those in what was then Upper and Lower Canada, and in Nova Scotia and New Brunswick, hard upon the first faint outlines of a political structure, did not, however, bear witness to any popular movement. The early universities were not so much creations of the state—it would, in any case, be inaccurate to use the word *state* about any of the forms of political control exercised in British North America at the time; they were rather creations of a small privileged group who embodied authority in the colony—the ecclesiastical hierarchy in either the Roman Catholic church or the Church of England and the officials, chiefly officers in the British forces, minor aristocrats, and bureaucrats versed in the ritual of the law. And the university was viewed as a means of preserving and inculcating a set of values that guaranteed the stability of society. The French-Canadian colleges were *citadelles nationales* whose function was to produce the religious and political elite by which the theocratic society of Quebec could be preserved. And the founders of the three king's colleges had a similar goal in mind, although the society they sought to preserve existed only in a distant land now that the first attempt to establish it in North America had been frustrated, so they believed, by the fanaticism and self-absorption of the American colonists. In what remained of British North America, they were determined that this would never take place. Harris cites two passages that give the intellectual tone of the times, a mixture of pious respect for orthodoxy and a nervous and bitter fear of what had happened only a few hundred miles away across a shadowy and undefended border. The first is an address to Sir Guy Carleton, governor-in-chief of British North America, sent to him in 1773 by five clergymen still resident in New York.

The founding of a College or Seminary of learning on a liberal plan in that province where youth may receive a virtuous education and can be qualified for the learned professions, is, we humbly conceive, a measure of the greatest consequence, as it would diffuse religious literature, loyalty and good morals among His Majesty's subjects there. If such a seminary is not established the inhabitants will have no means of educating their sons at home, but will be under the necessity of sending them for that purpose either to Great Britain or Ireland, which will be attended with an expense that few can bear, or else to some of the states of this continent, where they will soon imbibe principles that are unfavourable to the British tradition.[2]

The second letter, four years later, is from Bishop Mountain, who was to be a founder of McGill, to the lieutenant governor of Quebec.

Let me be permitted, then, to suggest the danger which may result to the political principles and to the future character as subjects of such of our young men among the higher ranks as the exigency of the case obliges their parents to send for classical education to the colleges of the United States. In these Seminaries, most assuredly, they are not likely to imbibe that attachment to our constitution in Church and State, that veneration for the Government of their country, and that loyalty to their King, to which it is so particularly necessary in the

2. Ibid., p. 28.

present time to give all the advantages of early predilection in order to fix them deeply both in the understanding and the heart.[3]

The charter gained for King's College in 1827 by the Anglican bishop of Toronto, John Strachan, delivered the college up bound and obsequious to the Church of England. The Anglican bishop of the diocese was the visitor with final judicial control of the university; the president of the university must be a clergyman in holy orders in the United Church of England and Ireland; the executive government of the university consisted of a council, made up of the chancellor, the president, and seven members, who were required to be members of the Church of England and to subscribe to her articles; and degrees in divinity were restricted to persons in holy orders in the Church of England. Yet Strachan maintained, with the weight of evidence on his side, that the statute was the most open and liberal that had ever been granted by the crown, since it imposed no religious subscriptions or tests on students or graduates, other than those in divinity.

The promptness with which universities in Canada were founded is laudable and gives an early note of intellectual refinement in what was otherwise a hard and barren scene. But the concept of the university was thrust upon the colonies by a small group of like-minded adherents, and it was established more as bulwark against the enemy without—the evil and misguided American revolutionaries—than as a source of new wisdom. The infant Canadian university was not sustained, as were the early American foundations in New England, by a sense of mission— the revelation of God's word to the New World. However, the French-Canadian colleges were, one might argue, exceptions. Certainly their founders approached their educational task with dedicated zeal. But the French colleges were not thought of as sources of new truth or entrusted with a missionary task. They were regarded as branches of the church, to explicate what was already known to those who had no doubts about the ultimate nature of the world.

Thomas Chandler Haliburton, a Loyalist Tory who feared and

3. Ibid., p. 29.

despised the American Revolution at the same time that he admired the intellectual vigor and moral strength of those who inspired and sustained it, compared the Canadian universities in an unflattering way with the American universities.

Scarcely had the ground in the neighborhood of Boston been cleared, when the General Court founded a college, which they afterward called Harvard, in token of gratitude to a clergyman of that name, who bequeathed a considerable sum of money to it. The town of Newtown in which it was situated, was denominated Cambridge, the name of the *alma mater* of many of the principal people in the colony. In this respect, they showed a far greater knowledge of the world, and of the proper course of education, than the inhabitants of the present British colonies. They first established a university, and then educated downward to the common schools, as auxiliary seminaries, which were thus supplied with competent teachers; while duly qualified professional men and legislators, were simultaneously provided for the state. In Canada, there is an unfriendly feeling toward these institutions, which people, who play upon popular prejudice or ignorance, endeavor to foster, by representing them as engrossed by the sons of the rich, who are able to pay the expense of their own instruction, without assistance from the public treasury; and that all that is thus bestowed, is so much withdrawn from the more deserving but untrained children of the poor.[4]

The book in which this passage occurs, *Rule and Misrule of the English in America,* came out in 1851, and Haliburton reflects his awareness of the faltering course of the Maritime universities, whose progress by the middle of the century had not borne out the enthusiastic self-assurance of their founders. Throughout the whole of British North America, universities had not enlisted great popular support and, what was more immediately crucial, the support of elected representatives, a condition that was not changed by the popular surge leading to Confederation and the setting up of a federal state.

The state of American universities up until the Civil War was not greatly different. Richard Hofstadter quotes a comment made by Longfellow in 1823 and suggests that it could be applied to

---

4. Thomas Chandler Haliburton, *Rule and Misrule of the English in America* (New York: Harper and Brothers, 1851), pp. 190–91.

the colleges of 1860. "What has heretofore been the idea of a university with us? The answer is a simple one:—two or three large brick buildings—with a chapel, and a president to pray in it."[5] But the American situation changed dramatically after the 1860s in a post–Civil War flowering of revolutionary ideas. This was the era of the proliferation of state universities and land-grant colleges established with a sense of responsibility to society, of swift secularization, enormous growth in support, from both government and private individuals, and it saw the implantation, chiefly from German sources, of the idea of research as a prime function. The Canadian universities, during the latter part of the nineteenth century, continued on their placid way, faintly aware of what was going on south of the border, but not greatly influenced by it. Canadian universities were thought of as interesting but exotic growths, not closely related to the compelling problems of every day, and this attitude was reflected in the actions of government.

In one area the universities intersected sharply with the political life of the country—the interrelationship between religion and education. In French Canada the concern was central and overpowering, but it was like the heavens, omnipresent, full of interesting and colorful variations, but fundamentally unchangeable. In English Canada, however, where from the very beginning sects multiplied and vied for power and authority within this life and in the next, religion and higher education made up a powerful political mixture. In the United Canadas during the forties and fifties and, after Confederation, in the province of Ontario, the interrelationship between religion and education was a dominant issue, finally resolved in a manner that prepared the way for an orderly development and that reflected a typically Canadian way of containing and reconciling apparent opposition.

The problem had two closely related phases. The first question was, should the state associate itself with a particular religious

5. Quoted in Richard Hofstadter and Walter P. Metzger, *The Development of Academic Freedom in the United States* (New York: Columbia University Press, 1955), p. 374.

body in its support of higher education? It became abundantly clear in an area where Presbyterians, Methodists, and Baptists were more numerous and more vocal than the adherents of the Church of England, that the answer would be No. Second, how did one make sure that sectarian energy and conviction, strong and unquenchable, did not fragment and weaken the intellectual life? In the incisive words of a supporter of secularization and concentration, the danger existed that we would establish "schools not of *science*, but of *sect*, in which the minds of our youth will be steeped for years in the gall and vinegar of partizan distrust and animosity, and from which the educated, and therefore influential, members of the community will come forth in yearly bands, only the better qualified at the public cost, to be public pests, and to wage an incessant war with the nurslings of rival Seminaries."[6]

The government solution was contained in two bills, the Baldwin Bill of 1849, which proclaimed the secularization of King's College, and the Hincks Bill of 1853, which established the distinction between university and college—the former an examining and administrative body, the latter a teaching body, which could be either an undenominational creation of the state or a creation of a religious body. The college concept remained a theoretical concept until it was embodied in the University of Toronto Federation Act of 1887, which provided the basis by which full teaching colleges of the Church of England, the Methodists, and the Roman Catholics could enter the university, preserving their distinctive emphasis while drawing upon the increasingly rich and varied resources of the state institution.

In this treatment of the sectarian problems, repeated elsewhere in Canada, one finds a typical Canadian solution. The state proclaimed its belief in secularization and yet found a means, indirectly, of supporting the sectarian principle. In recent years the state has gradually enforced a stricter secularization policy, and religious foundations in both English and French Canada have found it more comfortable to rid themselves of overt re-

6. Peter Colin Campbell, *Thoughts on the University Question* (Kingston: Chronicle and Gazette Office, 1845), p. 13.

ligious control. But from the middle of the nineteenth century on there has never been in Canada, to the same extent as there was in the United States, a clear separation of the secular and the religious. In the United States educators followed the doctrine of the Enlightenment, which certainly for the great private universities and the newer state foundations isolated religious life— a valuable, powerful, but untidy area—from the working of the practical intellect. (For many sectarian universities, which stressed a Christian rather than an intellectual training, the principle worked in reverse.) In Canada there was more uniformity and a typically Victorian compromise whereby religious doctrine and moral instruction existed in friendly tension with the secular outlook in the same or associated institutions.

This continuing alliance between religion and education, strong, omnipresent, but in English Canada never explicitly defined, left behind, even after it had weakened and lost its legal force, a tradition that exercised a various and pervasive influence. It helps to account for the college tradition—directly in French Canada where the collèges, small, intimate communities, existed away from the university campus in a rural or small-town setting under the immediate control of the church; indirectly in English Canada, where the college usually had church sponsorship and emphasized the role of the residence, inseparable from the college, as an instrument of moral and social instruction. The religious connection meant a heavy emphasis on the humanities, particularly on classics (increasingly supplanted by English literature in the twentieth century) and philosophy, both of which were congenial to the religious spirit, although not necessarily to sectarian orthodoxy. By the end of the nineteenth century, philosophy had become the dominant subject in both English and French universities, and it nourished the best teachers and scholars: John Watson of Queen's, George Paxton Young of Toronto, J. Clark Murray of McGill, William Lyall of Dalhousie.[7] The rise of the social sciences in this century has diminished the role of philosophy, but it still retains a central role in Canadian

7. Harris, Higher Education in Canada, p. 135.

universities—stronger, I believe, than in American universities, at least on a comparative quantitative basis. When English studies rose to a position of dominance in the humanities by the second decade of the twentieth century, they carried with them from the nineteenth a tradition with strong philosophical emphasis. It is significant that the two Canadian writers who had made the greatest international impact—Marshall McLuhan and Northrop Frye—have close college connections, McLuhan with the Roman Catholic College of St. Michael's, Frye with Victoria College, the voice of thoughtful Methodism in the nineteenth century and since then an exponent of Protestant dissent. (William Blake, the subject of Frye's first major book, would have found in Frye's college of the thirties and forties a sympathetic environment.) Both McLuhan and Frye have moved into systematic analysis and philosophical generalization from and through literary studies, and both can, on occasion, assume a prophetic stance.

No doubt, particularly in French Canada, the religious connection imposed constraints and tethered speculation. To a lesser extent, this was also true in English Canada. But the sectarian diversity of the university also reduced the chances of a heavy, central authoritarianism and blunted the clumsy forays of the state. I recall from the early days of my administrative career a vivid illustrative incident. The "red Dean" of Canterbury, Hewlett Johnson, was denied a platform in the central hall of the University of Toronto, chiefly because of quiet but steely protest from the board of governors; but he found a friendly reception in Trinity, the Church of England college, where he expounded his pastoral communism to a large, sympathetic, but critically alert student audience.

The state, as I have pointed out, was much concerned throughout the nineteenth century with resolving the rival educational claims of religious sects. But in the vital area of financial support, it adopted a wary and frugal approach. The British North America Act of 1867 assigned education to the provinces. The fathers of Confederation had primary and secondary education in mind, since the universities, although numerous enough for a nascent nation (there were eighteen degree-granting colleges in 1868), did not form a coherent system and were of interest only to a small minority. The province, although accepting responsibility for the universities, concentrated on primary and secondary school education and left the universities to their own devices. Private benefactions did not flow in, as in the United States, to fill the financial gap, except modestly at Dalhousie, Toronto, McMaster, and Queen's, and generously (by Canadian standards) at McGill. And the financial drought did not cease until after World War II. When compared with the private and state universities and colleges of America, Canadian universities thus occupied a hazy middle ground, not treasured sufficiently by wealthy individuals and the public to achieve a private status, yet not able to look to the state for systematic and reliable support.

The financial history of the University of Toronto, which shared with McGill the largest responsibility for higher education in Canada, spells out the nature of the financial problem, although it should be remembered that in national terms Toronto enjoyed a modest affluence. A special commission of 1906 led to an act that laid the foundation for a new academic autonomy in the creation of an independent lay board and in conferring on the president final powers of academic appointment. The commission also recommended that the university should receive for operating revenue a sum equal to 50 percent of the provincial succession duties. The government accepted the recommendation but in 1914, with the grim prospect of war, decided to limit the amount of the annual grant to $500,000 in the event that 50 percent of the succession duties exceeded this amount. Another commission appointed in 1920, this time confined to financial matters, reaffirmed the recommendation of the earlier commission. The government turned down the recommendation, and "over the ensuing 20 years the amount of the annual grant averaged $1,500,000, approximately one-third the amount that would have been allocated had the succession duty formula been followed."[8]

The policy of the provincial governments toward the support of universities, certainly in Ontario and the Maritimes, arose from

8. Ibid., p. 362.

the determined survival of too many universities in a sparsely settled country. But it arose also from an official lack of enthusiasm for higher education, particularly for its humanities-centered, frankly elitist character. The state did not see in universities agents for social progress and broad democratic enlightenment, as was increasingly the case in the United States. In the seventies and eighties the provinces, like the states in the United States, were inclined to set up their own institutions for the study of agriculture and engineering, the two professional disciplines with the most practical message for developing economies; somewhat later they did the same for teacher training; and the universities were slow to absorb these professional studies.

The social sciences, also with a practical message, although less audible, were slow to develop in Canadian universities. I find a nice Canadian irony in the fact that the man who dominated the social sciences during the first two decades of this century in what was then generally regarded as the leading Canadian university, McGill, made his real and abiding reputation as a humorist. Stephen Leacock did not have a high opinion even of the subject he taught. "Take enough of that mystification and muddle," he wrote, "combine it with the continental area of the United States, buttress it up on the side with the history of dead opinions, and dress it, as the chefs say, with sliced history and green geography, and out of it you can make a doctor's degree in Economics. I have one myself."[9] Leacock was far less relaxed about the latest arrivals in the social science family. Psychology, he thought, was a pretentious bore, asserting that it could bring new life to almost any subject in the curriculum. Sociology was "a sort of windy first cousin to religion with a letter of recommendation from Herbert Spencer"[10] and, in a less acerbic vein, "a wonderful subject of reflection for riper years, but hopelessly artificial as a class study for youth."[11]

9. Stephen Leacock, "Has Economics Gone to Seed?" in *Too Much College* (New York: Dodd, Mead & Co., 1946), p. 60.
10. Stephen Leacock, "Teaching the Unteachable," in ibid., p. 142.
11. Stephen Leacock, *The Boy I Left Behind Me* (New York: Doubleday, 1946), p. 162.

Graduate work and systematic research were also slow to develop. The federal government made indirect contributions here through a system of bursaries, studentships, and fellowships instituted by the newly established National Research Council in 1917–18, but only to the natural sciences. In the view of provincial governments, the universities were advanced instructional seminaries; research and graduate work, particularly in the humanities and social sciences, had little appeal; and until the forties there was a good deal of lassitude in the universities themselves. Graduate studies, in the opinion of many senior scholars, belonged to the old European universities and to the generously endowed senior foundations in the United States. The Canadian task was to concentrate on undergraduate studies, particularly through the honors course, an intensive four-year program that combined specialization with a degree of liberal education and provided a firm foundation for advanced work elsewhere.

In this atmosphere of state indifference and institutional lassitude there was little support for innovation. Signs of activity began to appear in the thirties, but in general one can say of pre-World War II Canadian universities that they confined themselves to competent undergraduate programs (with some peaks of excellence) in the traditional subjects and in the principal professions. For modest innovations, especially in the humanities and social sciences, and for the development of national organization concerned with scholarship, they relied heavily on American support, especially from the Carnegie and Rockefeller foundations. It would be appropriate, I have speculated, for the Canadian government to set up a special extraterritorial awards division, and to confer companionships of the Order of Canada on the current presidents of the Rockefeller and Carnegie foundations as a recognition of the sustained and discerning contribution made by those two foundations to Canadian higher education.

By the beginning of World War II the Canadian universities had established themselves firmly in the national consciousness as sound institutions that merited support. There was a network of established universities, most of them with nineteenth-century antecedents, and they attracted a student body that represented an unchanging cross-section of society, a little over 4 percent of the university age group. In English Canada the universities rested on a theoretically democratic basis, since the secondary schools that prepared for university were free and placed no positive barrier to attendance. But the French-Canadian universities occupied a pinnacle of economic and social elitism. Until 1929 the classical colleges enjoyed a monopoly on secondary education and general arts; they were biased toward a literary education, and, more important, depended on student fees. This monopoly was not effectively broken until the fifties.

There was no coherent pattern of financing in the university world. The provinces acknowledged responsibility but pursued arbitrary and unrealistic policies; and the federal government confined itself to a few indirect forays into graduate studies and research, almost wholly in the sciences. Graduate studies were peripheral and unorganized; the university was thought of as a popular museum with anterooms for social activity and the acquisition of professional skills; research was largely the personal idiosyncrasy of unusual individuals, and the institutions acknowledged no corporate responsibility in this area.[12] Yet the universities effectively controlled the world of learning. There was no tradition of individual scholarship outside the universities. The Royal Society, which had been founded in 1882 as a center for scholarship in all branches of learning, had become, in effect, a university preserve.

During the war years the universities stood still, and for several years immediately afterward they were too busy looking after a flood of veterans to indulge in self-analysis. The great changes came in the fifties and the sixties. In this respect Canada was no different from the universities in the United States, and indeed throughout the world; but the changes in Canada were more

12. The general assessment of Canadian scholarship in the humanities and the social sciences in 1949 given in *The Report of the Royal Commission on National Development in the Arts, Letters, and Sciences* (Ottawa: Printer to the King's Most Excellent Majesty, 1951) is accurate: "We have, it seems, some able scholars, but no consistent and representative Canadian scholarship emanating from the country as a whole and capable of making its contribution to Canadian intellectual life and to that of the western world" (p. 161).

sudden and cataclysmic than they were in the United States, partly by contrast with what had gone before, partly because of a major national shift in emphasis. In the fifties and sixties the country accepted the universities as partners in social development and change. In a sense, this amounted to the Americanization of the universities, a belated recognition of general principles associated with the revolution that the United States had been gradually implementing over the last two centuries. One very significant difference, however, was that the much larger American higher educational system now covered a vast range of institutions with much greater variation in quality.

The impetus for the change in the place of learning and the arts in Canada—transformation is a more accurate word for so vast and vital a movement—came from the federal government. The instrument of change was the Royal Commission on the National Development in the Arts, Letters, and Sciences, established by the Liberal government early in 1949, one of the first acts of the new prime minister, Louis St. Laurent. Politically, the commission was regarded primarily as another in a long series of investigations of the role of broadcasting in Canada, now given new dimensions by the imminence of television. But the broadcasting issue was to be placed in a broad context, as part of a cultural pattern and as an aid to national self-understanding. The universities were not specifically mentioned in the Order of Council establishing the commission, but in the final report they are the dominating institutions—the key to development in every aspect of the national life. "They are," the report declared, "local centres for education at large and patrons of every movement in aid of the arts, letters and sciences. They also serve the national cause in so many ways, direct and indirect, that theirs must be regarded as the finest of contributions to national strength and unity."[13] In the final recommendations of the commission, the universities were principal beneficiaries. The government acted immediately on a recommendation for federal subsidy of univer-

13. Ibid., p. 132.

sities based on the population of each of the provinces, and in the eventual carrying out of the major central recommendation, "a Council for the Arts, Letters, Humanities and Social Sciences," the universities fared magnificently. One-half of the initial endowment was devoted to their building needs in the humanities, social sciences, and arts, and a major part of the other half was devoted to their *needs in advanced* scholarship.

Why did the universities, not even listed in the initial cast of performers, finally take over the star role? One could draw up a list of factors, common in the United States and far more potent there—the postwar leap in the birth rate, the great veteran surge into the universities, the gradual movement of universal education beyond the secondary school, the vaulting technological expansion set off by the arms race. These played their part in Canada, but there were other reasons, too, peculiar to the country and to the times.

Before World War II the universities, as I have pointed out, had modest government support and no direct federal recognition. But on the national scene they had been building up, with no conscious intent or deliberate contrivance, an influential and pervasive band of supporters, interpreters, and apologists. Perhaps the greatest concentration of civil servants with a university bias was in the Department of External Affairs, which, during the thirties and forties—as demonstrated by the career of L. B. Pearson, once lecturer in history at the University of Toronto, at that time minister of external affairs in the St. Laurent government—had seemed to provide a more exciting alternative to the academic life. The prime minister, Louis St. Laurent, had been a professor of law at Laval University, and in both manner and matter was an exemplar of the strong strain of liberal humanism in the French-Canadian educational tradition. While the commission was still actively in session, he spoke about the universities in this way at a University of Toronto convocation: "The universities are, without question, among the most precious of our institutions . . . essential though it is to provide for the training of scientists and of men and women for the professions, this is not the highest national service the universities perform. Their highest service is to educate men and women in that liberal human tradition which is the true glory of our Christian civilization. The first task of a true University is to keep alive the flame of civilization itself."[14]

Certainly the composition of the commission virtually assured a university emphasis. Three out of five were active members of universities, widely known as defenders and expositors of the academic life: Dr. N. A. M. MacKenzie, President of the University of British Columbia; the Most Reverend George-Henri Lévesque, Dean of Social Sciences at Laval University; and Dr. Hilda Neatby, Professor of History at the University of Saskatchewan. The chairman of the commission, the Right Honorable Vincent Massey, despite his long career as a diplomat and as a party man discreetly walking the corridors of power, had always held education, and especially higher education, close to his heart. The two years he had spent at Balliol following graduation from the University of Toronto had both clarified and reinforced his devotion to liberal education, which he thought of as grounded in the humanities and as the guardian, expositor, and nourisher of the arts. In his youth he had been a lecturer in history and a dean of residence at the University of Toronto; he had directed the fortune left in trust by his grandfather to educational goals; he had been a member of the board of governors of the University of Toronto for many years; and, on his return from London, he had been elected chancellor of his alma mater. The commission, which was to bear his name, was not likely to take a cool, utilitarian view of the function of the universities.

The commissioners were, in a sense, regional representatives, but they had a national outlook. Of particular importance was the strong French-Canadian support, given concrete expression by the prime minister, Father Lévesque, and by a close adviser to the prime minister, Maurice Lamontagne. All these men stood for a liberal federalism. The revolution in Quebec was just be-

14. Notes to an Address, University of Toronto, 27 October 1950, National Archives, R. G. 33, 28, vol. 1A.

ginning, but it was in its quiet and least parochial form; it was still possible to think of one Canada in which a devotion by both English and French to learning and the arts would be a strong bond of unity.

Although the initiative for the rehabilitation of the universities came from the federal government, that impetus was not sustained, nor, given the constitutional facts, could it have been sustained. When in the early sixties the full scope and cost of university expansion became apparent, the provinces finally stirred in their long slumber of indifference and assumed control. The federal government relinquished direct support, although its indirect financial contribution grew immensely. By the Federal-Provincial Fiscal Arrangements Act of 1967, the federal government made a contribution to the provinces of 50 percent of postsecondary operating expenditures. But this money—$422 million in 1967 compared to $99 million distributed to universities in Canada under the old system of per capita grants—became provincial money under provincial control, and the federal pressure in higher education lost its immediacy. The federal government was like some distant and benevolent uncle who made stunning gifts to his indigent nephews but never saw or visited them.[15]

The responsibility for the educational revolution had now passed to the provinces, and they pursued it with vigor and with no great endowment of sophistication. They were most deeply concerned with the widening of accessibility, without having an equally tender concern for quality. They were not enthusiastic about the universities' passion for research and graduate studies, although during the sixties they accepted the utilitarian argument of the universities that only by the development of graduate studies and research could the universities produce the staff that was so urgently required. The quantitative gains were enormous. No country increased more rapidly the enrollment ratios in post-

15. The contrast here with the United States is striking. There a belated development of federal support for universities has led to increasing government interference to achieve social goals.—[Editor]

secondary institutions for the twenty-to-twenty-four group.[16] Graduate studies moved from the peripheral to the integral. In 1961, full-time graduate enrollment in all Canadian universities was 6,500 and part-time, 3,800; in 1974–75 the comparable figures were 37,350 and 24,000, a sixfold increase. In 1973–74 nearly 2,000 doctoral degrees were granted, compared to 300 in 1960–61. This growth was facilitated by the great increases in fellowship aid through the Canada Council. Between 1960 and 1970 the council's resources for the arts, humanities, and social sciences grew from approximately four million to approximately thirty-five million dollars.

I have referred to these changes as the "Americanization" of Canadian universities. By endorsing a policy of open accessibility and the concept of the social value of new knowledge, Canada was, one might say, at long last accepting in its educational practices some of the concepts implicit in the American Revolution. Many of the criticisms of this development were not that Canada was too hasty in adopting these changes, but that she had been too cautious and hesitant. Students protested endlessly against the persistence of economic barriers to full accessibility, and the universities, suddenly recognized as centers of research, were indignant when research support failed to maintain its momentum.

16. The external examiner's report of the Organization for Economic Cooperation and Development completed in 1975 gives the following table:

Enrollment Ratios for the 20-24-Year Age Group, Selected Countries (percentages)

	1960	1965	1969
Canada	13.5	20.9	25.5
France	7.4	13.9	15.9
Japan	8.6	11.9	15.8
England & Wales	6.2	8.7	9.8
USA	32.2	40.4	48.4
USSR	11.0	29.5	26.5

By now the gap between Canada and the United States has, I should think, narrowed greatly.

What then had happened to the conservative, antirevolutionary concepts that had dominated higher education in Canada—the bias to languages and philosophy, the emphasis on thoroughness in the undergraduate degree, and the untroubled merging of the religious and the secular? These had, to the regret of many, disappeared, consumed in the fire of change. But there were deep and troubled questionings of the Americanization process. First, there was a questioning of the technological takeover of the administration of universities—administration conceived of as the most efficient way to get quantitative results. The takeover had two phases: business control of the individual university through a lay board and the development of systems for universities within a given political jurisdiction. At the beginning of the present century the Canadian universities had elected for the American solution of a clear-cut division between academic and lay control, with the latter possessing the ultimate power. But the disturbances of the late sixties, which in Canada had a tough reformist core beneath the fashionable trappings of romantic outrage, shifted the ultimate power within the university back to staff and students and brought the prospect of a self-governing community. This development coincided, however, with the growth of government power within a coordinated university system and the rise of a militant faculty trade unionism, so that the institutional changes were muted. Following British patterns, faculty participation in university government had always been somewhat greater in Canada than in the United States. So there still remains the potential for institutional assertion based on a consciousness of academic community—the last hope, it seems to me, for the survival of institutional autonomy.

The second questioning, more clearly articulated and more passionately stated, was of the shift that had taken place in the national background and formal educational training of staff. During the sixties when the demand for new staff was at its greatest, Canadian graduate schools, particularly in the social sciences, were just beginning to turn out a few doctorates, and the demand in these subjects was met in considerable part by turning to the United States. The result, according to a good deal of critical comment now given official verification in the report by Tom Symons for the Association of Universities and Colleges of Canada, entitled *To Know Ourselves,* was the "Americanization" of certain subjects—the use of textbook material drawn from American experience and of assumptions developed in American graduate schools and the denigration, either by omission or by contemptuous dismissal, of Canadian material and attitudes. The subject is complex and confusing, whether approached through statistics or theory, but the discussion in Canada, prolonged and intense, will leave its mark. There will be, as a result, an attempt in Canadian universities to shift the balance between the national and the international (for "international," some would say "American") to the national both in hiring practices and in curriculum emphasis. For the first fifty or sixty years of their existence, Canadian universities remained outside a continental pattern by reason of their strong European ties; then they were gradually drawn into that continental pattern, I would argue for sound and compelling reasons. Now they will begin a process of cautious withdrawal. But the withdrawal will not mean isolation; it will mean, one hopes, the development of a self-consciousness and a self-awareness that will sharpen and strengthen the Canadian universities' distinctiveness in a North American context.

In their future development, the universities of the seventies will have one crucial strength that was not present in the pre-expansion days. The Canadian universities now have, for the first time in their history, a solid scholarly core. It is true that some advances had been made in the sciences before the era of expansion; but with scholarship in the humanities and social sciences sustained only by the efforts of a few individuals, university libraries were in general adequate only for undergraduate work, and a good many fell short even of that standard. When in 1962 Edwin Williams of Harvard did a survey of "resources of Canadian university libraries for research in the humanities and social services," he reported a pervasive poverty. Only Toronto's library could be properly described as a research resource. Williams observed that "there is a greater disparity in Canada than in the United States between the largest of the university libraries and the others. Toronto is more than twice the size of the next largest Canadian University library, McGill; but Harvard is only fifty percent larger than Yale." Now in a little over ten years the picture has changed. Toronto's preeminence has been maintained both in facilities and in the number of books; but there are at least a half dozen other university libraries that can qualify in several areas as research centers. The establishment of a national library in 1953 and its eventual consolidation along with the archives in a central building in Ottawa has brought bibliographical coherence to the national scene.

Even the university press, often one of the first sacrifices in an economy drive, has survived and prospered. Until 1936 Toronto was the only university press; now, as the result of spirited activity in the sixties, there are nine others, of which four—British Columbia, Laval, McGill-Queen's, and Montreal—have large enough publishing programs to be admitted to the Association of American University Presses. These presses have the main responsibility for scholarly publishing in Canada. Without them and a few senior commercial presses, Canadian scholarship would have to turn to foreign houses. Indeed, for many specialized studies of Canadian problems, there would be, without the university presses, no outlet at all, since neither English nor American presses have shown any tenderness for Canadian subjects. The university presses have also made possible a whole new generation of scholarly periodicals, which now provide a national focus for each major discipline.

The scholarly world, like the universities, has become far more highly organized. The Royal Society, often criticized in the past for its leisurely and unprofessional ways, is now surrounded by learned societies based on strict disciplinary criteria. Presses, scholarly periodicals, and national organizations stimulate scholarship and facilitate its publication; presidents' reports now close with a crescendo of articles and books produced by staff members.

Scholarship, like the universities in general, has been Americanized. And, as in the United States, it has attracted a good deal of criticism both within and without the university for its excesses and pretensions. But scholarship has nonetheless reinvigorated the universities, and if a national strategy in research finally emerges from the discussions of federal bodies and the nondoctrinaire interchange between federal and provincial authorities, the universities may regain the central position that they briefly occupied in the fifties and sixties. They still retain a characteristic that served them well in that period, a national organization that brings together the old and the new, the big and the small, the centers of learning and the custodians of general education. They lack, it is true, the qualitative edge that the private universities in the United States give to the upper end of the spectrum of higher education in that country. But they have the advantages of more uniform standards and of being able to move together in a common cause. Ironically, this institutional democracy brings them closer than their American counterparts to the spirit of '76.

The expansion of the Canadian universities in the sixties—in number of institutions and students, in diversification of curricula, and in financial support—was paralleled by the expansion of the literary arts in the number of active writers, books published, and financial support available. Margaret Atwood, herself a new major writer of the sixties, in a general survey article in the *Times Literary Supplement*, described the changes in the literary scene as "a literary expansion of Malthusian proportions."[17] She was referring to poetry, which has always been the dominant force in Canadian literature, certainly in English-Canadian literature, but her generalization would apply to all other areas—to fiction, formerly dominated each year by a few familiar, established writers, with a scattering of adventure stories, domestic romances, and didactic tracts, now with a steadily growing group of important figures and the yearly appearance of new, experimental writers; to criticism, particularly of books about Canadian literature; and to biography and journalism, where the authors approached Canadian subjects, often of a startlingly contemporary

17. Margaret Atwood, "Poetry in the Buffer Zone," *Times Literary Supplement*, 26 October 1973, p. 1305.

character, with an unapologetic vigor. Atwood's "Malthusian revolution" must be put in its proper perspective. Canada still remains a minor power in the English literary world. The report of the Royal Commission on Book Publishing that appeared in 1972 pointed out that "the annual British and American output of new books is made up of approximately 91,000 titles; the number of new titles added to *Canadian Books in Print* each year is about 1700."[18] If the output of books in French in France and Canada were added to this, the proportional Canadian contribution would shrink almost into invisibility. Still, the quantitative leap in Canadian publishing is remarkable. To go back only as far as 1948, nine years preceding the setting up of the Canada Council, is to reenter the period of Canadian literary colonialism. In that year, according to the statistics presented by the Massey Commission, English-speaking Canada published fourteen books of fiction, thirty-five books of poetry and drama, and six general books.[19]

As I have implied, the quantitative explosion was accompanied by a qualitative improvement. Within Canada there was, for the first time, an acceptance of a book by a Canadian writer as having as much importance for the literate reader as a book by an American or English writer and, if the subject matter was also Canadian, a good deal more appeal. Suddenly there was a literature that could be taken for granted as worthy of attention and criticism. In its report for 1971–72, the Canada Council observed that "this was the year it became fashionable to have a few Canadian books on the coffee table, to casually mention the latest Atwood or Aquin in mundane conversation." Northrop Frye in his conclusion to the third volume of *The Literary History of Canada,* as undeviatingly brilliant as anything he has written on Blake or biblical mythology, expresses the sense of national relief and self-confidence. "For well over a century . . . discussion about Canadian literature usually took the form of the shopper's dialogue: 'Have you any Canadian literature to-day?' 'Well, we're expecting something in very shortly.' But that age is over, and writing this

18. *Canadian Publishers and Canadian Publishing* (Ontario: The Queen's Printer for Ontario, 1972), p. 222.
19. Ibid., p. 228.

conclusion gives me rather the feeling of driving a last spike, of waking up from the National Neurosis."[20] This internal self-confidence was balanced by an increasing external recognition. Edmund Wilson's book, *O Canada, An American's Notes on Canadian Culture* (1966) had prepared the way. It was much abused in Canada, but its critical comments, although often superficial and outrageously biased, were also often brilliant and perceptive. I know of no successor to Wilson's book in either the United States or the United Kingdom, but critical comment in reviews has become more frequent, better informed, and more enthusiastic. The distinguished English critic William Walsh has written essays on Klein, Birney, and Anne Wilkinson in which he sees them as accomplished (and often brilliant) poets working in full awareness of their European antecedents. The international market in Canadian literature shows signs of buoyancy. Wilson had a roster of Canadian favorites: Morley Callaghan, Hugh MacLennan, Marie-Claire Blais, Andre Langevin. In Europe, Earle Birney, who has been writing fine poetry now for thirty years, has been suddenly discovered and laureated, and in the United States Margaret Atwood and Margaret Laurence enjoy a modest vogue.

The efflorescence of the literary arts, like the expansion and strengthening of the universities, corresponded in time with the establishment and early activity of the Canada Council. For the universities, the Canada Council was the most important part of a federal initiative that led to widespread support; for the literary arts, the Canada Council was much more important, since it turned poverty into a modest security. It is true that most of the Canada Council money for the arts went for performance and the sum allotted for the support of writers was comparatively small. (In 1971–72, of approximately $12 million allotted to the arts, the writers received in fellowships approximately $800,000.) But Canada Council grants to writers have provided an escape from the pressures of the market and have enabled good books

20. Carl F. Klink, ed., *Literary History of Canada; Canadian Literature in English,* 2d ed. (Toronto: University of Toronto Press, 1976), p. 319.

to be completed that otherwise would have been abandoned. The method of making awards, by setting up panels of established writers and critics outside of the council, has been sound, and Canada Council policies in writing have avoided political interference and stifled philistine protest.

I referred to the expansion of the universities as a process of "Americanization." The same generalization cannot be made about the expansion of the literary arts. The move to state support was not an imitation of an American model. The American National Endowment for the Humanities was not founded until 1965. More important, the expansion and vitalization of Canadian literature owed little to American influences and models. In this respect, it was following a pattern that had dominated its entire development.

If one considers Canadian literature (either English or French) in its full extent, it emerges as part of European rather than of American literature. The same generalization could be made, of course, about American literature until about the middle of the nineteenth century. But gradually thereafter American literature acquired its own accent and sense of tradition, and it might seem to have been inevitable that Canada would be swept into an American literary environment. There were American-Canadian associations—Archibald Lampman admired Longfellow as a sonneteer and writers like Oliver Wendell Holmes and Thomas Bailey Aldrich, who stood for a Victorian neoclassicism, and the phenomenon of the Canadian expatriate writer casually absorbed into American literature appeared early with Charles G. D. Roberts and Bliss Carman. But the dominant tradition in Canada was European. The best poetry in English—and poetry has always been the dominating genre in Canada—was written by those who were grounded in the classics, as were Lampman and Roberts, or in a wide range of European literatures, as was Duncan Campbell Scott; and they thought of themselves as being in a British tradition, of belonging, however indirectly, to the world of Keats, Tennyson, Arnold, and Swinburne. The best poetry of the nineteenth century was "academic" poetry, poetry that emerged from close study of classical texts, whether ancient or modern litera-

ture. The major poets were university graduates who retained
their university connections, a characteristic of the literary economy that still persists. A test case for the strength of American
influence was the poetry of Walt Whitman, in which the revolutionary republic seemed to find its authentic voice. But although
Whitman had some interesting Canadian associations—his earliest biographer was a Canadian, Maurice Richard Bucke, who
lived in London, Ontario, and who declared in his book that
"Song of Myself is the most important poem that has so far been
written at any time, in any language,"[21] and Whitman traveled in
Canada and wrote in typical rhapsodic manner about what he
saw[22]—he inspired no imitators and received much vituperative
criticism in the Canadian literary periodicals.[23]

The same European tradition continues into the twentieth
century. Pratt is often assumed by American and British critics
to be a simple narrative poet entranced by bigness and the crash
of events, a teller of tall tales in a folksy manner. But a moderately
careful reading of his poetry and some understanding of his background and interests reveal an artist with a broad metaphysical
sweep, toughened by his early professional work in the psychological theories of Wilhelm Wundt and biblical criticism and later
by his acquaintance with science and evolutionary speculation.
All this was combined with a knowledge of English poetry so
intense that influences from a wide variety of sources—from the
Elizabethans, Thomas Hardy, the Irish playwrights—are completely absorbed in his own individualistic style. The same scholarly eclecticism, with a predominantly European base, is to be
found in Pratt's younger contemporaries—Klein, Birney, Reaney,

21. Maurice Richard Burke, Walt Whitman (Philadelphia: David McKay,
1883), p. 159.
22. "The young native population of Canada was growing up, forming a hardy,
democratic, intelligent, radically sound, and just as American, good-natured and
individualistic race, as the average image of best specimens among us" Works of
Walt Whitman, ed. Malcolm Cowley (New York: Funk & Wagnalls, 1968), vol.
2: The Collected Prose, 1968, p. 162).
23. A review of Whitman in The Canadian Monthly and National Review (1
March 1872), p. 279, refers to Whitman's "rampant bestiality" and contends
that what he writes "so far from being poetry . . . is not even verse." This article
is representative of the general tone of Canadian criticism, although there were
occasional Whitman admirers, Charles G. D. Roberts among them.

Scott, Smith, LePan, Finch—who still constitute the strength of modern English-Canadian poetry. The process can be seen at work most powerfully in Klein, Smith, and Birney, who are more patently scholarly poets than Pratt. Each writes poems that are clearly imitative, like inspired teachers illustrating a style or manner—Klein, of Keatsian romance or Byronic satire, or Joyceian word play; Smith, of seventeenth-century metaphysical poetry; Birney, time and time again of medieval alliterative poetry. But the scholarship and imitativeness are completely absorbed in their best poems, in which the clever imitations and learned echoes disappear in a passionate personal statement.

My examples of the European literary consciousness come from poetry, which is the dominant genre and the area of major achievement. The novel is still, by comparison, undeveloped, although the senior writers—Callaghan, MacLennan, Richler, Laurence, Buckler, and Davies—have firmly consolidated their position within Canada and have attracted an increasing amount of critical attention outside the country. Even in this limited tapestry, the predominant strands are European. Edmund Wilson was fashioning a garland of praise that no Canadian critic would have devised when he placed Callaghan in the company of Chekhov and Turgenev. But he was right, as he usually is with writers he admires, in seizing upon the essence of Callaghan, a writer whose novels "center on situations of primarily psychological interests that are treated from a moral point of view, yet without making moral judgments of any conventional kind."[24] Wilson's generalization about Callaghan could be extended, with strong individual variations, to the others in the group of writers I have mentioned. All are sensitive to the Canadian environment—MacLennan makes the creation of a social environment a major task —and yet the general impression left by the prose fiction is that of a private world, where human motives and emotions are explored and dissected. The novels lack the detail, the solid recreation of a particular society that one finds in the American natural-

24. Edmund Wilson, *O Canada, An American's Notes on Canadian Culture* (New York: The Noonday Press, 1966), p. 4.

ists. Like the poetry, although less clearly, they are more a part of European than of American literature. Robertson Davies's recent trilogy—*Fifth Business, The Manticore,* and *World of Wonders*—illustrates this Canadian bias. In a sense the novels constitute a social history of Canada between the two world wars. But social history is only a connecting strand; the colorful elements are Jungian analysis and the metaphysics of good and evil, with Canada seen as a strand in the European cultural pattern.

This non-American quality of the literature, indeed, an active resistance to American influences, is a negative way of establishing distinctiveness. But it did not create a strong national literature devoted to the expression of national ideals and sentiments. Edmund Wilson complained that this left Canadian literature in English in an enfeebled state, unimpassioned, with no clear criteria for criticism or satire. He much preferred Canadian literature in French, which in the nineteenth century unashamedly celebrated the virtues of land, language, and religion, and in the twentieth fought for French *culture* against American materialism. Wilson's delight in a strong nationalistic bias in literature and his complaint about its absence in English Canada have been shared by many Canadian critics. It was, for instance, the gravamen of the Massey Report's severe (and rather sketchy and ill-informed) comment on the inadequacy of our literature and its failure, when compared with Canadian painting, to project the national consciousness.

But the absence of a strong national drive in the literature is not a complete liability. Indeed, one might say that our writers were thereby expressing a national self-doubt, an absence of a faith that Canada was a new land with an immaculate revelation, moving toward great predestined goals. And if this did not produce a robust literature of ringing assertion, it did nourish a vein of quiet contemplation and a tradition of ironic humor. The ironic humor, which permeates the work of Haliburton and Leacock, is a major ingredient of the novels of Richler, Davies, and Atwood and of the comic and satiric verse of many poets—Birney, Smith, Scott, Reaney, Purdy, Nowlan come to mind. The irony often arises from our ambivalent relationship to the United States, an assertion of independence founded on the possession of powerful but obscure moral virtues along with an actual acceptance of the American style in our daily life. The classical scene in this ironic tradition is in Margaret Atwood's novel *Surfacing*. At a northern lake, near the border of Ontario and Quebec, to which the heroine and her brittle friends have come for a brief sanctuary, they meet only two other people—two fishermen, "two irritated-looking businessmen with pig faces." They are, the heroine concludes, Americans, indifferent to their surroundings, callously destructive, not like so many others of their countrymen "humourless and funny and inept and faintly lovable like President Eisenhower." Then, in a scene of brilliant reversal, the Americans identify themselves as Canadians, one from Sarnia and one from Toronto, who have assumed that young people "with the hair and all" are "Yanks."[25]

Although ironic humor, a quizzical contemplation that is self-deflating, is a steady undercurrent in Canadian literature, there is also a more positive, assertive note. The best writers have not worried about the "identity" problem. They assume the distinctiveness of the tradition in which they write and the existence of the country that has produced that tradition. It is true that this national self-confidence does not have the certitude of writers in an older nation, what Van Wyck Brooks describes as "that secure and unobtrusive element of national character, taken for granted, and providing a certain underlying coherence and background of mutual understanding."[26] Often their national self-assurance becomes a search for its meaning or, more simply, a search for a home that is known to exist but whose qualities are not easily deciphered. "The country reveals itself only slowly even to those who love it most," writes Douglas LePan, whose poetry is often a brilliant foray into national self-revelation, "and much of its character still remains ambiguous."[27] The search for national self-

25. Margaret Atwood, *Surfacing* (Toronto: McLelland and Stewart, 1972), pp. 66, 128.
26. Van Wyck Brooks, "America's Coming of Age," in *Three Essays in America* (New York: E. P. Dutton, 1934), p. 84.
27. "The Dilemma of the Canadian Author," *The Atlantic* (November 1964), p. 161.

revelation is also a search for personal self-revelation. Klein, for instance, discovered his Canadian subject after a lifetime devoted to portraying the tortured and heroic course of Judaism. In his final, climactic poem he confronted industrialized, philistine Canadian society—a society whose seers are "the local tycoon . . . epical in steel," the orator making a pause, "the don who un-rhymes atoms"—and still emerged with a belief in the power of the poet, "the 12th Adam taking a green inventory in a world but scarcely uttered." Margaret Laurence's latest and most ambitious novel, *The Diviners,* is also about the artist in Canadian society, the search for an imaginative and emotional core that she finds, not in effete academe or in the great Canadian mirage, a rugged and romantic Scotland, but in the little western town of her youth, a society at once constricted and cruel, and warm and vital.

The writers I have mentioned are nationalistic in the sense that they are devoted to their country and concerned about its fate. And devotion and concern do not rule out a tone of criticism, often as in the political poetry of Earle Birney, bitter and despairing. But there is not among the major writers a strong strain of anti-Americanism, in Carl Berger's felicitous and accurate phrase "that faithful consort of Canadian National feeling."[28] This might seem unusual, since Canadian writers, unlike academics, do not enjoy an easy and familiar relationship with their American contemporaries and they are more immediately aware than the academics of the American domination of the whole field of popular culture. Certainly there have been spirited responses, especially in the popular philosophical essays of George Grant and in such writers as Dennis Lee and Dave Godfrey. Grant has his literary disciples, who see in Canada an outlying fortress that must fall before the inexorable march of American technology. But for the most part Canadian writers take a less despairing view and follow the independent course they have always elected, untroubled by American fashions, indifferent also to American

28. "Internationalism, Continentalism, and the Writing of History," in *The Influence of the United States on Canadian Development: Eleven Case Studies* (Durham, N.C.: Duke University Press, 1972), p. 49.

achievements, seeing themselves and their country as a continuing part of a European tradition.

What general conclusions can we draw from looking at the place of learning and the literary arts in the light of American revolutionary experience? There is a basic reservation about any conclusion. Universities everywhere are stubbornly conservative institutions, and they have great capacity for resisting change, even in a generally revolutionary setting. They have a deep-seated fear of violence, and violence and revolution are insepa-rable. The literary arts, too, are not necessarily part of a revolu-tionary scene. They have their own inner life that often seems to be independent of political and social change. It is difficult, then, to estimate the impact of a social revolution on higher education and the literary arts.

In estimating the impact of the American Revolution on Ca-nadian higher education and the literary arts, one is looking at an emotional rather than an intellectual phenomenon. To Canadians, the Revolution meant a repudiation of European ties, and they were determined to resist the spread of this attitude across the border. Canadian universities and the literary arts grew up in this atmosphere. For the universities, it meant for many decades a position of respectable obscurity with, however, some accompany-ing assets—an emphasis on the humanities, a tolerant and philo-sophical attitude toward the place of religion in higher education, and a devotion to undergraduate education. The late embracing in this century of two cardinal American ideas, offsprings of revolution in a new land—the right of all citizens to as much edu-cation as they could absorb and the power of new knowledge to change society for the better—broke the slow evolutionary move-ment of Canadian universities and turned them overnight into American institutions. There are now professed doubts about this process and the question before the Canadian universities now is whether they have the inner strength to modify the powerful American influence.

The literary arts, initially, like the universities apprehensive of American revolutionary experience, were more successful in maintaining their independence of American influence. They were, of course, not institutionalized, and this reduced the amount of direct influence; and there was little exchange even on an individual basis. English-Canadian literature grew up with a strong European bias. Although the writers concentrated increasingly on the immediate world around them, they did not see it in a rhapsodic, national light. Canada was not a new land created by revolutionary fiat, but a union of the old and the new, the primitive and the sophisticated—a subject for amused and ironic contemplation. For the literary arts, then, the response to the American revolutionary experience, although negative, was a determining factor in creating a sense of self-sufficiency and in sustaining a steady, unspectacular, evolutionary growth.

10

Evolution and Revolution as Aspects of English-Canadian and American Literature

A. J. M. Smith

Until the revolutionary revival in the fifties, sixties, and seven-ties of the present century, one of the most distinguishing features of Canadian art and culture, and a sadly limiting one, was the spirit of colonialism that showed itself particularly in literature, poetry especially. "Colonialism," I noted as long ago as 1948, "is a spirit that gratefully accepts a place of subordination, that looks elsewhere for its standards of excellence and is content to imitate with a modest and timid conservatism the products of a parent tradition."[1] One of the most enfeebling results of colonialism is the feeling of an inescapable inferiority that it engenders. E. K. Brown in his classic *On Canadian Poetry*, published in 1943, said that the colonial attitude of mind "sets the great good place not in its present, nor in its past nor in its future, but somewhere out-side its own borders, somewhere beyond its possibilities."[2] Thus one of the fruits of colonialism may be a turning away from the despised local present, not toward the mother country but toward an exotic, idealized crystallization of impossible hopes and "noble" dreams. A vague romanticism seems to be encouraged by a colonial sense of inferiority. This is well illustrated by the preface to a book of poems by a New Brunswick author, Peter John Allan, which was published in London in 1853. The verse showed strong influences of Byron, Moore, and Shelley. "My lot," wrote the poet, "having been cast on the wrong side of the At-

1. A. J. M. Smith, ed., *The Book of Canadian Poetry*, 2d ed. (Chicago: University of Chicago, 1943; Toronto: W. J. Gage, 1943), p. 14.
2. Edward K. Brown, *On Canadian Poetry* (Toronto: Ryerson, 1943), p. 14.

lantic in a colony where the Muse cannot find a resting place for the sole of her foot—in its very little capital, whose politics would be a mere private scandal to a European ear, and where society is strangely limited—can it be a matter of surprise that I should have sought for relaxation from more severe studies in the amiable foible of verse making?"³ To consider the realities of life around him as too modest or too coarse for the attention of poetry is one of the temptations of the poet in a colony, particularly if he thinks himself the inheritor of a long and elaborate tradition.

The romanticism engendered by the colonial spirit was not necessarily an exotic one. Sometimes it led to impossible hopes and a fervid nationalism, as can be seen in the prefaces to the two first Canadian anthologies, Dewart's *Selections from Canadian Poets* (1864) and Lighthall's *Songs of the Great Dominion* (1889), or in the introduction to Standish O'Grady's *The Emigrant: A Poem in Four Cantos* (Montreal, 1842), where you will find these words: "This expanded and noble continent will no doubt furnish fit matter for the Muse. The diversity of climate, the richness of the soil, the endearing qualities of a genial atmosphere must no doubt furnish a just excitement to the poetic mind, and arouse the energy correspondent with a richness of scenery, which the contemplative mind will studiously portray."⁴

This is perhaps closer to the enthusiasm of early American poetasters than to the colonial musings of a Peter John Allan. The Reverend Edward Hartley Dewart, whose *Selections from Canadian Poets* has already been mentioned, remarkably anticipated E. K. Brown's analysis of the consequences of colonialism. An ardent advocate of nationalism, he lamented the absence of a national poetry that would triumph over sectionalism and provide the "cement" that would hold a politically united nation together. He saw the spirit of colonialism as the chief obstacle to the creation of a national literature and thus to a confederation of the various colonies.

A second and even more vital factor that has characterized

3. Quoted in A. J. M. Smith, *Canadian Poetry*, 3d ed. (Toronto: W. J. Gage, 1957), p. 13.
4. Ibid., p. 11.

Canadian art and literature and pointed to some of the main differences between American and Canadian poetry has been the loneliness and sparseness of the Canadian landscape and the indifference and, indeed, the malevolence of nature, which has induced what Northrop Frye has not hesitated to call "stark terror." The true frontier for the Canadian writer, unlike the American, is not the West but the North. There is nothing (until recently) that could be called revolutionary about Canadian poetry. A colonial is not one who has launched a successful rebellion; you cannot rebel against nature.

The geographical, climatic, and other environmental conditions as they affect the poet, particularly the Canadian poet, have been best stated by Professor Frye. "It is not a nation, but an environment that makes an impact upon poets," he wrote in his "Preface to an Uncollected Anthology."[5]

[A]nd poetry can deal only with the imaginative impacts of that environment. A country with almost no Atlantic seaboard, which for most of its history has existed in practically one dimension; a country divided by two languages and great stretches of wilderness, so that its frontier is a circumference rather than a boundary; a country with huge rivers and islands that most of its natives have never seen; a country that has made a nation out of the stops on two of the world's longest railway lines; this is the environment that Canadian poets have to grapple with, and many of the imaginative problems it presents have no counterpart in the United States, or anywhere else.

One of these problems, and perhaps the greatest, is the uncompromising hostility of the northern landscape and the hostility of nature. Looking through a large anthology of Canadian poetry on historical principles published in the early forties, Frye found "the outstanding achievement to be the evocation of stark terror. Not a coward's terror, of course, but a controlled vision of the causes of cowardice. The immediate source of this is obviously the frightening loneliness of a huge and thinly settled country."[6] Here, Frye notes, the horror of nature and the unconscious horrors of the mind coincide, and he cites as his chief exemplar

5. Northrop Frye, *The Bush Garden* (Toronto: Anasi, 1971), p. 164.
6. Ibid., p. 138.

nearly all the best poetry of E. J. Pratt. This applies certainly to
Pratt, to Birney's *David,* to passages in such early poems as
Heavysege's *Jephtha's Daughter,* Mair's *Tecumseh,* and Craw-
ford's *Malcolm's Katie,* and to the poems of the northern lakes by
Wilfred Campbell, but it seems to me to leave out much of the
best, and much more placid, poems of Roberts and Lampman—
although Frye can find examples even in these two poets to justify
his theory. Certainly he is right when he remarks, "As compared
with American poets, there has been comparatively little, outside
Carman, of the cult of the rugged outdoor life which idealizes
nature and tries to accept it. Nature is consistently sinister and
menacing in Canadian poetry."[7] I would question only the word
consistently.

Another source of difference between Canadian and American
literature lies in the social status of the first settlers and in the
motives that led them to leave Europe and come to the New
World. For the Americans it was to escape an old and oppressive
society and create a new one; for the Canadians it was to protect
and retain the privileges that they had enjoyed in the mother
country and that were now threatened by the rise of mechanical
industrialization. Mrs. Moodie and Mrs. Traill were typical, and
the Scottish working-class poet Alexander McLachlan an exception, although even he later became an enthusiastic Canadian
nationalist. It will be convenient, however, before dealing with
these to consider the Americans.

Historians, literary critics, and philosophical commentators
from Crévecoeur and Tocqueville to George Santayana and
Henry Bamford Parkes have prophesied or recorded the development of American social, political, and cultural history as the
more or less inevitable consequence of the motives and character
of the original settlers, who founded the colonies in the New
World long before the Revolution. Crévecoeur's *Letters from an
American Farmer,* though published in England in 1782, was written before the Revolution. This former officer in Montcalm's
army, later a farmer in Pennsylvania, was unsympathetic toward

7. Ibid., p. 142.

the Revolution, although he took no part in any hostile act. His book is idyllic, and it describes (except when dealing with the western forest frontier) an almost Eden-like state of innocence, with "the American" as what the new school of Frygian critics in Canada would call the New Adam. The most fruitful part of the book for our inquiry is found in Letter III, "What is an American?" "What then is an American," he asks, "this new man? He is either an European, or the descendant of an European, hence that strange mixture of blood you will find in no other country." Here Crèvecoeur cites a family of his acquaintance whose grandfather is English, whose son married a French woman, and whose four grandsons married wives of four different nations. He then proceeds to his definition.

He is an American, who, leaving behind him all his ancient prejudices and manners, receives new ones from the new mode of life he has embraced, the new government he obeys, and the new rank he holds. He becomes an American by being received in the broad lap of our great *Alma Mater*. Here individuals of all nations are melted into a new race of men, whose labours and posterity will one day cause great changes in the world.[8]

This is clearly pre- but not unrevolutionary, and it concludes with a remarkably unclouded prophecy. The letter continues in an even more enthusiastic vein. Conditions in America are freer, less hampered, economically more profitable and dependent on individual effort and individual rewards, and, above all, *new*. The American, Crèvecoeur asserts, acts upon new principles and must necessarily entertain new ideas and form new opinions. "From involuntary idleness, servile dependence, penury, and useless labour, he has passed to toils of a very different nature, rewarded by ample subsistence. This is an American."[9] The rank of freeholder inspires the American with sentiments little known in Europe, and in describing this new class of American, Crèvecoeur suggests the first stages of the attitudes and feelings that made the Revolution probable, if not certain.

8. St. Jean de Crèvecoeur, *Letters from an American Farmer* (London: J. M. Dent & Sons, 1912), p. 43.
9. Ibid., p. 44.

The early knowledge they acquire, the early bargains they make, give them a great degree of sagacity. As free men they will be litigious; pride and obstinacy are often the cause of law suits; the nature of our laws and governments may be another. As citizens it is easy to imagine that they will carefully read the newspapers, enter into every political disquisition, freely blame or censure governors and others. As farmers they will be careful and anxious to get as much as they can, because what they get is their own.[10]

This is Emerson's "embattled farmer" seen before the battle. The American freeholder, in striking contrast to the European serf he originally was, finds that the rewards of his industry "follow with equal steps the progress of his labour; and his labour is founded on the basis of nature, self-interest."[11] Crèvecoeur, it is clear, is an agrarian conservative. His background, however, was that of the French Enlightenment, and from the presence of economic self-reliance and unlimited natural resources waiting to be exploited he foresaw the development of a new American psychology and the creation of a new and necessary system of jurisdiction and government, but he did not wish to see it brought about by a violent revolution.

A more acute mind than Crèvecoeur was Alexis de Tocqueville, who in the second part of his *Democracy in America* (1840) devoted a chapter to "The Influence of Democracy on Language and Literature," which touches our concerns very closely. According to Tocqueville little influence of the Revolution had as yet been felt. "The citizens of the United States are themselves so convinced that it is not for them that books are published, that before they can make up their minds upon the merit of one of their authors, they generally wait till his fame has been ratified in England."[12] The small number of serious literary works published in America, he affirmed, were English in substance and more so in form. (This complaint, I must break in to say, was common in Canada as late as the twenties of the present century.) Tocqueville concludes, "The inhabitants of the United States have then at present, properly speaking, no literature." Such writing of

10. Ibid., pp. 45–46.
11. Ibid., p. 44.
12. Alexis de Tocqueville, *Democracy in America*, ed. Henry Steele Commager (New York: Oxford University Press, 1947), p. 279.

value and originality that does exist is the work of the journalists, who "speak the language of their countrymen, and make themselves heard by them."[13]

The critic finds that the causes for this state of affairs must be sought in several peculiar circumstances independent of the democratic principle. The two most important of these were the American's contempt for the past—for history, that is—and his purely practical view of nature. "Democratic nations care little for what has been, but are haunted by visions of what will be. Democracy shuts the past against the poet, but opens the future before him." And as for Nature: "Americans are insensible to the wonders of inanimate Nature. . . . They do not perceive the mighty forests which surround them till they fall beneath the hatchet. Their eyes are fixed upon another sight . . . its own march across these wilds—drying swamps, turning the course of rivers, peopling solitudes, and subduing Nature."[14] Nothing so petty or trivial (that is, antipoetic), Tocqueville concludes, as the life of a man in the United States. He feels that their mainly English origin had slowed the development of an indigenous literature among the Americans; he has no doubt that the new environment, the task of exploiting the vast resources of nature, and the new system of democracy will eventually lead to the development of a literature, and an original one. What is to be expected of such a literature he describes in a crucial passage.

Let us transport ourselves into the midst of a democracy, not unprepared by ancient traditions and present culture to partake in the pleasures of the mind. Ranks are there intermingled and confounded. Knowledge and power are both infinitely subdivided. . . . Here then is a motley multitude whose intellectual wants are to be supplied. These are new votaries . . . have not all received the same education: they do not possess the same degree of culture as their fathers, nor any resemblance to them—nay, they perpetually differ from themselves, for they live in a state of incessant change of place, feelings, and fortunes. . . . It is from the bosom of this heterogeneous and agitated mass that authors spring. . . . I must expect to find in the literature of such a people but few of those strict conventional rules which are admitted by readers and writers in aristocratic ages.

13. Ibid., p. 280.
14. Ibid., pp. 291–92

. . . Among democratic nations each new generation is a new people.[15]

Tocqueville sees little that is native in the *Waverly*-like novels of Cooper or the Goldsmithian essays of Washington Irving, even though the subject matter of both is undoubtedly American, but he is remarkably farsighted in his view of what is to come. He says that American readers and the writers who will please them have no time or inclination to appreciate the more delicate beauties of literature. They require books that can be quickly read and easily understood. Above all, they must have what is unexpected and new—"rapid emotions, startling passages—truths or errors brilliant enough to rouse them up, and to plunge them at once, as if by violence, into the midst of a subject."[16] In addition to these effects, Tocqueville notes what is to be expected of the remarkable commercial instinct of the American settler, and he does not conceal his dislike of what he foresees.

Democracy not only infuses a taste for letters among the trading classes but introduces a trading spirit into literature. In aristocracies, readers are fastidious and few in number; in democracies they are far more numerous and far less difficult to please. . . . The ever increasing crowd of readers, and their continual craving for something new, insures the sales of books which nobody much esteems.[17]

Launched into this vein of prophecy our observer becomes sapient and full of interest, although his own point of view is antirevolutionary rather than revolutionary. In a curious anticipation of Noah Webster and Henry L. Mencken, he added that while the American men of letters might be said "to live more in England than in their own country . . . such is not the case with the bulk of the population." He draws the conclusion that "it is not to the written but to the spoken language that attention must be paid" if we wish to understand "the modifications the idiom of an aristocratic people may undergo when it becomes the language of a democracy."[18]

15. Ibid., pp. 280–81.
16. Ibid., p. 281.
17. Ibid., p. 282.
18. Ibid., p. 284.

To Tocqueville, as for Crèvecoeur, these consequences, foreseeable in the future, did not derive from the Revolution, but from democracy, which itself resulted from the motives of immigration, the character of the immigrants, and the new conditions they found or made in the New World, particularly in the colonies south of Canada. In Canada, the British military, ecclesiastical, and commercial establishment after the conquest chose to encourage, if not to perpetuate, the authoritarian regime of the past. The Revolution itself was not a cause but a consequence.

One does not, of course, need to go back as far as Crèvecoeur or Tocqueville to find the whole course of America's revolutionary cultural history attributed to the motives and characteristics of the early settlers. Another brilliant foreigner, as idealistic as Crèvecoeur and as ironic as Tocqueville, the philosopher George Santayana, paints a portrait of "the American," not only as he originally was but as he inevitably became, that is not very far removed from theirs. "The atmosphere of the new world," he observed in his *Character and Opinion in the United States* (1920), "produced in intellectual matters a sort of happy watchfulness and insecurity. Never was the human mind master of so many facts and sure of so few principles."[19] He continues, writing what might be thought of as a conclusion to what Crèvecoeur began in his chapter "What Is an American?"

To be an American is of itself almost a moral condition, an education, and a career. . . . The discovery of the new world exercised a sort of selection among the inhabitants of Europe. . . . The fortunate, the deeply rooted, and the lazy remained at home; the wilder instincts or dissatisfaction of others tempted them beyond the horizon. The American is accordingly the most adventurous or the descendant of the most adventurous, of Europeans. It is in his blood to be socially a radical, though perhaps not intellectually.* What has existed in the past, especially in the remote past, seems to him not only not authoritative, but irrelevant, inferior, and outworn. . . . But his enthusiasm

---

* This seems to be not true of the founding fathers. They were intellectually radicals, but socially conservative.

19. George Santayana, *Character and Opinion in the United States* (New York: W. W. Norton, 1934). p. 163.

for the future is profound. It is the necessary faith of the pioneer.
. . . The optimism of the pioneer is not limited to his view of himself
and his own future; it starts from that.[20]

John Adams too had shared the opinion we have been considering that it was the motivation and the character of the first
settlers that made the Revolution and everything else not only
possible but inevitable. Henry Bamford Parkes quotes a significant brief passage from the *Works*, published in 1856. "The
Revolution was in the minds and hearts of the people; a change
in the religious sentiments of their duties and obligations. . . .
Who then was the author, inventor, discoverer of independence?
The only true answer must be the first emigrants."[21] The name
Santayana gives to the American spirit, however, is not democracy or independence, but materialism. Perhaps they were the
same thing, the first in the field of politics, the second in that of
economics and business. "The most striking expression of the
American's materialism," Santayana continues, "is his singular
preoccupation with quantity," and, a little farther on, "love of
quantity often has a silent partner, which is diffidence as to quality. The democratic consciousness recoils before anything that
savours of privilege, and lest it should concede an unmerited
privilege to any pursuit or person, it reduces all things as far as
possible to the common denominator of quantity."[22]

Later analysts also saw the social, political, and cultural development of the United States as a process of natural selection.
Henry Bamford Parkes, from a point of view not unlike Crèvecoeur's agrarian conservatism, and Russel Nye, from a liberal
point of view that owes a good deal to F. J. Turner and Parring-
ton, agree that the special conditions that brought a certain type
of European to the New World were responsible for the revolutionary creation of a unique society made up of unique individuals. Parkes spoke of the "selective process," which favored
energy, adaptability, and capacity for endurance. In the course

20. Ibid., pp. 168–69.
21. Henry Bamford Parkes, *The American Experience* (New York: A. A.
Knopf, 1947), p. 86.
22. Santayana, *Character and Opinion*, pp. 185, 187.

of centuries these qualities became established as suitable to the new environment and as characteristically American. America was a state of mind, he declared, not merely a place. In his book *This Almost Chosen People*, Nye has emphasized the early American idealism, optimism, and faith in progress. He wrote, of course, entirely without the irony of a Santayana. "The Revolution," he declared,

marked a great step forward in the acceptance of the doctrine of progress in America, for it seemed to those who led it that it meant the creation of a new kind of government unique in the history of the world, based on natural law. . . . The rapid growth of the new nation and its apparently limitless resources for further growth encouraged even greater optimism. The frontier and the relatively open society of the new country allowed each man to believe that he could improve his condition and make his fortune by his own efforts.[23]

This was hardly the hope of the British North Americans. English Canada began as the result of the conquest of New France, and it is tempting to think that a colony occupied to a great extent by disbanded soldiers and their officers might show a more aggressive attitude than a nation of farmers and merchants. But it soon became apparent, as we see in the first "Canadian" novel, *The History of Emily Montague*,[24] an epistolary social comedy of life in Quebec City just after the British occupation, that the temper of the English authorities, officers and gentlemen and Anglican clergymen, was thoroughly conservative and not at all unsympathetic to the former French military and ecclesiastical establishment. It was the Revolution, of course, that marked an irreparable split between the two countries—one glad for almost a hundred years to remain a colony, the other quickly becoming an independent, progressive, and materialistic state. Before the Revolution, however, Crèvecoeur had seen little difference between the two colonies, except, as did Haliburton also, in conservative Nova Scotia; but when war finally broke out, the role of the well-to-do Loyalists was neither unimportant nor un-

23. Russel Nye, *This Almost Chosen People* (East Lansing, Michigan: Michigan State University Press, 1966), p. 3
24. Frances Moore Brooke, *The History of Emily Montague*, 4 vols. (London: J. Dodsley, 1769).

heroic. Before the end of the fighting some fifty thousand Loyalists fought on the side of the British in every important engagement, and at the end of the war it is not surprising that many of them suffered persecution and the loss of their property.

The Loyalists who entered Nova Scotia before 1783, most of them from around Boston, were designated by the governor, Lord Dorchester, as United Empire Loyalists. These were the largest number who came to British North America. They had suffered heavily for their stand during the war, and they were outraged and bitter. By birth and education they were confirmed Tories and looked upon the triumph of the American mob pretty much as Burke was to look on the excesses of the French Revolution. Besides, they had been hurt where they were most sensitive. Their property had been confiscated, and it was to reestablish themselves as landowners and capitalists that prominent men like Jonathan Odell, Jacob Bailey, and the Winslows, all of whom became notable as writers and educators, came into the Maritime colonies.

Most of the Loyalists were Congregationalists, and their pastors and schoolmasters were Harvard men. It is not surprising that some of them still thought of themselves as "American." When the Puritan Jacob Bailey was forced to leave his parish in Maine and sail in a chartered schooner across the Bay of Fundy to Halifax, his vessel pursued by an American privateer (to make matters worse, on a Sunday), he spoke of the Americans as "my countrymen." He wrote in his *Journal of a Voyage from Pownalboro to Halifax* (1779) as follows:

I am persuaded that my countrymen exceed all mankind in a daring and enterprising disposition. Their bold and adventurous spirit, more especially, appears with distinguishing *éclat* when they are engaged in any unjust and vicious undertaking, and their courage commonly increases in proportion to the badness and villainy of the cause they endeavour to support. Let a New England man once throw off the restraints of education, he becomes a hero in wickedness, and the more strict and religious he has been in his former behaviour, the greater will be his impiety in his present situation. It has often been remarked by foreigners who have engaged in commerce with our Puritans that when they first come abroad no people alive have such a prevailing aversion to profane swearing, and yet they quickly become the most docile scholars in the school of vice, and make the greatest proficiency in every species of profanity. They openly ridicule their former attachment to devotion, and are very ingenious in framing new and spirited oaths, and when they have an extraordinary mischief to perform they always choose to perpetrate it on a Sunday.[25]

A second group of settlers in Canada consisted of half-pay officers from the armies of Wellington and their wives, who received grants of land primarily in English Upper Canada at the end of the Napoleonic wars. These and others of the same class, the younger sons of impoverished gentlemen and their families, settled in the bush and tried to make a garden of it. We have a record of their hardships, their failures, and their successes in the writings of the two Strickland sisters, Mrs. Susanna Moodie and Mrs. Catherine Parr Traill. The Moodies and Traills came to Canada in the early thirties and after a short time settled on a large tract of land near the town of Peterborough. The story of their hardships and adventures in clearing the wilderness and making a new home is set down by Mrs. Moodie in *Roughing It in the Bush, or Forest Life in Canada,* which although written much earlier was not published until 1852, and by Mrs. Traill in *The Backwoods of Canada* (1836).

Mrs. Moodie published a second and much happier book in the following year, called *Life in the Clearing,* which brought up-to-date what had turned out to be a success story. Her first book was filled with bitterness and homesickness, while the second is an account of difficulties overcome and moderate wealth and moderate fame achieved through hard work, courage, and an obdurate sense of British integrity and rightness. The vigor of some of the narratives and the concreteness of some of the descriptions give these books a value much greater than Mrs. Moodie's generally undistinguished verse and sentimental fiction, but what gives them a special interest to the social historian is the quite unself-conscious sense of superiority based on class, sex, and race that they reveal on every page.

25. Quoted in A. J. M. Smith, ed., *The Colonial Century* (Toronto: W. J. Gage, 1973), pp. xviii–xix.

There is nothing whatever of the exuberance and enthusiastic hope that Crèvecoeur and Tocqueville saw in the attitudes of the American settlers. *Roughing It in the Bush* opens with a pessimistic introduction calculated to allay "the fever of immigration" and expose the lying allurements of land jobbers and loan sharks. The very first sentence states,

In most instances, emigration is a matter of necessity, not of choice; and this is more especially true of the emigration of persons of respectable connections, or of any station or position in the world. Few educated persons, accustomed to the refinements and luxuries of European society, ever willingly relinquish these advantages, and place themselves beyond the protective influence of the wise and revered institutions of their native land, without the pressure of some urgent cause. Emigration may, indeed, generally be regarded as an act of severe duty, performed at the expense of personal enjoyment, and accompanied by the sacrifice of those local attachments which stamp the scenes amid which our childhood grew, in imperishable characters upon the heart. Nor is it until adversity has pressed sorely upon the proud and wounded spirit of the well-educated sons and daughters of old but impoverished families, that they gird up the loins of the mind, and arm themselves with fortitude and dare the heartbreaking conflict.[26]

The Moodies' early hardships, their dislike of their neighbors, who were earlier settlers of the lower orders, chiefly Irish or Scotch, and their sense of the bush as a prison house all appear in *Roughing It in the Bush.*

The contrast in tone with *Life in the Clearing* could hardly be greater. In the second book, Mrs. Moodie and her husband are living in the thriving river town of Belleville, well established, prosperous. She is reconciled to her new home, a true Canadian. The poet and critic Margaret Atwood, thinking of the contrast between the two attitudes, in a recent volume of poetic interpretations, *The Journals of Susanna Moodie,* makes a significant comment.

If the national illness of the ·United States," she writes, "is megalomania, that of Canada is paranoid schizophrenia. Mrs. Moodie is divided down the middle: she praises the Canadian landscape but ac-

26. Ibid., p. 160.

cuses it of destroying her; she dislikes the people already in Canada but finds in people her only refuge from the land itself; she preaches progress and the march of civilization while brooding elegiacally upon the destruction of the wilderness.[27]

Almost the same could be said of Mrs. Moodie's sister, Mrs. Traill. *The Backwoods of Canada* tells very much the same story. Both writers are extremely class-conscious, made more so, indeed, by their early experiences in the bush. "This is a fine country," wrote Mrs. Traill, "for the poor labourer, a grand country for the rich speculator; a hard country for the poor gentleman, whose habits have rendered him unfit for manual labour."[28] The impression one gets from American commentators, is that only the poor laborer and the rich speculator went to the United States, while the poor gentleman remained loyal to the British flag.

One of the most critically interesting episodes in Mrs. Traill's narrative, unaccountably omitted from the modern reprint in the widely used New Canadian Library, is the story of an encounter with a young Scottish engineer on the steamer taking the new settlers up Lake Ontario. It is worth quoting at some length.

We were rather entertained by the behaviour of a young Scotchman, the engineer of the steamer, on my husband addressing him with reference to the management of the engine. His manners were surly and almost insolent. He scrupulously avoided the least approach to courtesy or outward respect: nay, he even went so far as to seat himself on the bench close beside me, and observed that "among the many advantages this country offered to settlers like him, he did not reckon it the least of them that he was not obliged to take off his hat when he spoke to people (meaning persons of our degree), or address them by any other title than their name; besides, he could go and take his seat beside any gentleman or lady either, and think himself to the full as good as them."

"Very likely," I replied, hardly able to refrain from laughing at this sally; "but I doubt you greatly overrate the advantage of such privileges, for you cannot oblige the lady or gentleman to entertain the same opinion of your qualifications, or to remain seated beside you unless it pleases them to do so." With these words I rose up and left

27. Margaret Atwood, *The Journals of Susanna Moodie* (Toronto: Oxford University Press, 1970), p. 62.
28. Catherine Parr Traill, *The Backwoods of Canada* (London: C. Knight. 1846), pp. 139–40.

the independent gentleman evidently a little confounded at the ma-
noeuvre: However, he soon recovered his self possession, and continued swinging the axe he held in his hand, and said, "It is no crime,
I guess, being born a poor man."[29]

Mrs. Traill's husband joined in the banter, and they got onto
the subject of the advantages or disadvantages of rude or gentle-
manly manners, which provoked the poor engineer to ask, "Pray,
what makes a gentleman?" This gave his courteous tormentor the
chance to reply, "Good manners and good education. . . . A rich
man or a high-born man, if he is rude, ill-mannered, and ignorant,
is no more a gentleman than yourself."[30]

Another radical young Scotchman who emigrated to Canada
was the poet Alexander McLachlan, and his sentiments at first
were not unlike those of the insubordinate engineer. McLachlan's
background was very different from that of the Moodies and
Traills. His experiences as a poor weaver in Glasgow filled him
with the egalitarian sentiments of the Chartist movement. He
writes in his earliest poems of the horrors of poverty in an industrial metropolis.

> Where bloated luxury lies,
> And Want as she prowls the streets
> Looks on with her wolfish eyes.

His verse is nowhere keener than in his description of the modern
city, with

> Its palaces reared to gin
> And its temples reared to God;
> Its cellars dark and dank,
> Where never a sunbeam falls
> Amid faces lean and lank
> As the hungry-looking walls.[31]

Another of McLachlan's early poems is called "Young Canada, or
Jack's as Good as His Master," which shows something of an

29. Ibid., pp. 83–84
30. Ibid., pp. 85–86.
31. Cf. A. J. M. Smith, *Towards a View of Canadian Letters* (Vancouver:
University of British Columbia Press, 1973), pp 42–45.

American spirit of Utopian enthusiasm that in his case, however, was to lead to development in his later years of an ardent love of his new home in Canada, just as it did in the case of Mrs. Moodie. Even the radical early song from McLachlan's *Emigrant* begins and ends with the "conservative" or "middling" or "Canadian" desire to have it both ways.

> I love my own country and race
>   Nor lightly I fled from them both,
> Yet who would remain in a place
>   Where there's too many spoons for the broth
>
> .   .   .   .
>
> Old England is eaten by knaves,
>   Yet her heart is all right at the core;
> May she ne'er be the mother of slaves,
>   Nor a foreign foe land on her shore.[32]

Here there is nothing American at all. As Northrop Frye commented, "there is nothing of the typical American identification of freedom with national independence: the poet is still preoccupied with the old land and thinks of himself as still within its tradition. There is even less of the American sense of social inequality."[33] During the Civil War, however, McLachlan went so far as to write an "American War Ode," in which his humanitarian radicalism found expression in a hymn that was neither Canadian nor imperialist.

> The spirit of Washington
>   Stalks from the grave,
> And calls on his children
>   Their country to save. . . .
>
> Where backwoodsmen triumphed
>   O'er tyrant and King:
> There still the long rifle
>   For freedom can ring.[34]

32. In all three editions of A. J. M. Smith, *The Book of Canadian Poetry* (Toronto, Chicago, 1943) and *The Oxford Book of Canadian Verse* (Toronto, New York: Oxford University Press, 1960).
33. Frye, *Bush Garden*, p. 168.
34. Smith, *Canadian Letters*, p. 45.

But such ideas were exceptional and even in McLachlan we can find others that are impeccably and almost fulsomely loyal to Britain. The Crimean War, the birthday of the Queen, the visit of the Prince of Wales, the Fenian raids—these and like subjects inspired not only McLachlan but other poets like McGee and Sangster as well.

Tocqueville, we may remember, had expressed the view that the busy, practical American felt that "fine letters" were not for him and that only in the work of journalists and political orators was an American literature being born. Mrs. Traill in Upper Canada expressed similar sentiments about the same time, but unlike the Franco-American observer her tone is neither objective nor approving. After describing in romantic terms the beauties of the winter woods, where the snow-enshrouded tree stumps seemed to her like ghosts or wood nymphs, she remarks, "As to ghosts or spirits, they appear totally banished from Canada. This is too matter-of-fact a country for such supernaturals to visit. Here there are no historical associations, no legendary tales of those that came before us. Fancy would starve for lack of marvellous food to keep her alive in the backwoods. We have neither fay nor fairy, ghost nor bogle, satyr nor wood-nymph. . . . No Druid claims our oaks" and so on and so on. I quote this because, while the same observation can be found among American critics and historians, there it is not a lament but almost a source of pride. Mrs. Traill continues, "I heard a friend exclaim, when speaking of the want of interest this country possessed, 'It is the most unpoetical of all lands; there is no scope for imagination; here all is new. . . . The only beings I take any interest in are the Indians, and they want the warlike character and intelligence I had pictured to myself they would possess.'" "This," adds Mrs. Traill, "was the lamentation of a poet."[35]

There was one American writer, however, who expressed a similar view; suprisingly enough, it was Cooper. In his *Notions of the Americans* (1828) Cooper cites the paltry rewards of literary effort in the United States as one of the reasons for the sluggish

35. Traill, *Backwoods of Canada*, p. 153–54.

development of a native literature, but then he goes on to say that a "second obstacle against which American literature has to contend is the poverty of materials. . . . There are no annals for the historians; no follies (beyond the most vulgar and commonplace) for the satirist; no manners for the dramatist; no obscure fictions for the writer of romance; no gross and hardy offences; nor any of the rich artificial auxiliaries of poetry."[36] Turning to fiction and speaking perhaps of his own practice, Cooper denies realism and favors romance. Apparently, he felt that democracy did not lend itself to literary expression, although he did recognize that American novelists have all been successful or the reverse just as they have drawn warily, or freely, on the distinctive habits of their own country.[37]

An original American—even a revolutionary—literature was to appear, sooner than most of the early commentators had expected, in the work of the great New Englanders, Emerson and Thoreau, and somewhat later in that of Melville, Whitman, and Twain—and I would not be prepared to deny, that of Henry James. An early statement of what such a literature might be like is found, as might be expected, in Emerson's *The American Scholar*, an address delivered, as a matter of fact, ten years before Cooper's pessimistic appraisal. Emerson said, "If there is any period one would desire to be born in, is it not the age of Revolution when the old and the new stand side by side and admit of being compared. . . . I read with some joy of the auspicious signs of the coming days, as they glimmer already through poetry and art, through philosophy and science, through church and state." He goes on:

One of these signs is the fact that the same movement which effected the elevation of what was called the lowest class in the state, assumed in literature a very marked and as benign an aspect. Instead of the sublime and beautiful, the near, the low, the common, was explored and poeticized. . . . The literature of the poor, the feelings of the child, the philosophy of the street, the meaning of household life, are

36. R. E. Spiller, ed., *James Fenimore Cooper, Representative Selections* (New York: American, 1936). pp. 15–16.
37. Ibid., p. 18.

the topics of the time. . . . It is a sign of new vigor when the extremities are made active, when currents of warm life run into the hands and feet. I ask not for the great, the remote, the romantic. . . . I embrace the common, I explore and sit at the feet of the familiar, the low. Give me insight into today, and you may have the antique and future worlds.[38]

This is original—and very American—at least in its dismissal of the past, although not in its lack of enthusiasm for the future. Emerson and the men of his generation and the next expressed a strong faith in the immense potentialities of American democracy and progress. But some of them, particularly Hawthorne, Thoreau, Whitman, and Melville, went far more deeply into the psychic realities of American feeling than the social and humanitarian realism anticipated by Emerson in the passage just quoted. These, and of course the Emerson of *Nature* as well, wrote in symbolic terms that made their emotional experience, although profoundly American, universally significant.

Melville, like Emerson, was able to indulge high hopes for the appearance of a strong and original American literature. In a sketch entitled "A Select Party," thinking no doubt of himself, he describes "a young man in poor attire, with no insignia of rank or acknowledged eminence," who learned that the only way to reach posterity "is to live truly and wisely for your own age." This is the American writer, he declares, "for whom our country is looking anxiously into the mist of Time, as destined to fill the great mission of creating an American literature, hewing it, as it were, out of the unwrought granite of our intellectual quarries. From him, whether moulded in the form of an epic poem or assuming a guise altogether new as the spirit itself may determine, we are to receive our first great original work."[39] To be contemporary, to be modern, to be new. This is the task nature and history alike impose on the American artist, but in fulfilling it, Melville made a new adaptation of an old form. For *Moby Dick*, as Richard Chase is not alone in pointing out, accepts the universal convention of

38. From William R Benét and Norman H. Pearson, eds., *The Oxford Anthology of American Literature* (New York: Oxford University Press, 1938), p. 482.
39. Francis O. Matthiessen, *American Renaissance* (London, New York: Oxford University Press, 1941), p. 244n.

the classic epic. "It celebrates customs, techniques, occupations, ideals, and types of heroic humanity which are characteristic of the culture in which they appear. . . . We must have heroes, nobility, and these will be the heroes of the American nineteenth century—hunters, explorers, captains of industry (for Ahab *is* one of these and the *Pequod* is a beautifully efficient factory for the production of whale oil)."[40] The skills and occupations stressed are not the martial skills of the *Iliad* nor the political and moral skills of the *Aeneid* nor the theological virtues of *Paradise Lost*, but the triumphant techniques of subduing nature.

It is only much later in Canadian literature and then almost only in the two greatest of the poems of E. J. Pratt—the tragic *Brébeuf and His Brethren* and the comic *Towards the Last Spike* —that a similar new and national development of an old tradition can be found, one that is in a similar way rooted in the contemporary culture of the poet. But these two poems have something else in common with Melville. They are, as Richard Chase said of Melville and, indeed, of the most significant American fiction from Hawthorne through Mark Twain, Henry James, Frank Norris to Faulkner and Hemingway, "shaped by contradictions and not by the unities and harmonies of our culture."[41]

These contradictions and paradoxes that revealed themselves in the work of the great American writers did not appear until much later in Canadian literature, largely because the development of Canada was more orderly, more evolutionary, and limited mainly to that narrow strip westward along the two great railway lines spoken of by Frye. It was not hastened by the strong spirit of materialism and individualism that was soon to change the character of the American Revolution, when the idealistic spirit of the "embattled farmers" and their intellectual leaders was to give way to new, progressive, and practical actions. I find much to agree with in the interpretation of Henry Bamfield Parkes, who wrote,

40. Quentin Anderson and Joseph A. Mazzeo, eds., "Melville and *Moby Dick*," in *The Proper Study: Essays on Western Classics* (New York: St. Martin's Press, 1962).

41. Richard Chase, "The Broken Circuit: Romance and the American Novel," in *American Critical Essays* (London: Oxford University Press, 1959), p. 313.

While Americans had believed in a universal freedom and equality, they also encouraged and applauded the competitive drive of individuals toward wealth and power. And in a complex industrial society this drive was directed less against nature and more against other human beings. Those individuals who succeeded in acquiring economic privileges did so by restricting the freedom of others; and the competitive struggle for power and prestige threatened to destroy the human warmth and open-heartedness that had hitherto been the special virtue of American society.[42]

With the expansion westward, the triumph of Jacksonian democracy, and the struggle for individual and corporate economic supremacy following the Civil War, the idealism and indeed the conservatism of the founding fathers and the makers of the Constitution resulted in what it is hardly an exaggeration to call a "betrayal" of the Revolution; an acknowledgment of this fact can be found scattered through the writings of writers as different as Emerson and Whitman. Whitman, indeed, as Norman Newman remarked in an article in *Canadian Literature* that in part contrasts Canadian and American poetry, "was glorifying a world which was disappearing, though he thought it the world of the future."[43] As a result, American literature became pessimistic, critical, and profoundly subversive, not only, of course, in the muckraking novel of the late nineteenth century and the naturalism or critical realism of the twenties, but also in the work of more

42. Parkes, *American Experience*, p. 12. In his chapter on "The Constitution" in the same book, Professor Parkes spells out the details. "The American Constitution, drafted by the Philadelphia Convention of 1787, was based on aristocratic and capitalistic principles. . . . By accepting the Constitution the people of the United States were virtually deciding that they should not remain a nation of small property owners, but that they should become a capitalistic people, possessed of the greatest wealth and power and of a high standard of living, but divided by the most extreme economic inequalities." "In 1787," he continues, "fifty-five men, almost all of whom were wealthy merchants, lawyers, or landowners, met behind closed doors at Philadelphia, in order to draft the charter of a new central government for the thirteen states. Most of them were agreed (according to Edmund Randolph) that 'the evils under which the United States labored' were due to 'the turbulence and follies of democracy,' and that 'some check therefore was to be sought against this tendency of our governments'" (pp. 116–17).

43. Norman Newman, "Classical Canadian Poetry and the Public Muse," *Canadian Literature* 51, p. 46.

intellectual writers like Henry Adams and George Santayana or Lewis Mumford or Carl Becker.

Now as I draw to a close, let me come back briefly to the Canadian scene. And once again, as at the beginning of this essay, I turn to Northrop Frye, the wisest and most comprehensive of Canadian critics, for a summing up, a comparison, and a contrast. In the long conclusion that he wrote for Carl F. Klinck's collective *Literary History of Canada* (1965), Frye put his finger clearly on the heart of the subject before us today. He pointed out that since Canadian literature began with an influx of defeated Tories after the American Revolution, its literature has always had "a strong anti-revolutionary bias." Norman Newman, in an interesting article, "Classical Canadian Poetry and the Public Muse," remarks similarly that "the two most important factors in the history of this country [Canada] have been the English-Canadian rejection of the American Revolution and the French-Canadian rejection of the French Revolution."[44] But with respect to the English writers at least, Frye goes much further in elaborating reasons and citing examples. The passage is worth quoting at length.

The Canadian radicalism that developed in opposition to Loyalism was not a revival of the American revolutionary spirit, but quite a different movement, which had something in common with the Toryism it opposed: one thinks of the Tory and radical elements in the social vision of William Cobbett. . . .

Or, he might have added, Joseph Howe:

A revolutionary tradition is liable to two defects: to an undervaluing of history and an impatience with law, and we have seen how unusually strong the Canadian attachment to law and history has been. . . . When more radical expressions [than in Haliburton] begin to creep into Canadian writing, as in the poetry of Alexander McLachlan, there is still much less of the assumption that freedom and national independence are the same thing, or that mercantilist Whiggery which won the American Revolution is necessarily the only emancipating force in the world. In some Canadian writers of our own time

44. Ibid., p. 40.

—I think particularly of Earle Birney's *Trial of a City* and the poetry of F. R. Scott—there is an opposition, not to the democratic but to the oligarchic tendencies in North American civilization, not to liberal but to *laissez-faire* political doctrine.[45]

That is to say, I suppose, that these writers are not revolutionary or radical, but socialistic.

But these conditions are changing, and we must remember that Frye's analysis, sapient as it is, was written more than a decade ago. Since the beginning of the seventies—inspired in part by the establishment of a number of new small presses, many of them subsidized and most of them an answer to the takeover of some of the best and long-established Canadian publishing houses (The Ryerson Press and W. J. Gage & Co. by large American corporations, and Macmillan in Canada by the large Canadian combine of Maclean-Hunter) fiction and poetry of a new, imaginative, and technically and morally revolutionary sort has been produced in hitherto unknown abundance. This has been the work not only of older and experienced writers like Robertson Davies, Margaret Laurence, and Irving Layton but also of a host of new younger novelists such as Dave Godfrey, Hugh Hood, Graeme Gibson, Margaret Atwood, and Marian Engel, and poets such as Michael Ondaatje (author of an experimental verse-and-prose drama, *The Collected Works of Billy the Kid*), Dennis Lee, Al Purdy, John Newlove, and Margaret Atwood again. The causes of this unprecedented outburst are various and complex. I can do no more here than suggest a few of the factors that have contributed to it.

Certainly the first factor, I think, is a new nationalism, a new assertion of independence, not from English imperialism but from American technocratic dominance in the fields of communications, industry, and economics. And along with this new self-interested pride has come also a sympathy with the emerging underprivileged nations of the Third World (with which some extremists like to think Canada has much in common), and this has produced some very remarkable tendentious Canadian litera-

45. Frye, *Bush Garden*, pp. 248–49.

ture in the African novels of Dave Godfrey, Margaret Laurence, and David Knight, and the poems of Knight and Dorothy Livesay. Livesay has also been a great encourager of the movement for the liberation of women and has edited an anthology descriptively entitled *Forty Women Poets of Canada*, which demonstrated that women writers have very consciously entered into the spirit of the new movement. Some of this work is revolutionary in a technical sense, but most of it may be called revolutionary in the purely spiritual sense that it makes so sharp, sudden, and intense a contrast to the spirit of subservience and (perhaps more than half-unconscious colonialism that characterized even the most serious Canadian literature up until the beginning of the sixties). Gone is the feeling of inferiority, and not only the younger writers feel today that they can find an adequate response to truly new, frank, and enthusiastic work published by native presses and local "little magazines."

11

The Quiet Revolution and Revolutionary Movements among Quebec French Canadians

Guy Rocher

Most papers presented at this conference compare Canada and the United States in various respects, with the explicit aim of shedding more light on both the distinction and the relationships between revolution and evolution in modern history. It happens that within the context of the North American society, Quebec recently witnessed the appearance and disappearance of revolutionary movements; at the same time, quite rapid changes were taking place, following patterns that can be called evolutionary. A description and comparative analysis[1] of those two processes in Quebec may be a contribution to reflection and research on the conference theme.

In the first section of this paper, I will give some historical data

1. The literature on the methodology, uses, and limitations of comparative sociology is very extensive. We can find a good part of it in Elina Almasy, Anne Balandier, and Jeanine Delatte, *Comparative Survey Analysis: An Annotated Bibliography, 1967–1973* (London and Beverly Hills: Sage Publications, 1976). Among many other works, let us mention especially R. M. Marsh, *Comparative Sociology: A Codification of Cross-Societal Analysis* (New York: Harcourt Brace and World, 1967); Talcott Parsons, *Societies: Evolutionary and Comparative Perspectives* (Englewood Cliffs, N.J.: Prentice-Hall, 1966); R. L. Merritt and S. Rokkan, eds., *Comparing Nations: The Use of Quantitative Data in Cross-National Research* (New Haven: Yale University Press, 1966); S. Rokkan, S. Verba, J. Viet, and E. Almasy, *Comparative Survey Analysis: A Trend Report and Bibliography* (The Hague: Mouton, 1969); S. M. Lipset, *The First New Nation: The United States in Historical and Comparative Perspectives* (New York: Basic Books, 1963); Ivan Vallier, ed., *Comparative Methods in Sociology: Essays on Trends and Applications* (Berkeley: University of California Press, 1971); Neil J. Smelser, *Comparative Methods in the Social Sciences* (Englewood Cliffs, N.J.: Prentice-Hall, 1976).

on the Quiet Revolution, which was not a revolution, but an evolution inspired by reformist objectives and strategies; and also on the revolutionary movements during the last two decades in Quebec, actions by radical movements that were inspired by a revolutionary ideology or ideologies and that had recourse to violence and terrorism. I will then propose some elements of a comparative analysis of those two processes, as they took place in Quebec. This will lead us to raise three questions that will be dealt with in the last three sections.

Some Historical Data

In this first part, let me briefly recall the main events that constituted what has come to be called the Quiet Revolution in Quebec and also outline the history of the Quebec revolutionary movements in the sixties. Although a considerable number of books and articles have dealt with the period, especially with the history and analysis of the so-called October crisis that took place in the fall of 1970,[2] this period of the history of Quebec is still not well known.

The Quiet Revolution is usually said to have started either in 1959 with the death of Maurice Duplessis, who had been the prime minister of Quebec for over twenty years and was a conservative and quite despotic nationalistic politician, or in June 1960 when the Quebec Liberal party won the election under the leadership of Jean Lesage with a platform of somewhat more progressive policies. Although it is not completely false, this way of dating the beginning of the Quiet Revolution is somewhat

2. Quite a number of things have been written on the so-called October crisis in Quebec and on the FLQ. Among many others, let us mention Ron Haggard and Aubrey E. Golden, *Rumours of War* (Toronto: New Press, 1971); Claude Ryan, *Le Devoir et la crise d'octobre 1970* (Montreal: Leméac, 1971); Fernand Dumont, *La vigile du Québec* (Montreal: Editions Hurtubise H.M.H., 1971); Gérard Pelletier, *La crise d'octobre* (Montreal: les Editions du Jour, 1971) (this book was written by and partly for a member of the Trudeau cabinet); J. W. Hagy, "Quebec Separatists The First Twelve Years," *Queen's Quarterly* 76 (1969): 229–38; G. Morf, *Le terrorisme québécois* (Montreal: Les Editions de l'Homme, 1970).

artificial. The Quiet Revolution was characterized by changes of mentality, attitudes, and values among the French Canadians in Quebec much more than by a change in the institutions and in the social structures as such. And changes in attitudes and values do not take place overnight. If one can use the distinction that sociologists make between culture and social structures, we could say that the Quiet Revolution was above all a cultural revolution, unmatched by equivalent changes in the economic institutions, in the political machinery, or in the general social organization of the society.[3] The industrialization and urbanization of Quebec had taken place at the beginning of the twentieth century and had continued to mid-century. During this period, French Canadians in Quebec lived through that industrial revolution but retained a preindustrial mentality. In the thirties and the forties, the gap between the industrial Quebec society and the preindustrial mentality of the French Canadians became ever more visible. After World War II, which had an outstanding impact in French Canada, the gap had widened still more, at least among certain sectors of the population, including intellectuals, union labor leaders, and some politicians.

Therefore the origins of the Quiet Revolution can be easily identified in the second half of the 1940s and at the beginning of the 1950s. Some union labor leaders then came into open conflict with the Duplessis regime, and also some academics, especially at the Faculty of Social Sciences at Laval University with Father Lévesque, the founder and first dean of that faculty; some groups of artists and intellectuals also challenged the dominant conservative philosophy of life in Quebec at that time. One journal called *Cité Libre* was the best interpreter of the new values that were emerging. Prominent among those who proposed and expressed the viewpoint of those restive minorities in that journal were Pierre E. Trudeau, Jean Marchand, and Gérard Pelletier. These later became ministers in the federal government and were the so-called French Power, first in the Pearson Liberal government and later on in the Trudeau government. At the June provincial

3. I have developed this idea in *Le Québec en mutation* (Montreal: Editions Hurtubise H.M.H., 1971).

election of 1960, when the Quebec Liberal party was elected under Jean Lesage, new values were finally emerging, although not yet fully developed. They could do so only because changes proposed by the Lesage government and made by it had been prepared by some fifteen years of underground work among the minority groups opposed to the Duplessis government and the conservatism and clericalism of Quebec society.

During the sixties, the changes that have come to be known as the Quiet Revolution centered around two main areas: the role of the Roman Catholic church and educational reform. The omnipresence of the church and its power up to the 1960s have been abundantly illustrated in the historical and sociological literature on Quebec.[4] Actually, the powerful status of the church in French Canada did not necessarily date back to the French regime, as is usually thought. Although strong enough in the first half of the nineteenth century, the Roman Catholic church in Quebec was then far from being as powerful as it was to become by the end of that century when the so-called liberal opposition to the church, very active among intellectuals and political men, had been crushed. The church gained tremendous power around 1870.[5] Thereafter, for almost a century, French Canadians in Quebec had the reputation of being strongly united by their common conservative religious beliefs and by the unchallenged authority of the Roman Catholic church. Yet it seems that the actual power of the church was deteriorating, for it took only a few years in the 1960s to bring about a drastic change. The fight of the Roman Catholic church against Lesage's creation of a Department of Education in 1963 was its last big struggle to retain the political and institutional power it had long enjoyed. After that, the church's political power declined so quickly that those who

4. On the power of the church in Quebec prior to 1971, see, for instance, Horace Miner, *Saint-Denis: A French-Canadian Parish* (Chicago: University of Chicago Press, 1939), and Everett C. Hughes, *French Canada in Transition* (Chicago: University of Chicago Press, 1941).

5. On this topic, see, for instance, Fernand Dumont and Guy Rocher, "Introduction à une sociologie du Canada français," in *Le Canada français, aujourd'hui et demain*, Recherches et Débats du Centre Catholique des Intellectuels Français (Paris: Librairie Arthème Fayard, 1961), pp. 13–38.

witnessed it were incredulous. At the same time, the church was losing its grip upon the mentality of the French Canadians.[6] The number of practicing Catholics dwindled rapidly, first among youth, but also largely among adults; and the number of priests and nuns also decreased rapidly. The church was losing the firm hold that it had had for decades over education, social welfare, public and private morals.

Education was the second major area that was deeply touched by the Quiet Revolution. As it had been almost completely in the hands of the Roman Catholic clergy at all levels for over seventy-five years, and since practically all schools and colleges, public as well as private, were sectarian, it is not surprising that education changed rapidly when the Roman Catholic church was undergoing drastic changes. But the sources of educational reform were at first not necessarily antireligious. They are to be found in the growing questioning of the traditional educational system of Quebec that had started at the beginning of the 1950s. The traditional educational system came more and more under attack because it was said to be unsuitable for the needs and requirements of modern industrial society and because it was felt to be one of the main impediments to the social and economic mobility of French Canadians in industrialized and urbanized Quebec. Educational reform came to be regarded as the main and necessary path to give French Canadians access to the industrial society that Quebec had now become. As long as the classical colleges, which had been inherited from the Jesuits' secondary institutions in seventeenth-century France, and the universities were open to only a small fraction of the young population, and as long as the majority of French Canadians were entering the labor market after or even before finishing elementary school, it was felt strongly that they would remain the cheap, unqualified labor that they had been for decades. This surely was the main concern of the Lesage government when it started its educational reform. And this concern became still more explicit in the report of the Royal Commission on Education in Quebec, the so-called Parent

6. See, for instance, Colette Moreux, *Fin d'une religion?* (Montreal: Les Presses de l'Université de Montréal, 1969).

Commission, which provided the government with the blueprint of a new educational system that was partially put into effect and that inspired, stimulated, and supported radical changes that took place in the 1960s in the Quebec educational system.

It is interesting to observe that it was precisely when the Quiet Revolution was still in its most euphoric period in 1963 that revolutionary movements made their first appearance in Quebec. Suddenly, recourse to violence, advocated by underground revolutionary groups, appeared on the Quebec scene. For seven years, from 1963 to 1970, several activist radical groups, the best known of them and also probably the most active being the FLQ (Front de Libération du Québec), had recourse to various violent ways of expressing their protest and of enhancing their viewpoints. Dynamite was stolen and used to make bombs; munitions and firearms were stolen either from the armed forces or from firearms dealers. Threats were uttered against various persons, especially politicians and businessmen. Banks were robbed with the avowed purpose of financing revolutionary movements. Each time, the radicals took care to stamp their deeds or claim responsibility in the hours following the incident.

During those years it was difficult to know whether the terrorist movements in Quebec were growing in number and organization or were stationary. Rumors circulated about a guerrilla army being formed and trained somewhere in the Laurentians, and some prominent figures gave credence to those rumors by wild statements about the quantity of firearms and ammunition that had been stolen. But there was no way to confirm or disprove the rumors.

From time to time young people were arrested, most of them allegedly belonging to the FLQ, and were brought to court, convicted, and jailed. Most were students or former students, all were pretty young. They were from various socioeconomic origins. But in spite of these arrests, the FLQ was clearly not dismantled, for new bombs kept exploding. Obviously, there was more than one FLQ cell, but it was impossible to know whether there were a great number or only a few.

It is possible to distinguish several periods in the short history of the terrorist movements in Quebec from 1963 to 1970. Using G. Morf's description of the different waves of revolutionary activities during that period,[7] Raymond Breton summarizes them in the following words:

In the first wave, the attacks were restricted almost exclusively to British and federal institutions and symbols (Wolfe and Queen Victoria monuments, military buildings, mail boxes, R.C.M.P. buildings). The second and third waves involved both a change in tactics and in targets. Instead of exploding bombs at various points, attempts were made to organize a revolutionary army. The second wave ended with the arrest of six persons calling themselves the *Armée de Libération du Québec;* and the third wave consisted in the formation of a military training camp for the *Armée Révolutionnaire du Québec.* According to Morf, such camps were to be established all across the province.

Breton goes on,

The violence of the second and third waves does not seem to have been terrorist in nature. Rather it seems to have been the by-product of attempts to acquire (through robberies) the necessary funds, radio equipment, and armaments for military operations. Not surprisingly, these two waves involved military depots, banks, firearms stores, and a radio station. An interesting development, however, is that a number of French-Canadian establishments were robbed (a Caisse Populaire, and branches of the Banque Canadienne Nationale and the Banque Provinciale). The fourth wave included a number of robberies for equipment but, importantly, now also explosions at companies with workers on strike. The same is true of the fifth wave, with further new targets: provincial government buildings, provincial political parties (explosions at the clubs of the Liberal and Union Nationale parties), municipal institutions (Montreal City Hall), and even a labor organization with moderate views. This last wave (before the kidnappings) seems to have been the most intense both in the number of explosions (or attempted explosions) and in the diversity of targets.[8]

The fall of 1969 was a turning point in the history of radical action in Quebec. It marked the sixth and last wave of violence,

7. Morf, *Le terrorisme québécois.*
8. Raymond Breton, "The Socio-Political Dynamics of the October Events," in *The Canadian Review of Sociology and Anthropology, La Revue Canadienne de Sociologie et d'Anthropologie,* 1972. Quoted from the special issue on "Aspects of Canadian Society," 1974, p. 51.

provoking a profound crisis that rocked Quebec. The government of Quebec, with the Union Nationale in office, put before the Parliament what was then called Bill 63, the purpose of which was to increase and make more explicit, if possible, the status of English as one of the two official languages in Quebec. There followed a campaign against the bill by all the nationalist French-Canadian movements, rightist as well as leftist, nonseparatist as well as separatist. This lasted several weeks. A huge demonstration to oppose the bill finally took place in Quebec City in front of the Parliament building. But in spite of all the protests, the bill was passed. The untimely enactment of that bill may be regarded as a deliberate provocation by the Quebec government. An outcome seems to have been that some extremist members of the FLQ decided to adopt a new strategy: bombs had not been enough, the time was ripe for still more radical action. Coming apparently from the FLQ, threats were heard of kidnapping political men, businessmen, and employers and also there was talk of political murders.

After at least a couple of unsuccessful attempts against diplomats in Montreal (the United States consul general and the Israeli trade commissioner), James Cross, the British trade commissioner in Montreal, was kidnapped in the first days of October 1970. Then, Pierre Laporte, minister of labor and immigration in the Quebec government—the newly elected Liberal government of Mr. Bourassa—was also kidnapped a few days later. Pierre Laporte was killed in circumstances that have never been clarified, while James Cross was finally discovered and freed by the police more than two months after his kidnapping. Some of the kidnappers were arrested, brought to court, and convicted. Those who had held James Cross, in exchange for freeing him, were permitted to leave for Cuba on condition that they must never return to Canada.

This was the most impressive *coup de main* of the FLQ. It created what is known as the October crisis, a crisis that was partly caused by the federal government's frightened recourse to the War Measures Act. Ottawa sent the army into Quebec on the assumption that there was a state of "apprehended insurrection."

But strangely enough, the FLQ disappeared with the earthquake that it had provoked. The kidnapping of Cross and Laporte and the violent death of the latter marked the FLQ's demise. It then became obvious that the FLQ consisted at that time of only a few people who were astute but not very well organized, with little or no funds, a very few arms, and no guerrilla organization behind them, except for a few friends and some more or less active sympathizers. So far, six years later, the FLQ has not yet revived, and there has been no further evidence of its existence or of its activities. Some of its former leaders are now law-abiding citizens, working in citizens' movements as social organizers. Others are still in jail or live more or less miserably in exile.

Comparative Analysis

After this brief historical outline, we will now devote the second part of this paper to a comparative analysis of the evolutionary and revolutionary processes that we have just described. If we first look at the *objectives* of the Quiet Revolution and of the revolutionary movements, it is easy to note that they were widely different. The Quiet Revolution was termed "quiet" precisely because it was reformist in both its objectives and its means. The revolutionary movements were radical in their objectives and violent in their means. Let us spell out a little more the meaning of those terms, keeping in mind that we are analyzing and describing here the ideologies of the Quiet Revolution and the revolutionary movements as expressed by the representatives of each of those two currents of thought themselves.

With regard first to economic objectives, the ideology of the Quiet Revolution conformed with the acceptance of capitalist industrial society as the North American type of modern life. One of the goals of the Quiet Revolution was precisely to enlarge and enhance the accessibility of French Canadians to the means and goods of that industrial society. It was believed that with the appropriate education, French Canadians would find the motivation to upgrade and qualify themselves in new fields that had been opened, by new technology and advanced scientific knowledge. The aim was therefore a leap forward into the new world of industrial society, in order to benefit from it not merely as marginal workers but as full-fledged participants.

The revolutionary ideology, on the contrary, was characterized by rejection of the capitalist society as being necessarily a source of injustice, inequalities, and exploitation, especially for French Canadians. The revolutionary movements were overtly socialist in their inspiration, although not clearly of the Marxist-Leninist school of thought. In other terms, they were leftist movements, with a more or less clear Marxist frame of reference and jargon. In many of their writings and statements there was a mixture of populism and Marxism, for instance, in the manifesto of the FLQ that was read on the public network of Radio-Canada as one of the conditions for the release of James Cross.[9]

When we look at political objectives, we find that the ideology of the Quiet Revolution was generally oriented toward greater autonomy of Quebec within the Canadian Confederation, so that the Quebec government could take a larger share of its responsibility (and regain some money from the central government) in matters that were regarded as having a great impact on the cultural and social life of the French-speaking community, namely in education, social security and welfare, immigration, communications, and also Northern Affairs. The Canadian Confederation was generally not questioned, nor was the Canadian constitution itself (the British North America Act of 1867). It was assumed that the BNA Act provided enough leeway for the Quebec government to implement its main economic, political, and social objectives. It was generally agreed that the federal government had increased its power largely beyond the limits that had been set by the BNA Act in 1867, due to the imperatives of the economic depression in the thirties and of World War II. The main objective now was for the Quebec government to regain the juris-

9. An English translation of the FLQ manifesto, which was read over the radio and television network of Radio-Canada on the 8th of October 1970, in partial fulfillment of demands made by the kidnappers of Mr. Cross, is found in Ron Haggard and A. E. Golden, *Rumours of War*, pp. 277–81.

dictions and financial resources that were clearly assigned to the provincial governments by the constitution and that had been progressively taken over by the federal government.

The political views of the revolutionary movements were in sharp contrast with the preceding. All the revolutionary movements were strongly separatist and were radically opposed to both the federal government and the Canadian Confederation. They started with a definition of Quebec as being the equivalent of a colony within the Canadian Confederation. Using the model of colonial domination in underdeveloped countries and also an analogy with the American blacks, French Canadians in Quebec were defined as "White Negroes" (and indeed, called themselves so) who had fallen under the hegemony of a Canadian English-speaking bourgeoisie, which was more or less allied with American capitalists and with a minority of French-Canadian petite bourgeoisie. Western capitalist society was questioned, not necessarily specifically, but through a critique of the Canadian and Quebec society. Therefore, in the eyes of members of the revolutionary movements, no good could come from either the federal government or the Canadian constitution because of the economic weakness of Quebec and of French Canadians. All ties must thus be cut. The only possible solution was to sever Quebec from the Canadian Confederation and to create an independent socialist Quebec nation-state.

The Quiet Revolution and the revolutionary movements can also be distinguished for their views on cultural matters. I think the Quiet Revolution can be characterized by a pluralistic ideology. The traditional ideology of Quebec was largely unitarian, in the sense that all French Canadians were considered or supposed to be Roman Catholics, sharing some common values on the family, the school, and the role of the church. Reacting against that past, which was recent, the ideology of the Quiet Revolution rested on the acknowledgment that the former unanimity of French Canadians (which was more or less implied) no longer existed and that they were now to develop an attitude of tolerance that they had not cultivated sufficiently in the past, but that was regarded as one main characteristic of modern societies.

This attitude of tolerance was to be applied to all religious beliefs, cultural subgroups, and various other kinds of dissent.

The revolutionary movements also broke sharply with the recent past, but in a different way. Reaction against past unanimity turned them in a different direction that can be termed a "laicist" ideology. The revolutionary movements were remarkably antireligious and overtly opposed to the former domination of the Roman Catholic church in Quebec. They advocated a nonsectarian society and the immediate transfer to the state of the different powers and responsibilities that the church had progressively taken upon itself. More or less in line with the Marxist analysis of the role of religion in the capitalist societies, the revolutionary movements regarded the church and religion as having aided, abetted, and condoned the exploitation of French Canadians. No revolutionary process could therefore take place, and no drastic changes could be achieved, without the rejection of the clerical influence of the church and the utmost limitation of the public role of religion.

Turning now to the means of achieving these various objectives, there was a large gap between those advocated by the Quiet Revolution and those put forward by the revolutionary movements. On the whole, the Quiet Revolution relied on recourse to three more or less complementary means of action. One was the full use of the democratic process, in order to bring changes through parliamentary action. New legislation was drafted and brought before the Parliament of Quebec. And it was a more or less general practice that a great variety of pressure groups and social movements were heard formally by the decision makers. The ideology of participation in the process of decision making was put forward as one of the main means of implementing the democratic process.

Second, the Quiet Revolution was very largely inspired and achieved by a new class of civil servants, bureaucrats, and technocrats who became the main decision makers in Quebec. The Lesage Liberal government advocated the need of a strong Quebec (*"un Québec fort"*) to achieve the objectives of the Quiet Revolution. A strong Quebec was possible only if a new class of civil servant was developed and given power. Before the sixties, the civil service in Quebec had a poor reputation, being regarded as mostly filled by political patronage, by men of little competence, and more devoted to the politicians than to policy-making. The Lesage government brought radical changes in that respect by injecting into the provincial administration the fresh blood of young technocrats, most of them recruited among the academics and intellectuals who had prepared and blueprinted the Quiet Revolution in the fifties. These were the architects of the new legislation. They saw to its implementation and they engineered new social, economic, and political institutions.

Finally, the third and foremost means of achieving the Quiet Revolution was to be a drastic reform of the educational system in Quebec. As already pointed out, until 1960 Quebec's educational system had been completely in the hands of the Roman Catholic church. It was based on a large network of private institutions at the secondary and the university levels, and it was still inspired by the educational ideas of the eighteenth century. The development of a new and diversified educational system, wide access to the schools for all those who had the ability and the taste for education, and the reorientation of the curriculum in line with the modern industrial society, were regarded as the three conditions necessary to open the road to full participation by French Canadians in the benefits of industrial Quebec.

The views of the revolutionary movements on the ways and means to be used in a "separate Quebec" were in sharp contrast with what has just been said. On the whole, their position can be characterized by complete distrust of the parliamentary democratic process, which they regarded as being dominated by a privileged economic class. Politicians, civil servants, and businessmen were all said to have common interests. No policy could be devised, no legislation could be passed that would clearly favor the working class and the underprivileged. The latter were necessarily fooled when they thought they could rely on the parliamentary process and the bureaucracies to protect and enhance their interests. There was therefore only one way to bring about needed radical changes—by developing a greater political consciousness among the Quebec masses, by contributing to violent upheavals that would shake the ruling classes, and by preparing a revolution that would bring down existing institutions.

I suppose that another big difference between the Quiet Revolution and the revolutionary movements has by now become clear. It is that the Quiet Revolution was the ideology of the dominant political group, for it is hard to believe that it was the ideology of a majority of French-Canadian Quebeckers. On the other hand, the revolutionary ideology was shared only by a minority of people and groups, the latter mostly young people who were very clearly marginal in the Quebec society, even among its youth. We can probably argue that the revolutionary ideology was marginal and held only by a minority because we know that it resorted to violence. But one could also hold that the revolutionary movements had recourse to violent means precisely because they were marginal. The relationship can be seen both ways, since one always finds a kind of vicious circle between revolutionary activities and marginality. It is in that sense that some extreme revolutionary acts are called "terrorism."

Terrorism as such has not yet been studied much by sociologists, and it is still ill-defined. This is one case where I believe that a value-free social science is clearly not possible. Terrorism will be defined with the bias and prejudice that one feels naturally about the use of violence and terror as political weapons. Even more than war, resort to terror by its very nature raises emotions that are generally negative, precisely because the purpose, explicit and conscious, of terrorism is to create panic and fear by making danger present everywhere and at the same time keeping it always concealed.

Moreover, terrorism sometimes seeks to say more in symbolic terms than by what it really does. In some cases, recourse to terror is aimed at disorganizing the political and/or economic structures of the society in the hope that the people and groups responsible for social order will quit and so leave the road open to the revolutionaries. This means that terrorism must then be very well organized and largely spread throughout a society, must be in a position to achieve that end, or must at least aim in that direction. This has been especially the case in colonial countries, where the imperialist authorities were a minority that was geographically concentrated in some specific offices and in some residential districts.

But most of the time terrorism does not reach that stage, and its aim is then more to bring a message rather than to disorganize society. Hijacking is clearly one case in point. I think that it is this second type of terrorism that Thomas A. Thornton had in mind when he defined terror as "a symbolic act designed to influence political behavior by extra-normal means, entailing the use or threat of violence."[10] On the other hand, it is the first type of terrorism that is so well described and analyzed by Brian Crozier in his book, *The Rebels*, when it means the equivalent of what can be called a state of "internal war."[11]

In Quebec, unlike many other colonial countries such as Cuba, Angola, China, and South Vietnam, terrorism never achieved the stage of an internal war. There were attempts to create a revolutionary army, but, as we have seen previously, this dream never materialized in Quebec. In the last phases of its existence, the FLQ was trying to shift from the symbolic use of terrorism to a more military one, with the hope of creating a state of internal war. In spite of several attempts to achieve that end, and despite some effective actions in that direction (such as robberies of banks, of firearms, of military armaments), this objective was not achieved. The FLQ itself was, in the end, the last victim of its own action.

But, then, the question that comes to mind is the following: How is it that the FLQ failed in its revolutionary action? This is one question that we will try to answer. But in order to answer that question, we must first answer another one: Why did the revolutionary ideology exist at all in Quebec? But since the FLQ and the revolutionary movements in Quebec appeared in the

10. Thomas Perry Thornton, "Terror as a Weapon of Political Agitation," in *Internal War. Problems and Approaches,* Harry Eckstein, ed. (New York: The Free Press of Glencoe, 1964), p. 73.

11. Brian Crozier, *The Rebels: A Study of Post-War Insurrection* (London: Chatto and Windus, 1960).

wake of the Quiet Revolution, one must finally answer a third question: How can we explain the Quiet Revolution of the sixties in Quebec?

We now have three questions to answer. Proceeding chronologically, if not logically, we will first deal with the last question and then proceed to the second and finally to the first one.

The Quiet Revolution: Why?

In an article that in other ways recalls the imperialistic role that the United States had played in the Third World, Lucian W. Pye opens the way to answering the question of why the Quiet Revolution took place in the sixties. "The relative immunity to insurgency of highly complex industrial societies, at the one extreme, and of homogeneously integrated traditional communities, at the other, points to the crucial reason why the problem of insurgency is so closely related at this time in history to the transitional and underdeveloped new nations of the world. The process of social and psychological disruption that accompanies the downfall of traditional societies opens the way to a host of sharp cleavages within such societies."[12]

After World War II, Quebec was precisely no longer a "homogeneously integrated traditional community." During the previous decades, Quebec had become an urban and industrialized society, with a rapidly declining minority of French Canadians living on farms and in rural villages. On the other hand, Quebec was in the process of becoming a "complex industrial society," without still being an advanced and highly complex one. Although it was a more advanced industrial society than many of the new nations in Asia and Africa, it was still in the "transitional" stage of a society in the process of being industrialized. Economically speaking, in terms of industries and finance, Quebec has been, and still is, lagging behind the province of Ontario. It doesn't have the large diversity of industries that is to be found in

12. Lucian W. Pye, "The Roots of Insurgency and the Commencement of Rebellions," in Eckstein, *Internal War*, pp. 163–64.

Ontario, and it suffers from an unbalanced economic development because of the high concentration of its industries in the
metropolitan area of Montreal at the expense of the rest of the
province, which is not the case in Ontario. On the other hand,
one can say that it is a more advanced industrial society than the
Maritimes and some Prairie provinces.

But, more significantly, it is in sociological rather than economic terms that postwar Quebec can be regarded as a transitional industrial society. Alexis de Tocqueville gives us an interesting lead as to what happened in Quebec in the fifties and the
sixties. In his introduction to *De la démocratie en Amérique*,
Tocqueville compared the state of democracy in France and in
the United States. He said that in France, the democratic revolution had taken place in what he called "le matériel de la société,"
which, in his language, meant the political structures of the
French society. But he added that the democratic revolution had
not reached the laws, ideas, habits, and customs of the French.[13]
The French democratic revolution was therefore incomplete, and
it was hard to know in what direction French society would move
in the future. Tocqueville said that he had discovered that the
democratic revolution was much more advanced in the United
States, in the sense that it had taken place not only at the political
level, but it had also penetrated and permeated the daily life of
the Americans, their spirit as well as their legislation. What
Tocqueville called "le principe de la démocratie"[14] ("the principle
of democracy"), which was the egalitarian principle, had developed in the United States more than anywhere else in the
world "et, marchant avec les moeurs, il a pu se développer
paisiblement dans les lois."[15] With his extraordinary lucidity,
Tocqueville added that democracy was in his view not necessarily
an absolute good because he thought there was no such thing as
an absolutely good democracy. But he had finally reached the
conviction that, in Europe, "nous arriverons, comme les Améri-

---

13. Alexis de Tocqueville, *De la démocratie en Amérique*, ed. J. P. Mayer,
abridged ed. (Paris: Gallimard, Collection Idées, 1968), pp. 29–30.
14. Ibid., page 37.
15. Ibid., page 37.

cains, à l'égalité presque complète des conditions."[16] It was this irreversibility of the trend toward more and more democratic societies, a trend that could be observed over several centuries, according to Tocqueville, that brought him to the conclusion that the consequences of the democratic revolution in the United States had to be well understood, in order to forecast and, if possible, modify the future of the European societies.

I think this observation by Tocqueville can help us understand the origins of the Quiet Revolution in Quebec. There are two ways in which this analogy applies. First, I have developed at length in Le Québec en mutation the idea that after World War II, Quebec had become a highly industrialized society, with the economic structure of an advanced industrial society. But the French Canadians, at least a large number of them, had maintained a preindustrial mentality, or at least the external visible elements of a traditional mentality. Their vision of the world, their attachment to the orthodox Roman Catholic beliefs, their strong family ties, their lack of capitalist ethics, their acceptance of the dominant role of the clergy, were among the main elements of the ethos of the French Canadians up to the 1950s. Because of those views—and I am sure that the causal relationship could be reversed and still be true—the French Canadians were not active elements of the development of industrial Quebec. They contributed the labor force, part of the technicians, and the professional bourgeoisie, but they did not provide the capital and the dynamic agents of the current changes.[17]

Second, just like nineteenth-century French as described by Tocqueville, it could be said of Quebec French Canadians that they were living in democratic political structures without having the habits, the customs, and the ideas of a fully democratic society. For them, as for the French of the nineteenth century, the democratic revolution was not completed and they were still clinging to some values of the ancien régime.

After World War II, Quebec was still a "transitional" society because of the unbalanced development between its political and

16. Ibid., page 37.
17. Rocher, Le Québec en mutation, Introduction.

economic structures on the one side and the ethos and culture of the French Canadians on the other. Quebec was structurally urbanized, industrialized, and democratic, but culturally pre-industrial and still partly imbued with the spirit of the ancien régime. Quebec was surely one of the most interesting cases where the folk and traditional society survived in what was in other respects a modern industrialized society. The same situation still prevails even today in several areas of the United States and in other parts of Canada. But it was more striking in the case of the French Canadians because of their homogeneity in terms of ethnic origins, language, and religion.

After World War II, the cleavage between industrial and democratic structures on the one hand and a preindustrial mentality on the other became wider and wider. This is probably a case where Ogburn's theory of the "cultural lag" could be applied as one possible explanation of social change, or rather of cultural change. The notion of strain used by Parsons is also useful here. "*Strain* . . . refers to a condition in the *relation* between two or more structured units (i.e., subsystems of the system) that constitutes a tendency or pressure toward changing that relation to one incompatible with the equilibrium of the relevant part of the system. If the strain becomes great enough, the mechanisms of control will not be able to maintain the conformity to relevant normative expectations necessary to avoid the breakdown of the structure."[18] Such is, according to Parsons, the main "endogenous" source of change in the social system. If we use Parsons's paradigm of the four functional subsystems of the social system, we can say that what we can call the structural changes that had taken place in Quebec were located in the economy-adaptation subsystem and in the policy-goal attainment subsystem, but that the latency-pattern maintenance and tension management subsystem lagged behind the two others, and that this was also partly true, although to a lesser extent, of the integration-societal community subsystem. In other words, the law was more advanced

18. Talcott Parsons, "An Outline of the Social System," in *Theories of Society,* T. Parsons, E. Shils, K. D. Naegele, J. R. Pitts, eds. (New York: The Free Press of Glencoe, 1961), 1:71.

in the direction of the industrial and democratic society than the culture and mentality of the French Canadians.

The strain created by this "cultural gap" first appeared among some groups of intellectuals, probably at the end of the 1940s, but definitely in the first half of the 1950s. From those sources, which were then rather peripheral to the Quebec French-Canadian society, it spread progressively but quite rapidly to some other groups, especially to the labor unions and to the Liberal party of Quebec. It is the latter that was finally to be the more visible, though not necessarily the more coherent, agent of the Quiet Revolution of the 1960s.

The Revolutionary Movements: Why?

It was precisely when the Quiet Revolution was at its height and in full swing in 1963 that the FLQ made its first appearance using violence, threats of violence, and a violent language. After having heard of violence elsewhere in the world and having read about it in the newspapers, the Quebeckers were suddenly confronted with terrorism as part of their daily life. Probably, as always occurs, their first reaction was one of incredulity accompanied by a profound feeling of malaise. It seemed unbelievable that people of our own ethnic group and nation would have recourse to violence for political purposes. Terrorism is good for others, for instance, Africans or Palestinians, but not for us! A subtle process of the denial of reality takes place at first. For instance, it was currently said and believed that the FLQ was probably made up of strangers, French leftist fanatics or "Pieds noirs" from North Africa, or at least that the FLQ was inspired by such strangers. Those perceptions were reinforced by the fact that the first FLQ member to be arrested was in fact a Belgian. But as time goes on, a community learns to live with terrorism and also with the idea that it is not the work of strangers but of its own people, maybe of one's relatives or of one's students or former students.

I think I am right in saying that terrorism first appeared to

Quebeckers, French-speaking as well as English-speaking, as a "corps étranger." Whether the FLQ was made up of strangers or of Quebeckers was somewhat immaterial to the feeling that was widespread in Quebec that it was built on the model of revolutionary movements in some distant countries and that it was not and would never be a genuine Quebec institution. But then, as it maintained itself over time, one had to try to explain how it was that it actually existed and was largely constituted of French Canadians. Later, one had to try to understand why it was active for a period of seven years.

In my judgment, the most systematic attempt to deal with this problem in sociological terms is Raymond Breton's. According to him, the appearance of the FLQ was part of "widespread confrontations over the distribution of power and influence" that accompanied the Quiet Revolution, to the point that "there is hardly a single institutional sphere that has remained unaffected."[19] Breton lists what he calls the various "arenas" of conflict. These were the fields of education and of health and welfare, the federal-provincial network of relationships, work organization, an increased tension in the relations between the French Canadians and the other ethnic and linguistic groups in Canada, an increased tension within Quebec between various citizen groups and the governments and between students and the faculties and administrators of their institutions. He notes that those conflicts were not peculiar to Quebec but that they were more intense in Quebec than in the rest of Canada.

But how is it that in the context of this redistribution of power and influence some people came to use terrorism as a political weapon? Breton provides us with some explanations. The first one is what he calls the "dialogue de sourds" between the separatists and the federalists. As he points out, "a social political option such as the separatist one makes more difficult the use of the usual (legitimate) channels of conflict resolution. Given this kind of situation, we would expect a higher probability that some groups

19. Raymond Breton, "Socio-Political Dynamics," p. 38.

on each side of the issue will advocate the use of more extreme (non-legitimate) tactics to affect the course of events."[20]

Second, Breton puts forward the hypothesis that the different separatist movements that existed at that time and that were not already unified, as they came to be by the end of the 1960s under the Parti Québécois, were unable to integrate and control their radicals. At first, as is pointed out by Breton, new associations and parties are not structured enough to cope with their more radical elements, who may then decide to create their own group, with a more radical ideology and using more violent means. Later on, the situation within associations and parties changes, but they then may become "too structured and rigidly controlled from the top,"[21] thus pushing the more extreme elements to break with the official party or association in order to go their own way. Finally, Breton reasons that after the first wave of terrorist action, the FLQ was engaged in what he calls "an escalation of violence" that was largely due to the failure of the previous phases to gain public support in the French-Canadian community and to inspire positive feelings in its favor.

Breton's explanations are quite valid, provided we take for granted that there were radicals among the French Canadians at the beginning of the sixties. It is true, as Breton points out, that there were "widespread confrontations over the distribution of power and influence" in Quebec in the sixties. But why did some separatists become radical and why did they decide to have recourse to terrorism, while many others did not? This is the question that Breton's hypotheses do not really answer. For this is a question for which there cannot be, at least for the time being, any clear and definite answer. We can only suggest plausible interpretations. Let me try some lines of explanation.

I think first that the cultural crisis that I have already mentioned provides us with some elements of explanation. The rapid change that took place in the cultural realm of the French-

20. Ibid., p. 49
21. Ibid., p. 50.

Canadian community brought with it the questioning of many traditional moral values. The acceptance of terrorism as a political weapon came to be symbolically associated, in the eyes of some youth, with the most complete rejection of the traditional ethics. Terrorism might therefore have been more profoundly related to a moral revolution than to a political one. For instance, for the extreme leftists of the journal *Parti Pris*—which was the main channel of expression of the young radicals of the 1960s— the Quebec of tomorrow was to be politically independent, economically socialist, and socially and culturally a nonsectarian society ("une société laique"). Of those three options, the last one was surely the most radical in terms of Quebec's long-standing religious traditions. This third option was the chief break with the traditional way of thinking in Quebec. It marked the most profound change of attitudes among the youth. The ideal of political independence had never been completely foreign to French Canadians; socialism was regarded as unacceptable, but not necessarily on ethical grounds. But when it came to complete religious neutrality in a society that had been under the aegis of the clergy and religion for over a century—this was the most important shift that was proposed. Recourse to terrorism was precisely in that line of thought, or better, it was seen as the logical end result of that line of thought. Therefore, we can hypothesize that for a certain number of youth in that period, when many moral values were being questioned, recourse to terrorism was the symbol of the most complete revolt against the past and the most radical break with the traditional values that had been associated with the economic subordination of Francophone Quebeckers and with many political frustrations.

One can see a confirmation of the value crisis that shook Quebec in the 1960s in the reformist movements among the Catholics that ran parallel to the radical movements. Whereas the latter were outside the Roman Catholic church and also against it, the former were taking place within the church and were part of it. They aimed at profound changes in the moral and dogmatic outlook of the church, as well as in the social doctrine and positions of the church in matters like capital-labor relationships, family planning and the use of contraceptives, the obligation of celibacy for the priests, the reform of the Roman Catholic liturgy. Laymen as well as priests, nuns, and brothers, adhered to those reformist movements, taking positions that were quite d'avant-garde compared to what was still regarded as acceptable in the Roman Catholic church in most countries at that time.

A second line of explanation has to do with the notion of "relative deprivation." Starting in the fall of 1959 with the Sauvé government, and then with the Liberal government of Jean Lesage, new aspirations were raised with regard to educational accessibility, occupational mobility, standards of living, and the relative autonomy of the Quebec government and of Quebeckers in North America as well as in Canada. But with the development of a separatist political option, the Lesage government, which was driven by the tide of the Quiet Revolution that had been prepared during the fifties, came to be regarded by some—especially among the youth—as being too moderate in its political aspirations and its economic as well as social reforms. What had now become possible, thanks to the educational and economic reforms of the Lesage government, appeared to some to be too little and too late when compared to all that had seemed to be possible. Therefore, the Lesage government, which at first appeared to be running too fast ahead of the population and which was in fact running ahead of at least a large proportion of the French-Canadian population, was suddenly bypassed by a minority that wanted more drastic reforms in order to meet higher aspirations for themselves and for the whole of Quebec.

Finally, it must be pointed out that, unlike what took place before the American Revolution in 1774 and 1775, the revolutionary ideology and the radical movements in Quebec were not born of repressive actions on the part of any of the governments. There were no "Intolerable Acts" passed by the Canadian and Quebec parliaments, and there was no harassment of the French Canadians. On the contrary, the FLQ made its first appearance not long after the backward and quite despotic Duplessis regime was over and when the more liberal and more progressive Lesage government was at its peak. Revolutionary movements may see the light in the trail of a liberal government as well as in a re-action against an oppressive one.

Failure of the Radical Ideology and Revolutionary Movements: Why?

We have already seen that the terrorist movements and the radical ideology died with the most violent wave of their exis-tence, the kidnapping of James Cross and Pierre Laporte. How can we account for that unexpected end precisely when the FLQ seemed to be more active than before?

Can we say that it was an effect of the War Measures Act? Obviously, it could have been exactly the reverse. As has been illustrated many times in many circumstances, repression of vio-lence usually provokes more violence and the vicious circle be-comes tighter and tighter. Because almost five hundred persons were arrested unnecessarily and held in jail incommunicado for days and weeks, and because the Canadian army was used in the streets of Montreal, a very hostile reaction to both the federal and the provincial governments for their brutal reaction was gen-erated in some quarters. And this hostility was so acute and quite enough largely spread that it might have given birth to new revo-lutionary movements and to new waves of terrorism. And I can say that this was the expectation at that time. But contrary to those expectations, nothing of that sort happened and there has been no political violence in Quebec since 1970.

In the article previously quoted, Raymond Breton contributes one explanation of that fact when he says that the revolutionaries were led to an "escalation of violence" because of the successive failures of their actions. I don't think that Breton uses this as an explanation for the end of violence, because Breton didn't deal with this problem. But I think it casts an interesting light on what happened. It is quite true that there was such an escalation of violence, from the bombs in the mail boxes to the Armée de Liberation du Québec (ALQ), finally to political kidnappings and murders. But the escalation of violence had a negative effect, not only on the general public opinion and population, but probably also on the members and sympathizers of the FLQ. That is why in the end the two small cells that kidnapped Cross and Laporte were desperately isolated, deprived of money and of effective support. When the kidnappings were done, and as long as Cross and Laporte were in the hands of the FLQ, one might have thought that the cells that were responsible for those actions were part of a vast network of members and sympathizers, or that they were carrying out a well-prepared plot. This was precisely the reasoning of the federal government when it proclaimed the War Measures Act and jailed some five hundred people. But there was no plot of insurrection and there was no guerrilla support. As has been suggested above, the successive waves of violence had progressively exhausted the FLQ's and ALQ's small reserves of men, energy, and imagination.

A second reason for the failure of the radical ideology rests again in the moral sphere of the French-Canadian society. The traditionalist and religious mentality of the French Canadians was still too alive and also too spread out in the society to accept radical actions readily. The French Canadians in the sixties were willing to live with a certain number of changes in ethics and values, but the leap into radicalism was too great for them to make suddenly. For several decades, they had been fed with a conservative social doctrine of peace and order, of acceptance of all inequalities, of respect of any authority, and of the recognition of private property, especially of small private property. Lipset has been seeking the reasons that socialism has never taken root in North America.[22] Some of the reasons that serve to explain that fact in the United States and the rest of Canada also apply to Quebec, and there are others that I have already dealt with in other publications.[23] One of those obvious reasons is the influence

22. S. M. Lipset, *The First New Nation* (Garden City, N.Y.: Doubleday Anchor Books, 1967); *Revolution and Counter-Revolution*, rev. ed. (Garden City, N.Y.: Doubleday Anchor Books, 1970); *Agrarian Socialism: The Cooperative Commonwealth Federation in Saskatchewan* (Berkeley: University of California Press, 1950); with J. H. M. Laslett, eds., *Failure of a Dream? Essays in the History of American Socialism* (Garden City, N.Y.: Doubleday Anchor Books, 1974).
23. Rocher, *Le Québec en mutation,* Introduction.

of the Roman Catholic church and of its doctrine on the social thinking of the French Canadians. It is surely this lack of socialist as well as of radical tradition in French-Canadian culture that explains the almost universal negative reaction to the actions of the FLQ, their lack of real support in the population, and their escalation of violence when their successive failures to gain support finally generated. It would surely be interesting at this point to compare Quebec with Northern Ireland, where the IRA and the provisional IRA have had enough following among Irish Catholics to survive and maintain an active rate of intervention for several years.

A third reason for the failure of the radical ideology has to do with the economic structure of Quebec. In contrast with Ireland, Quebec is economically part of the northeastern part of North America, being economically and financially associated with New England. The standard of living of the French Canadians, their ways of life, their aspirations are practically the same as the New Englanders, or just a little lower. In that respect, I think the young radicals of the 1960s made a false analysis of the revolutionary potential existing at that time among the French Canadians. They hypothesized that the Quiet Revolution was a sign that the French-Canadian working class was ripe for radical action, or at least for acceptance and support of radical intervention. But we know that such is not the case in North America, and maybe throughout the Western world. In a book that was on the whole badly received by the American social scientists and historians, both Marxists and non-Marxists,[24] Barrington Moore has effectively documented the fact that the only modern revolutions that have succeeded were revolutions by a peasant class against the coalition of landed lords and an urban bourgeoisie.[25] Such was not the situation in Quebec, where the rural class has become numerically less and less important, although it has gained in organization and aggressiveness. But obviously the

24. Jonathan M. Wiener, "The Barrington Moore Thesis and Its Critics," *Theory and Society*, 2 (Fall 1975): 301–30.
25. Barrington Moore, Jr., *Social Origins of Dictatorship and Democracy* (Boston: Beacon Press, 1966).

FLQ was not addressing the rural class, but the urban working class of the Montreal area.

It might also be that the radical ideologists of the 1960s made the mistake of taking French Canadians as a whole as "an ethnic class," to be analyzed on the model of the social class in the Marxist framework. This was a mistake that some of my best colleagues have also made,[26] and I think that it led the FLQ to believe that, apart from a tiny French-Canadian bourgeoisie, the whole French-Canadian community was ripe for developing the equivalent of a class consciousness in the face of the Anglo-Saxon exploiters, and finally to act as a revolutionary social class. But this belief neglected the complex system of social stratification or social classes that exists among French Canadians.

One final reason that can be brought for the failure of radical ideologies and actions in Quebec is that they lacked support from the generations of active adults of that period. Radical ideology and the radical movements were developed and supported by young people in their twenties, most of them either students or former university students who had dropped out and also some young former high school teachers. But those youths found no support for their ideology and actions among the men and women of the preceding generation. The latter had suffered from the authoritarianism and backwardness of the Duplessis regime, and they had dreamed of changes that would bring Quebec back into modern society. In the 1960s, they were therefore engaged, some of them very actively, in shaping the Quiet Revolution that they had prepared and dreamed of. They were not ready to follow young people whose actions they saw as disturbances of, and threats to, the process of the Quiet Revolution.

Moreover, they had not been trained to terrorist methods and street manifestations. In the faculties of law or in the new faculties of social sciences, or in the schools of administration or public administration that they had attended, they had trained themselves to be agents of change either in labor unions or in governmental offices or commissions, but surely not as under-

26. See, for instance, Marcel Rioux, "Conscience ethnique et conscience de classe au Québec," *Recherches Sociographiques*, 6 (January-April 1965).

ground revolutionaries and street demonstrators. Therefore, they had little or no sympathy at all for the radical ideologies, which they regarded as too extremist and also too ideological to fit their more "scientific" training. Most of them were also opposed to the use of violence and terrorism, which they regarded as foolish and desperate political adventures, with no future at all in Quebec.

Conclusion

In this paper, I have tried to document and interpret the double process that took place in Quebec in the 1960s, the evolutionary process that has come to be known as the Quiet Revolution, although it was not a revolution at all, and the development of the first phases of a revolutionary process that lasted seven years and finally came to an end in one of the greatest crises that Quebec had known. We have seen that those two processes took place almost concurrently, they ran parallel one to the other, and we can also add that they died out practically together. It is generally agreed that the Quiet Revolution was almost over by the end of the 1960s, precisely when the FLQ itself disappeared.

This suggests by way of conclusion that the two processes not only ran parallel but were in interaction with one another and that there were dynamic relationships between the two. The Quiet Revolution contributed to give birth to an ideology that was more radical than its own, and to violent movements that wanted to go faster than it did. But the recourse to terrorism contributed to crystallize the conservative opposition that developed in reaction against the changes brought by the Quiet Revolution. However, it would be a gross mistake to attribute the growing resistance to the Quiet Revolution among the French Canadians solely to the action of the terrorist groups. But it is most probable that their action, and, still more, what they presented as their program, came to be regarded by an increasing number of conservative French Canadians as a predictable outcome of the Quiet Revolution in the coming years. It was feared by many of those people that the Quiet Revolution was leading

Quebec not only to its independence, but also to socialism and to an atheist ϲociety.

In 1964, the conservative segments of the French-Canadian population had been defeated in their battle to oppose the creation of a Department of Education. For a while thereafter, they were quiet, but they gained an unexpected victory in 1966 when the Lesage government was defeated. This was the beginning of the slowing down of the Quiet Revolution, an objective that was explicitly expressed by the new prime minister of Quebec, Daniel Johnson. Shortly afterward, the leftist "independentist" party, the RIN (Rassemblement pour l'Indépendance Nationale), was absorbed by the new more moderate Parti Québécois and disappeared. In order to gain some support in the population, the latter did all it could not to be identified with the radicals of the FLQ.

After 1970, the Bourassa government made some changes, especially in the field of health and welfare. These had in fact been prepared and planned in the 1960s. But besides that, the Bourassa government contributed in its turn to anesthetize the last remnants of the Quiet Revolution. On the whole, over a very short period of time, less than two decades, sociologists can find in Quebec an interesting example in contemporary history and on a small scale, of how an evolutionary process may give birth to a revolutionary one and how the latter finally contributes to the death of the former.

12

Some Conclusions about the Revolution-Evolution Problem

Richard A. Preston

In his opening address to the Duke Canadian Studies Center Bicentennial Conference on Revolution and Evolution, Robin Winks asserted that the American Revolution was something more than a mere secession from the British Empire. He noted that the experiences of 1775–83 were a basis for later claims that American history was unique and for theories of "exceptionalism." This is a useful starting point for an investigation of the effect of the Revolution on the United States that would contrast it with the consequence of the absence of revolution in Canada. Seymour Martin Lipset, in the concluding session, went much farther than Winks in this same direction. He implied that revolution in America generated liberal influences that have reached all mankind, although the effect has since been upstaged (many would say spuriously) by the Russian Revolution. Canada's rejection of the 1776 rebellion, "the great refusal," Lipset believes to have been a counterrevolution that served to retain European feudally originated class divisions and privileges in the country for a long time; and it was therefore out of line with the liberal egalitarianism that the United States had fathered. So, he says, at least until the time of Confederation, Canada was a conservative society. Lipset holds that ever since the Revolution Canadians have had to defend their position by justifying their divergence from the American tradition. These two opinions thus both restate a common assumption that the Revolution and absence of revolution produced two different societies in North America.

So simplistic an explanation cannot, however, be taken as definitive, and Winks and Lipset did not intend it to be.[1] For the effects of separation, apart from the principles espoused by the revolutionaries, cannot be completely ignored. Secession permitted the United States to engage in experimentation that would otherwise have been very difficult, if not impossible; and although some of that experimentation implemented principles stated by the Revolution, this was not necessarily the case. Furthermore, as Charles Beard states in his historic study of the making of the Constitution, American society became stabilized to a considerable degree soon after the Revolution. Despite Jefferson's rhetoric noted in the introduction to this book, American views on society soon departed substantially from an unqualified acceptance of the concept of a right to revolt, the primary claim in 1776. On the other hand, it is well established that, because of Canada's retention of the British connection, certain features of British political and cultural life continued to shape Canadian society, and economic ties with Britain were maintained even after the latter abandoned mercantilism and adopted free trade.

Britain's political revolution had occurred in the seventeenth century, and the concept that further change should and could be by legal evolutionary processes was firmly established. This had an important influence on Canadian attitudes. Failure of the rebellions of 1937–38, which drew inspiration from the United States, and the subsequent development of responsible government appeared to prove that a Canadian revolution was not necessary. By the twentieth century the country had achieved independence and a democratic society without an American-type

1. In a paper prepared for a bicentennial symposium organized by the American Academy of Arts and Sciences and the Royal Society of Canada, Professor Lipset compared American and Canadian development in greater detail than in this paper and made some reference to the question of revolutionary versus evolutionary origins. Discarding what he called a "bias" toward the theory that the differences were significant, he was impressed by the theories of Louis Hartz and Kenneth McRae that Canada, like the United States, was a splinter society of Liberal Enlightenment and that observable differences were more in form than in content (Seymour Martin Lipset, "Radicalism in North America: A Comparative View of Party Systems in Canada and the United States," *Transactions of the Royal Society of Canada*, ser. 4 [1976]: 4:19–55).

revolution. Some believe that Canada had in consequence the advantage of a greater degree of stability. But those who stress the universal significance of the American Revolution can claim that the example of the United States was also important in Canada. An alternative theory might be that acceptance of that example was not the chief impulse, that in fact the American Revolution itself had been caused by a breakdown in communications within the eighteenth-century empire, and that it had been inspired by British seventeeth-century precedents that it had, indeed, vigorously asserted. Without reviving an old historical debate about the origins of the Revolution,[2] we obviously need to ask to what extent development in the United States implemented the principles of the Revolution and to what extent it was merely facilitated by the fact of secession. Contrast with Canadian experience might help to throw light on that complex problem. Comparative study of various areas of change may reveal whether any generalizations can be made.

Conclusions derived from research in specialized areas must take into account certain other causal factors mentioned in the introduction to this book. To recapitulate, there were differences between the United States and Canada, for instance, in the time of development, differences between environmental factors that derived from geography, and in the human factor caused by immigration. There were also similarities caused by the circumstance that both the United States and Canada have been evolutionary, rather than revolutionary, societies. Interpretation of the effect of these various factors must inevitably qualify conclusions drawn from specific comparisons. An even more difficult problem is posed by potentially divergent opinions about the nature of the societies themselves and of the way they are to be

2. As the causes of the American Revolution were deemed to be outside a discussion of the contrast between its effects and the evolutionary development of Canada, an excellent paper given by Gerald Gunderson at the Bicentennial Conference was not included in this volume. A review essay by J. M. Bumsted, "Dependence and Interest: The Political Economy of the First British Empire," *The Canadian Review of American Studies* 6 (Spring 1975): 99–109, and Joseph Ernst, "Political Economy and Reality: Problems in the Interpretation of the American Revolution," ibid., (Fall 1976): 109–18, are recent surveys of this complex problem.

interpreted. Americans and Canadians may not agree on the dominant qualities or the distinctive characteristics of their respective countries. Scholars and disciplines can also vary in their philosophical approach to human problems. There can thus be important subjective or unspecifiable factors that will make agreement on conclusions difficult, if not impossible. When analysing the results of the special studies that are included in this book, and when going on to undertake further exploration in other fields, these considerations must be borne in mind. Nevertheless, the use of a Canadian model can help to establish the degree to which American development was a product of the Revolution.

Although it had economic causes and consequences, the Revolution was primarily a political act in which the most important element was not violence but its consequence, a disruption breaking legal continuity. A useful starting point is therefore an examination of the results of the Revolution for the structure of law, on its theoretical framework, and on its practical application. Canadian scholars, especially Professor Kenneth McNaught of the University of Toronto, making comparisons of the United States with Canada, have asserted that there has been less respect for law and order in American society.[3] However, in his paper at the Bicentennial Conference, James Ely argued that despite the separation, and although Jacksonian democrats thought that English legal precedents should be swept away and replaced by "Republican law," those precedents nevertheless continued to be

3. K. McNaught, "The American Impact on Canada," *Canadian Geographic Journal* (January-February, 1976): 4–13.
McNaught noted elsewhere that there *has* been a record of collective violence in Canadian history as in other western states, but that in Canada it tends to be a consequence of racial and religious contention rather than of pressure for socioeconomic change or of deprivation ("Collective Problems in Canadian History: Some Problems of Definition and Research," *Report of the Proceedings of a Workshop on Violence in Canadian Society*, Centre of Criminology, University of Toronto, 8 and 9 September 1975, p. 175). But in an article that made contrasts with American experience, he argued that in dealing with clearly political cases Canadian courts have demonstrated confidence in the legitimacy of an evolving Canadian society and have firmly rejected the use of violence by any other entity than the state ("Political Trials and Canadian Political Traditions," *University of Toronto Law Journal* [1974]: 168–69).

followed to a remarkable extent. He said that the Revolution was undertaken, not to overthrow English law, but to limit the extent and manner of its application in the colonies. The Revolution removed the imperial veto on legislation and permitted reformers to simplify legal procedures in land law and criminal law. But that process had been operating before the Revolution occurred. It can thus be argued that the Revolution did not introduce new principles and that it may not have accelerated legal developments that had been facilitated by the separation. Indeed, there were persistent efforts to bolster the use of English common law in the United States because it was seen as a "highly improved system of reason." Although there were difficulties in adopting English statutes and great variations from state to state, the process was carried on to a remarkable extent, even though political separation was absolute. Ely's paper suggests that the consequence of the Revolution for this all-important sphere of legal continuity was much less than might have been expected.

In a prepared commentary on Ely's paper, McNaught said that he agreed with its conclusion that law in a republican society was remarkably similar to that in a monarchy. But he thought that this evaluation seemed to be more at the rhetorical than the substantive level. However, he suggested that the paper had pointed to fundamental errors in the conceptual framework erected by Louis Hartz, Daniel Bell, Seymour Lipset, and others who had excluded conservatism from Lockean America. McNaught said that Tocqueville's disciples have misunderstood him. They have argued that the Revolution forced conservatism underground and concealed it beneath the rhetoric of revolution and egalitarianism. On the contrary, he felt that there was even less evidence of a release of legal reforms as a result of the Revolution than Ely suggested; they would have emerged anyway, as they did in Bentham's England. Transatlantic interchange proved effective in developing legal ideas and practice. He contended that the Revolution had little to do with the evolution of law and politics in the United States.

McNaught noted that there was also intracontinental exchange. He said that he could see no evidence of Hartzian congealment and claimed that Canada could evidently borrow as easily from the revolutionary republic as from England; but of course Canadians could appeal more openly to the principles of law and order than could the conservative lawyers who dominated the profession in the United States. Indeed, if an American case suited their purpose better than an English one, Canadian courts used it, especially to oppose labor movements. In McNaught's opinion lateral international currents were more significant than substantive changes derived from the War of Independence—which he was not convinced was a revolution.

In a spontaneous contribution from the floor, Professor Sydney Wise of Carleton University said that there was no adequate study of the "reception statutes" in colonial legislatures that adopted English law for Canadian purposes. He noted, however, that there were instances in which English law was rejected, for example, in Upper Canada, the English Poor Law. Primogeniture was also not received in Upper Canada, nor was entail, except in primogeniture in the case of intestacy. Where there was discussion of the adoption of English law, as in New Brunswick, debate was vigorous. Forces in America lining up to reject primogeniture after the Revolution matched similar forces in the Canadian colonies. This was so also with the abolition of slavery, seen by some as evidence of a greater liberalism in monarchical Canadian colonies that drew from English example. However, in each colony there was a fierce debate on the slavery issue; and when slavery was abolished in Upper Canada in 1792 it was only for the issue of slaves then living. The last slave there died in 1833. With regard to Blackstone, whose influence in the United States Ely had noted, Wise said that the significant difference in Canada was that while Blackstone was the Bible of American lawyers, in British North America he was also the lexicon of the politicians who drew upon his *Commentaries* for arguments supporting a conservative political and social system in the colonies. Thus there seemed to be a considerable degree of consensus at the conference in favor of the belief that the Revolution had had a minimal influence on legal continuity and that Canada and the United States had had remarkably similar experiences in the adoption of English law.

As a political act either of separation or of revolution, the impact of the American Revolution of 1776 can also be measured in many other spheres, for instance in political ideology, in the shape of political leadership, in political institutions, in the coercive power of the state, and in the cohesion of the state. One might also ask how federal development, an obvious point of comparison with Canada, was affected. Finally one might be concerned to know whether the Revolution gave incentive to the use of force and further military solutions. In each of these cases, comparisons with the process of nation building in Canada would be possible. But only two problems could be considered at the Bicentennial Conference: the process of achieving political decisions and the operation of the party system. These are among the most important, although not the only important, elements of the political structures.

Professor Henry Albinski argued that party systems are shaped by the political system in which they operate and that modern parties are widely assumed to have had their origin in the United States immediately after the Revolution when lack of a feudal system and of class domination brought other issues to the fore. He suggested that the Revolution was "the touchstone for legitimatizing democratic ideals." A wave of libertarianism, land reform, ecclesiastical change, and decriminalization affected the growth of the party system. In contrast with what was said in the session on legal development, he voiced the belief that, while the United States possessed this touchstone, Canada lacked it. In Canada parties were, he argued, highly factional and a true party system did not develop until the end of the nineteenth century. He said that the conservatism of the Loyalists, the Family Compact, and the British imperial presence induced Tory qualities of limitation and hierarchy. Because English Canada was a plural sectionalized society, the confident congealed party system developed slowly. French-Canadian quasi feudalism had a similar impeding effect. For Albinski, party development is apparently associated with liberalism. It might thus seem to derive from the Revolution. On the other hand, the defeat of the Canadian rebels in 1837 set back its growth north of the border. In Canadian eyes the American party system was associated with republicanism and factionalism.

Albinski showed that both Canadians and Americans regarded each other's system as "factional," meaning presumably "not based on principle or ideals." It seems that, for Albinski, a true party system exists when a democratic majority can express its voice, and it develops where there is a high sense of national mythology expressing a popular ethos. So, he says, after Confederation the Canadian party system shouldered the nation-building task to an extent not duplicated in the United States. But Canadian political leadership has been low-keyed and accommodationist. By contrast, the American party system was more florid, perhaps pretentious. However (and here Albinski quoted a New Zealand professor, H. A. Morton), he said that the achievements of the Canadian system were more noteworthy: independence, social reform, economic development, and individual liberty without a major revolution or a civil war.

Albinski's paper thus appears to challenge a widely held assumption that the first true party system was sparked by the Revolution. He shows that in Canada evolution produced a party system, although at a later date. What the Revolution in the United States had thrown up was the concept of popular sovereignty, and that naturally affected the nature of parties. But, one might ask, is a party system without popular sovereignty any the less a party system? It is, of course, not a party system in the modern fully democratic sense. Any society in which a constitutional process makes change of government possible might have a party system. However, as Albinski demonstrates, European politics with multiple parties based on alleged principle rather than, as in the United States, merely on "ins" and "outs," might be said to have truer party systems. But there appears to be little doubt that the preliminary climate for a party system was provided by the Revolution. What the Revolution developed seems to have been democracy rather than parties.

One measure of the efficacy of a political system that includes parties is its capacity to facilitate change, to cope with new circumstances. A comparison of the achievements of the results of revolution in America and of evolution in Canada in this respect should therefore help to measure the significance of the Revolution. Robert Presthus said that the American colonies' dramatic break with Europe and with feudal tradition led to enhanced possibilities of upward mobility and individual advancement on the basis of performance and to the encouragement of experimentation and modernity in the United States. These things he believed resulted in political integration despite regional variation. The Canadian experience was in his opinion "dysfunctional." It aggravated the problem of accommodating change. He found that, as the accumulated weight of traditional institutions in Canada had not been displaced by revolutionary, that is to say violent, change, Canada was deficient in civil rights protection and was plagued by elite domination; but it had a greater respect for law and order and a greater tolerance of minorities. The result was the attempt to achieve national political integration and identity with the economic union of disparate parts by elite accommodation.

For Presthus the striking contrast between Canada's evolutionary path of national development and the revolutionary tradition in the United States explains what he sees as Canada's incapacity to bring about social change with reasonable ease and dispatch. He also believes that Canada's adherence to elite accommodation led to protectionist tariff policies and to nationalism, which he says is a costly aberration in a rich nation. While the American experience of revolution and civil war had encouraged experimentation and modernity and had stimulated a vigorous industrial adaptation, the contrasting processes of evolutionary development in Canada have decisively slowed national integration and the growth of a sense of identity. Presthus thus argued that the tradition of the Revolution in America greatly accelerated the different development of the United States. He agrees in certain respects with Winks, Lipset, and Albinski, but disagrees with Ely. Nevertheless, it is noticeable that both McNaught and

Wise, Canadian scholars with a considerable knowledge of the American field, agree with Ely about the apparently relatively limited effect of the American revolutionary experience when it is compared with Canada's experience of evolution in the fields of law and politics.

A broad conclusion that may be derived from the legal and political papers presented at the Bicentennial Conference is that any significant difference between the United States and Canada that can be attributed to the Revolution must be ascribed to the secession rather than to the introduction of basic revolutionary change into American life. However, a national mythology based on ideas generated by the Revolution was a long-standing influence on the American perception of a preferred society. Some aspects of American political life, for instance its political structure based on the separation of the powers, were products of the time when the Revolution occurred rather than of the Revolution itself. The American style of political leadership also undoubtedly was affected by the existence of a prevailing mythology colored by the Revolution. But all these generalizations clearly need further research and analysis.

The same forces also operated on the American external outlook. At one and the same time the Revolution detached the United States from Britain and from Europe and made it possible for the Revolution to stand, and even to be offered, as an example to the oppressed of the world. But American influence outside the Americas was almost completely restricted to verbal encouragement and there was no far-reaching concept of a world revolution such as sprang from the Russian Revolution of 1917. Isolation thus worked both ways. Britain was the only enemy capable of attacking the United States, but British governments were usually not antagonistic to American liberal ideals and therefore often favored liberal causes. The American example was very pervasive. As long as the immigration gates were kept open to populate the North American continent in the nineteenth century, the passive American response to liberalism elsewhere was generally acceptable.

Canada's retention of ties with Britain seems at first sight to have shaped the Canadian foreign outlook in a different mold from that of the United States, but superficial appearances can be misleading. It is true that the colony depended on Britain for defense, principally against the United States. But it is equally true that, although more inclined than Americans to approve of British imperial ventures (in which few Canadians actually participated), Canadians as a whole were quite as much preoccupied as were Americans with the development of their country. In 1885 John A. Macdonald preferred to secure his grasp on the West at a time when he was refusing to lift a finger to get "Gladstone and Co." out of the hole into which they had blundered in Egypt. Despite their imperial connections, Canadians in the nineteenth century were not much less isolationist than Americans. Although Canadian imperialists got a satisfaction from membership in the British Empire, few were prepared to bear "the white man's burden."

Even though the American presence seemed to give cause, Canadians were about equally disinclined to prepare for war in North America. Until the British withdrew their garrison in 1870–71, many Canadians were prepared to think in terms of an active military defense against the United States in support of the garrison. But when left to their own devices with a mere promise of support in a future crisis, few were prepared to advocate peacetime preparation for defense. Instead, they came to think in terms of peaceful solutions. The lone Canadian imperialist venture was the occupation of what was regarded as a natural heritage, the West, an emulation of American manifest destiny.

Americans had been able to back their anticolonialist dislike for European imperialism in the nineteenth century only by sheltering behind the greatest empire of all, Britain's. The Monroe Doctrine was effective only with the support of the Royal Navy. But at the end of the century completion of manifest destiny in the West was followed by American imperialist expansion into the Caribbean and Pacific. English-speaking Canadians at that time similarly engaged enthusiastically in the imperialism of the Boer War. Canada became involved in the wars of the twentieth century earlier than did the United States. But

World War I cooled Canadian enthusiasm and by the 1920s Canada was marching in step with earlier American anticolonialism. After the second war, in conformity with the United States, Canadian policy leaned to international organization to keep the peace. After midcentury the record seems to show, however, that it was Canada that, in attitudes toward imperial ventures overseas, in participation in international peacekeeping, in motives for contributions to international aid, and especially in regard to wars in Asia, was more in character with the ideals of 1776.

These generalizations do not, of course, take into account all shades of American and Canadian opinion. More research is needed to discover when and how and in what sections of society an American-like anticolonialism came to be so widely accepted in Canada. But enough has been said to suggest that the Revolution of the thirteen colonies did not make a fundamentally different imprint on the outlook of the United States on foreign problems from what came in the course of time to be established in Canada by a process of evolution. Some have thought that Americans, having greater power, were more inclined to use the revolutionary tradition to assert hegemony over much of the Americas by force. But Canadians, although described in one catch phrase as an "unmilitary people," have shown themselves to be equally martial when the occasion warranted. It may be that, in external political attitudes as well as internal, the actual impact of the Revolution was chiefly in rhetoric and mythology.

Just as political scientists seek evidence of the effect of the Revolution by examining the consequences of and for political ideology, so economists stress the importance of economic factors. Dr. André Raynauld, at the time of the conference the president-chairman of the Economic Council of Canada, recalling the importance of economic considerations in the events that led to the American Revolution and thus created the United States, contended that one cannot hope to understand the differences between Canada and the United States "without an examination of the economic forces that have shaped the two societies." Noting certain features of the Canadian economy that sharply distinguished it from that of the United States—for instance, its greater dependence on primary products and foreign trade, the extent to which its industry is controlled by foreign interests, the greater involvement of the government in the economy, and the greater degree of Canadian public funding of social welfare—he asked how far these differences have been caused by the contrasting revolutionary-evolutionary tradition or were merely due to geography and climate.

Raynauld came to the conclusion that economic factors, and especially differences in size, account for differences between Canadian and American development. Political forces had slight impact and then only in the period between the two world wars. In other periods American fiscal policy, not the colonial relationship, was the more important factor. He then went on to show the significance of other revolutions that must be considered along with the political one, notably modernization and the rejection of medievalism, the technological revolution, and the scientific revolution. He showed that the impact of these revolutions on the United States and Canada did not differ greatly and were to some extent strengthened, rather than hindered, by the colonial relationship. He concluded by saying that Canada still has a dependent relationship but that this is caused by economic forces, not political.

Raynauld did not refute the historical evidence that what the Americans rebelled against was the new imperial political policy to raise taxes for defense rather than the greater stringency of the mercantilist code for economic purposes. Nor did he, of course, rule out political ideology in the causation of the Revolution and the shaping of development in Canada in a fashion different from the United States. What he demonstrates in his paper is that, just as the Americans in 1776 came to the conclusion that their economic interests could best be served by political independence, so Canadians, over a longer period, have come to the same conclusion. He minimized the importance of revolutionary ideology and of the evolutionary tradition in the making of these decisions. The different development of the United States had, however, been confirmed by the act of separation.

Raynauld's examination was limited by time and space to the study of trade, investment links, and the impact of technological and scientific revolutions on the economy. Other questions that could have been explored were whether the experience of revolution or the lack of it affected the varying attitudes of Americans and Canadians to their economic problems. Did a spirit of self-reliance come earlier in the United States because of the Revolution, or was Canadian dependence on government aid and intervention rather a product of the relatively greater magnitude of the task of developing a bigger country with less capital and people? How did the revolutionary experience affect economic leadership? Was greater American insistence on the primacy of private enterprise in all fields of economic endeavor a consequence of the act of successful revolution? Is it merely part of the Canadian myth that the difference between the two states derives from the separation and that greater government intervention in the Canadian economy is necessary to preserve the well-being, indeed the very existence, of the state? It would be possible to explore these questions in a number of economic fields, land policy, migration, banking, financial institutions, communication systems, and labor policies.

In reexamination of the Canadian mosaic that contrasts with the American idea of the melting pot, John Porter questioned whether revolution and evolution were meaningful labels. He noted that there was no sharp distinction between American and Canadian immigration policies, or American and Canadian desires to absorb immigrants, except insofar as Canada tried to attract immigrants in the nineteenth century by offering block grants of land for various nationalities, a practice forbidden by American law. Canada thereby facilitated preservation of ethnic values. But the concept of the mosaic, coined in the twentieth century, was aimed at ethnic harmony rather than at the preservation of cultural differences. French language rights had not applied to other peoples in Canada and indeed the French Canadians themselves had vigorously rejected any such idea of an extension. Porter says that a 1973 survey shows that, in general,

Canadians identify more closely with Canada than with their "origin" groups.[4]

Porter said that on the other hand the American idea of the melting pot is not as much a rejection of the past as might appear at first sight. It is not necessarily revolutionary. Revolutions are attempts to transform society radically. The one in 1776 was different in that it sought to transform society by the use of free institutions rather than by force. There was no concept at that time of changing people or of giving them a new culture. The idea of mass immigration did not come until the late nineteenth century. Porter argued that present-day trends in both Canada and the United States toward a greater awareness of ethnic differences stem from prevailing worldwide anticolonialism and, to a lesser extent, from the plight of the peoples of Eastern Europe. It has resulted in the United States in what Porter terms a "nation of nationals," and in Canada the promotion of multiculturalism. The real difference is between assimilation in the United States and accommodation in Canada. But a concept of universalism still pervades both countries, and this is a revolutionary option to which the United States conforms more closely than Canada.

Porter confirms that the revolution-evolution contrast does not account for certain differences in the sociocultural makeup of the two countries. But he did not discuss symbolism.[5] There are also many other problems in this field that should be explored to give a fuller answer. Are differences between the two countries in their self-perception of national identity and social cohesion in any way attributable to historic development and revolutionary-nonrevolutionary origins? Is the particular brand of a regionalism

4. Anthony H. Richmond, "Language, Ethnicity, and the Problem of Identity in a Canadian Metropolis," in *Ethnicity in the Americas*, ed Frances Henry (The Hague: Mouton, 1976), pp. 41–71.
John Goldlust and Anthony H. Richmond, "Factors Associated with Commitment to and Identification with Canada," in *Identities: The Impact of Ethnicity on Canadian Society*, Wsevolod Isajiw, Canadian Ethnic Studies Association, vol. 15 (Toronto: Peter Martin Associates, 1977), pp. 132–53.
5. In an article ten years ago Porter reported that vagueness about national symbols in Canada puzzled newcomers ("The Canadian Character of the Twentieth Century," *The Annals of the American Academy of Political and Social Science* 370 [March 1967]: 51).

found in Canada, and the consequent persistence of what J. M. S. Careless has called a congerie of "limited identities," a product of history as well as of geography? What can be said about citizen participation in public and political affairs and about the structure of family life? There are thus many areas where it would be possible to utilize the yardstick of a contrast between the revolutionary-evolutionary experience of the two countries to throw more light on the nature of both.

As the consensus of opinion among social scientists appears to be that contrast with Canadian experience suggests that the American inheritance from the Revolution is largely a mythology and a tradition that grew more freely because of the political schism, exploration of comparisons between American and Canadian development in the spheres of the intellectual and aesthetics might be profitable. For literature and the arts are foundation stones of national identity. It would be fruitful therefore to know whether the Revolution in 1776 brought a proclivity toward radical change in these fields in the United States that was not repeated in Canada. To discover this it would be useful to ask what was the effect of the Revolution, or of a continuing imperial relationship, on the arts, language, literature, education, and general intellectual development? How did the Revolution affect the relation of the church to intellectual and artistic endeavor? Was language affected by the separation? And how did lack of a revolutionary experience relate to plural culturalism in Canada as compared with the more homogeneous society in the United States? Answers to questions such as these would help to define more clearly the significance of the Revolution in American development. The graphic arts, architecture, and music are all areas that could also be investigated.

It was not possible to explore all aspects of humane letters and aesthetic endeavor, but two papers at the Bicentennial Conference made comparisons between the United States and Canada in education and literature. Claude Bissell, former president of the University of Toronto and also a distinguished scholar of Canadian literature in English, drew upon his vast practical experience of higher education and also his wide literary knowledge in a paper that had two distinct parts, the institutional and the intellectual. A paper by A. J. M. Smith, a Canadian who taught for many years in the United States, supplemented Bissell's literary contribution. By tracing literary development down to the recent present, these two papers further our understanding of the extent of the Revolution's influence in earlier periods.

While Bissell assumed that the spirit of 1776 was a vital force in both education and literature and that it stressed the power of knowledge to change society and the right of all men to as much education as they can absorb, Smith seemed to be less certain. Quoting Santayana, who held that the American spirit was not democracy but materialism, Smith argued that an original, even revolutionary, literature did not appear until Emerson, Thoreau, Melville, Whitman, Twain, and even Henry James. Crèvecoeur had noted an American desire to create a new society, but to do it without violence. Tocqueville had found that American writers after the Revolution had clung to borrowed English styles but had no real respect for the past; the French observer blamed democracy rather than the Revolution. Yet it might be argued that it was the Revolution that had made this democracy possible. However, as Bissell showed, although the colonies developed institutions of higher learning at an early date, at first to produce theologians and later to foster the classical, deistic bent of contemporary European enlightenment, American universities remained elitist (and, he might have added, in many cases also church-related) until more than a generation after the Revolution.

It is paradoxical that in view of this allegedly limited impact of the Revolution on the immediate development in American intellectual life, United Empire Loyalist toryism, licking the wounds of defeat, made Canadian literature antirevolutionary from the beginning. Bissell shows that this was an even stronger case in the universities and colleges. For Canadian writers the Revolution marked the cutting of American ties and a determination to resist the spread of American culture. In Canada this led to the failure of colleges to share the great changes that marked American education in the 1860s when secularism, populism, and a mixture of government and state support brought about changes that derived belatedly from the ideology of the Revolution of 1776. However, Canadian universities continued to enjoy a "respectable obscurity with accompanying assets" derived from the elitist tradition.

According to Bissell, it is only in recent times that Canadian higher education has accepted the prevailing American pattern with its aim to open universities to all who meet entrance requirements and at the same time, its emphasis on scholarship and postgraduate studies on a vigorous specialism. On the other hand, a contemporary parallel burgeoning literary output, radical in appearance, owes nothing to the American Revolution but has continued and invigorated the nationalist anti-Americanism of earlier Canadian writing. Smith, who carried the story of the development of poetry (generally the earliest literary form to respond to new forces) down to more recent times, argued that present-day Canadian literary effort is responding, not merely to the old nationalism, but to chords that are being struck universally by anti-colonialism and the Third World. Of course, it can be argued that this literary output is, after all, the legacy of the first modern revolt against European imperialism in 1776. But radical thought would hold that that American spirit had long spent itself and that the Russian Revolution, and more immediately the ideology of the New Left, are nearer sources of inspiration. We might note here Bissell's conclusions that the American Revolution had, after all, been an emotional rather than an intellectual phenomenon and that neither Canadian literature nor higher education has in fact been comfortable with the revolutionary syndrome.

These two papers on literature and higher education were concerned only with comparing American trends with the English-Canadian experience. To carry the inquiry into an investigation of French-Canadian literary development would call for preliminary study of the existence of common features in English and French Canada that could be ascribed to the absence of revolutionary influences. Reference to the bicultural problem was made in other fields, but it would be more difficult in this one. French Canada is, however, undergoing change that has interesting features identifiable as revolutionary; there has even been an uncharacteristic resort to violence. Guy Rocher's paper, "The Quiet Revolution and Revolutionary Movements among French Canadians," is therefore included in this volume to provide a parallel with the revolutionary-evolutionary theme, even though it is not a comparison with, or a discussion of the consequences of, the American revolutionary experience.

Rocher wrote before the Quebec election of November 1976. He was, therefore, not responding to the political victory of an avowedly separatist party in the Province of Quebec. Rather, he was concerned to contrast the progress of the Quiet Revolution, a radical process of modernization that was a cultural revolution without any parallel changes in economic institutions, with certain radical movements that had resorted to terrorism when they were frustrated because dialogue between the proponents of the Quiet Revolution and the federal authorities had been fruitless. Rocher shows that the Quiet Revolution failed because it did not bring a diminution of non-French economic domination; but the atheistic socialist ideology of the revolutionary movements was alien to the traditional moral code of Quebec. It had then given birth to ideologies that were more radical than its own. Rocher thus shows that the revolutionary-evolutionary syndrome is a complex one. The subsequent victory at the polls of the Parti Québécois, regarded as a step toward independence, may mean that it is still possible that the aftermath of the conflict of revolutionary violence and evolutionary development may be a political marriage or a compromise. Whatever may be the future for Quebec, something of this kind appears to have occurred in the United States subsequent to the Revolution, and something similar seems to have emerged over the course of nearly two centuries in Canada.

The conclusion that can be drawn from study of the papers presented at the Bicentennial Conference on Revolution and Evotion is broader and more general. As both Robin Winks and Seymour Martin Lipset suggested in their talks, comparative study of Canadian and American development can be a fertile source for understanding both countries. Throughout this concluding chapter, reference has been made to vast areas that need research and analysis. An important contribution that this book can make is to inspire scholars to move into a very profitable field of research. These papers suggest that the American Revolution was more effective as a mythology and model than as an active force in forming social, political, and cultural institutions. Even though there are clear distinctions between Canada and the United States (of which Canadians are usually more aware than Americans), nevertheless in the fundamentals of their separate existences there are similarities that set them apart from many other peoples and cultures. Whether these are due to the universal features of the Revolution or to universals that derive more generally from the growth of Western societies is a question to which further research may one day provide a more cogent or definitive answer.

Index